Liudmyla Kalabukha

Do
the OPPOSITE

Life and Sales
BEFORE and DURING THE WAR

D1666869

[100% Ukrainian experience]

Thank you for purchasing this book. No part of the book may be reproduced, scanned or distributed in any manner without written permission from the author, except in case of brief quotations used in books, articles or newspapers. Your support and respect for the property of the author is appreciated.

The author shall have neither liability nor responsibility to any person or entity with respect to any loss or damage caused, or alleged to be caused, directly or indirectly by any information presented in this book.

Kalabukha L.O.

Do the OPPOSITE: Life and Sales BEFORE and DURING THE WAR (100% Ukrainian experience)

Translated from Ukrainian: Zoryana Rixens, Yulia Yakovliuk, Mariia Khrushchinska

Cover design: Oleh Bondaruk

ISBN 979-885-472-437-1

Imagine finding a book that reveals your past, present, and future — who you were, who you are, who you aspire to be, as well as your goals and fears. That's precisely what "Do the OPPOSITE: Life and Sales BEFORE and DURING THE WAR", Liudmyla Kalabukha's third book, is about. It became the best book of 2023 according to the results of the 7th All-Ukrainian Lesya Martovych Literary Competition. Liudmyla Kalabukha is a business sales coach, "Best Blogger of Ukraine 2019" winner, and honorary UN Ambassador in Ukraine for women's entrepreneurship development.

Her first two books, "Start Saying NO" (which was listed among the TOP-10 best books of Ukraine in 2017 in the all-Ukrainian ratings) and "When to Say YES" (awarded the Best Book of Ukraine in the "Readers' Choice" category at the KBU Awards 2020), have become national bestsellers. These books are not only reviewed by readers but are also carried along in emergency bags into uncertain situations and read in shelters.

Based on specific examples and stories from contemporary Ukrainians, "Do the OPPOSITE" proves that there are things we cannot lose, even when we have lost everything. It shows that we are able to put ourselves together and endure what seems impossible.

This work is a piece of motivation, inspiration, and desire to live, despite failures, doubts, fear, and despair. It also gives clear and practical advice on sales BEFORE and DURING TIMES OF WAR. Take this advice and put it into practice!

All rights reserved
ISBN 979-885-472-437-1

©L. Kalabukha, 2022
©Flying Colors Publishing, 2023

[Translator's Note:
In this book, people's surnames and names
that are used derogatorily
are written in a lowercase letter,
as well as the words "russia"and "russian", as the war is ongoing]

Dedicated to all the people, both near and far,
who have ever thought kindly of me,
and shared their words of encouragement,
whether in writing or personally.
This is for you!

CONTENTS

CHAPTER 5. HOW THE MONA LISA BECAME THE MOST EXPENSIVE PAINTING IN THE WORLD, AND OLEH VASIUKOV'S SENSATIONAL STUDY — 121

CHAPTER 6. TURKISH-STYLE BUSINESS: HOW TO SELL A LOT, EXPENSIVELY, AND WITHOUT EXCEPTIONS — 133

CHAPTER 7. LIFE, DEATH, GASTRONOMIC HORRORS AND THE DECOLUMBIZATION OF MEXICO — 144

FOREWORD

"Mom, the war has begun!" a call at 8:00 a.m. from my daughter who lives in Kyiv.

That's how I found out.

I am settling, coordinating, and connecting everyone not only in Ukraine but also all over the world. On the 11th day, I see my friend's story on Instagram: "Here was my apartment in Irpin. We had managed to leave before the "orcs" started shooting at the house."

Our dialogue in Direct:
"Where are you going?"
"I don't know."
"Lviv, my house, will it suit you?"
"Yes."
"Waiting."

Walking in, he initially asked for two things: a yoga mat to meditate and stretch (after spending nine days in the basement) and a Wi-Fi password (to write to his clients that he is alive and that he will fully fulfill his obligations).

He asked how I was doing with my work.
"What work? It's war!"
"So, you've stopped working completely, then?"
"Yes."
"Aren't you ashamed? Day 12 and you haven't started working yet? Post stories immediately, write to customers, live-stream on Instagram, and help restore sales!"

Thank you, my friend; I know you're reading this.

It was thanks to you that on March 9, I held the first wartime webinar on how to sell and earn in wartime. Hundreds of people wrote that it became a lifesaver for them.

Since then, I've received thousands of messages from readers of my books "Start Saying NO" and "When to Say YES". They

13

told me that those books were the only ones they had been carrying into the unknown. They were reading in shelters during shelling, sometimes for the second and third time, finding strength and motivation not only to merchandise but also to live, no matter where the war threw them.

I was amazed when online bookstores started ordering my books in very large batches. It turned out that all books saved from the warehouses during shelling in Kharkiv and Kyiv were sold immediately, and within a month after the war had started, sales returned to pre-war levels. And I was even more amazed when everyone started asking about the new book, the release of which had been announced for May 2022.

Publish a new book during the war? Nonsense! Or maybe it is necessary?

I was rejecting this idea and then returned to it a hundred times. I was clinging to it like a lifeline during air raid alerts and after reading particularly terrible news.

I was reviewing the already written material and testing each pre-war short story for relevance: something has been deleted and something else has been added. With a sinking heart, I would contact all the heroes whose stories were ready (Kyiv, Kharkiv, Lviv, Warsaw) to find out where and how they were and to write about their lives during the war.

The title. Again, I didn't have a title for an almost-written book. Until, on the 138th day of the war, I woke up at night. No, not due to the air raid alert. But because the title came itself: I opened the file "Book 3" on the computer and renamed it "Do the OPPOSITE: Life and Sales BEFORE and DURING THE WAR".

What is it about?
How to ask for help so that it is given.
How to stop blaming yourself for mistakes, and survive losses, insults, and betrayal.
How to find the right solutions and opportunities even where there are none.
How to swim against the current and win after a hundred failures.

How to find what you've been pursuing for a long time.
How to get back what seems to be hopelessly lost.
How to survive.
How to live.
BEFORE and DURING THE WAR.
Are we going the same way?
Let's go!

CHAPTER 1

SALES AND LIFE

CONTACT WITH THE OTHERWORLD, AN AX, AND $1700 IN 30 MINUTES

"And now I will take an ax and start hacking you to death," she hissed, blocking the entrance to the corridor. "And you won't jump out of the window: we're on the fifth floor. And the window still needs to be opened. Think! Think what to do!"

I have noticed that in critical moments of life, I perceive the situation as if from the side. So even now, I am watching myself, 26 years old, in that cluttered kitchen in a neglected apartment. An unknown-aged woman in a greasy dressing gown is standing in front of me, blowing cigarette smoke straight into my face and repeating:

"Do you hear me? I'll hack you to death now! Pavlo! Bring the ax, we're going to hack her."

How did I end up there and what was I doing?! Instead of grabbing a knife or a stool (or what else do people do in such cases in thrillers?) I was sitting numbly and mentally unraveling this chain of events that led me here.

Two years earlier
Iryna was a hairdresser. And hairdressers are golden clients! They would always buy everything from me. Why? They would always have ready money, no matter the government or any crisis. Our women might die of hunger, but they would never give up going to the hairdresser!

So Iryna noticed this, gave up her career as a lawyer, and started cutting hair, styling, and coloring it. In addition to that, she opened a hair salon right on the first floor of the house where she lived. Even at the same entrance. The business went up: plenty of clients, enough money, and enough for my jewelry too. Once a month, she would steadily buy jewelry for herself and as gift for others. At that time, I used to sell on credit, and she paid on time, was friendly, and we always communicated perfectly.

One year earlier

Suddenly, Iryna announced that she was ending her career as a hairdresser and becoming a fortune-teller.

How come? She was trained by another fortune-teller: she would go to see her for two months, carefully noting everything in a summary. And when the time came, she started her private practice. In her apartment.

So, I came to the address I had known for a long time, not to the hair salon, but to her home. And what did I see?! There was a long queue from the first to the fifth floor of the building: women, men, and children were patiently waiting for the newly-minted fortune-teller Iryna to receive them. And I almost fainted inside. No, it didn't smell like sulfur from hell, there weren't rows of dried frog heads, and she wasn't flying on a broomstick.

Completely different!

The insane stench was simply knocking me off my feet, and I had never seen such a mess in my life. It seemed as if a rampage or a harsh search by the NKVD had just taken place here. The floor was "mined" with piles of dog shit of varying freshness, which (it seemed) did not bother anyone, and no one was going to clean it up either. Through the wide-open door, one could see the interior of a cluttered kitchen, with a stove dripping with finger-thick burnt fat and a table littered with food scraps and candy wrappers.

And if you think that I am exaggerating what I saw (such as a creative nature, artistically reinterpreting reality; or, as my relatives like to troll me, a science fiction writer ☺), well, I am still "under-exaggerating" — if, of course, there is such a word. It will now be!

In the middle of this chaos, there was Iryna, first a lawyer, then a hairdresser, and now a fortune-teller, sitting on a worn-out chair, in a stale dressing gown, with unwashed hair, and receiving her clients.

In the picture that was revealed before me, I was most impressed not even by the interior and its new makeover, but by the fact that Iryna, whom I had known as a sweet and kind woman, was rude to her clients, to those unfortunate people who were queuing on the steps of the entrance for several hours and, shifting from foot to foot (they were not offered to sit down), right in the corridor, surrounded by piles of dog shit, would speak about their troubles in trembling voices.

When I shyly asked why she would talk so harshly to her clients (they didn't come to her because of a good life: they were looking for help, support, or comfort), she explained:
"I'm so sick of it all! I'm pretty slammed. Even my husband quit his job where he worked as a mattress sales manager, so now the two of us roll the eggs and remove spoilage. However, we still don't have enough time. Do you see the queues?"

And suddenly she growled:
"Wait! Don't you see I'm talking?!"

A tearful woman, who looked into the room where we were sitting, literally flew out the door. She was just the one in front of which I jumped the line amid the disgruntled whispers of citizens. Simply in the best traditions of "I only need to ask a question". So what? I didn't need fortune-telling, but to collect the next payment for jewelry + to stock Iryna up with new jewelry so that her debts didn't end, and I had confidence in the future.

Moreover, I have a sin: I asked Iryna to help me in a difficult business situation.

This is how social evidence works: you see such a demand and think that she may have truly some chakras opened and have established contacts with the world beyond present reality.

And I just had two clients who, being unavailable, had not paid the money.

Let me remind you that it was back in the days without the Internet and smartphones, when, in a best-case scenario, I had a home phone number for communication. And often, it was only a work number. And the telephone was not always in the office where the person worked. You had to show miracles of communication and persuasion to invite the right person, sometimes from another floor or even building.

Iryna lit a candle, waved her hands in the air, rolled her eyes, and said in a guttural voice:
"The first one is decent, and will soon give you everything back. She will call you herself. You should just wait. But the other one will never give your money back: she is dishonest and just screwed you. Forget it, cut your losses."

And what do you think? Everything happened exactly the opposite way.

The first one, who was supposed to be decent, turned out to be a fraud. She borrowed a lot of money at work, borrowed things from a dozen other people besides me, quit her job, and disappeared. Then she was said to have moved out of the rented apartment, leaving a lot of debts for utilities. And the story with the second one, who should have never paid back the debt, because she was allegedly dishonest and screwed me, in general, roused half of Lviv.

The client, who I could not get in touch with, was a young, beautiful, intelligent teacher and a science candidate.

When I spoke with her, she seemed to be everything you should be, look like, and live like: a brilliant career, a happy marriage, a child, an apartment in a new building with designer renovations, foreign business trips, and travels. And suddenly she was gone. She just didn't wake up in the morning. Her husband and little son were sleeping next to her when she died in her sleep. She was 29 years old.

I learned about all this a few months after the funeral. Her sister called me. After the relatives have recovered a bit from their shock, they managed to settle the affairs of the deceased. They completely settled my accounts. We became friends and would often cry together, remembering the late Khrystyna, who had adored the jewelry bought from me. She kept repeating, "This is for my daughter-in-law."

How guilty I felt for believing this half-fortune teller who claimed such things about my client.

I am writing, but my heart is still heavy even now. I'm ashamed.

"Well, she made a mistake, your Iryna got confused. Who hasn't?" said a cheerful IT specialist when we started talking about magic and the afterlife. "I work for a US company, and we have just launched a fortune-telling web portal. It's not uncommon there."

We almost fell off the shelves (it all happened in the sauna at the yoga retreat).

"A fortune-telling web portal?" exclaimed the yoga retreaters all at once.

"Yep. One American alone invested $1 million in it. And I am the manager of that project, I assembled a team. The owner requires that all IT specialists are exclusively from Ukraine. I selected everyone myself, poached the coolest specialists from other companies, and we pay outrageous wages.

What a profitable venture!

In a year, the web portal crossed the break-even point, and for three months in a row, it has been making a net profit of $20,000. The projected annual revenue is $500,000, to which everything is allocated. Oh, how I wish I had some spare cash to start something like this in Ukraine. I would get rich."

There was a similar story. One office in the United States promised a 100 percent guarantee in determining the gender of the child before, during, and immediately after fertilization. Well, they were always wrong, just like your fortune-teller. But they arranged everything in such a cunning way: the results were reported verbally, no certificates were issued, and no files were sent. And when a mistake happened (and it would always happen), they confidently demonstrated to people that they had accurately predicted the gender that came out: "This is how it is written in our database, everything is honest. You simply didn't hear, didn't look carefully, or didn't understand us that way."

And they do it so cleverly that no one brought them to court. Yet ☺.

But the cheerful IT specialist at the yoga retreat will be there 20 years later, 20 years after I was sitting in a cluttered kitchen and a woman was standing in front of me threatening to hack me to death with an ax.

This was exactly the teacher of the fortune-telling science to whom my client Iryna went with the synopsis. She got interested in my jewelry and invited me to her place.

So I came. And here I sat, wondering how long it would take and how they would find my hacked body, as well as when and who my husband would bring as a stepmother to my child when he remarried. Honestly, such nonsense would enter my mind instead of dealing with the matter at hand.

"Relax, why are you so tense?" said the fortune-teller while my whole life flashed before my eyes like a movie. "I'm kidding. And you did well: stayed confident, and didn't lose your temper. Show me what you brought there. I'm in the mood to buy everything."

So you're probably thinking that I turned around and left offended. In addition, while standing at the door, I delivered a pathetic speech in defense of human rights. That is, my rights.

But I didn't say anything.

I kind of thought: so much time, nerves, and emotions were invested in this meeting. It seemed to have swept away. My life was no longer in danger. Maybe I would pick up a penny as restitution for moral harm.

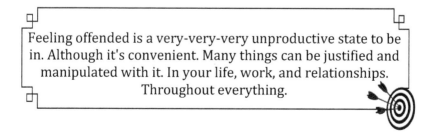

Feeling offended is a very-very-very unproductive state to be in. Although it's convenient. Many things can be justified and manipulated with it. In your life, work, and relationships. Throughout everything.

Friends, honestly, if I have to choose between the opportunity to teach someone good manners and the opportunity to make money, I will always choose the latter.

Feeling like a victim is a certain lifestyle, a vocation, a mission if you will.

Do you know what such people do? They find ways to make it so that they are offended everywhere, and everyone owes them. Because they were not noticed, treated, or invited to take a seat. The victim carefully observes everything and talks a lot about the good he does for everyone. And about human ingratitude. The victim will always notice that they have less on their plate than others, that they are interrupted in the middle of a sentence, or that they are looked at badly.

In life, it often happens that things are just the way they are. And it is a choice whether you pay attention to it, feel offended and underestimated, or do everything possible in any situation and get some benefit from it. It's our choice. Only ours, no one else's.

A Story from Kalabukha

In the harsh 90s, my friend Sashko worked as a manager in a company that installed telephone lines in large shopping centers. He hunted for the owner of one of these shopping centers for a long time, but nothing worked out. He didn't respond to any communication attempts.

Everyone around warned him that he had no chance. Furthermore, the owner had such a cold temper that he might even put his hands on his employees if they did not do things his way. But Sashko was seasoned. And everything was perfect with his motivation: many loans, a child, and a pregnant wife.

He went straight ahead. Miraculously dodging the guards, he entered the office of the hypothetical Ivan Ivanovych, and right from the doorstep began telling him how happy everyone would be if his company and he organized IP telephony for them in person.

Ivan Ivanovych, as everyone warned, immediately started swearing at him and threw him out of the door.

Sashko stood there, took a deep breath, and thought to

himself:

"I'm already here, I received a dose of negativity; what if he calmed down? I'll try to go inside one more time."

Ivan Ivanovych dropped the receiver in surprise when he saw Sashko again. And he wasn't just shouting this time: he started throwing decorative items at Sashko, having almost hit him several times as Sashko was running to the door.

Sashko was standing behind the door and thinking:
"Well, it definitely can't get any worse. I'm already here. I've put in so much effort. I've received so much negativity. I need the money badly. I won't give up. And according to the laws of sales, customer refusals and objections have to be worked through three times. With God's help."

He crossed himself and entered the office again.

Ivan Ivanovych's jaw dropped, literally. This time, he didn't yell or throw anything, but offered a chair to Sashko, sat opposite him, and said:
"I respect persistence and the will to win. You deserve that I at least listen to you. You've got five minutes."

At that time, Sashko concluded the biggest deal in the company's history. His bonuses were so big that he immediately paid off the loan for the car and partially paid in advance for the apartment. Sashko became a legend in the industry and was promoted.

That day I earned a total of $1,700. At that time, it was the salary that a teacher or a doctor would earn in two years. And I easily made that much money.

We immediately bought a car: it was just the missing amount. How did I do it? I always believe in and invest in each client. I didn't know if she would buy anything or not. And there, too, I gushed with glee that they had changed their minds about hacking me to death.

That was the second time I had been threatened with an ax (read about the first time in the book "When to Say YES").

It's a good thing everything worked out. But things could be different. I am convinced that working in sales is indeed one of the most dangerous professions in the world.

Which one is safe though? 😊

EBBS AND FLOWS

This is how it happens: problems appear just out of the blue. The number of broken deals, people that let you down, confused you, didn't show up, didn't pay, or simply forgot about your arrangements is growing like a snowball. No matter where I go, no one is around. No matter what I start, nothing works.

The War
So, when your world is collapsing and death and danger are around, you rally to hold on for as long as you can, then as long as you need to, and then bang! You break down over some trifle, such as a faulty electric kettle, from which the check was lost, and they refuse to replace it. You are ashamed, but you still sob over such a pittance. Why? Because this is already the tenth problem of the day. And the day is only getting started.

During one of these periods, I read about an interesting theory of ebbs and flows.

What is it about?

Life energy cannot be maintained at a high level all the time. It has its ebbs and flows, just like the sea. Our energy also recedes. Leaving us no matter what we do.

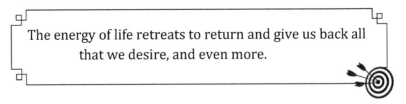

The energy of life retreats to return and give us back all that we desire, and even more.

The ebb has just begun. Yes, it is untimely and inappropriate, but as they say in Lviv, there is no other option.

It's necessary to accept it and ride it out. During this time, you need to pause to preserve what you have. Be happy about the little things. Be grateful for all the good things you have. Don't take it for granted. Look around. Listen to yourself. Conduct a kind of audit of what is going on.

How can one do it?

We have a following custom: sitting down before leaving. We've finished packing, everything is in luggage, and we're excited and curious. We sit quietly for a minute, focus, and our condition changes! We leave cool-headed and cautious.

Similarly, during low tides, when everything falls out of hand, you must stop and "sit down". Take a stroll in the park. Look at the trees, recall your childhood, and listen to the birds. Listen to yourself. Or, sit in a café and observe the people around you. Lay down to take a nap in the middle of the day, simply because you feel unbearable fatigue and you want to do it. Turn off the phone. And, without feeling guilty about the 100 thousand cases that require your immediate assistance, sleep sweetly and blissfully. Don't talk to anyone. Don't watch TV or swipe your phone. Leave the world behind. Sit in a comfortable chair with a relaxing book, or just lie down and listen to yourself and the sounds that appear to fill the silence in your home.

This is such a simple and accessible method of emotional "zeroing". It helps during low tides and is simply necessary before important events in life such as an exam (which should not be prepared for at night), an interview, a trip, competitions, and public speaking. Even before the date you've been looking forward to for so long.

Just know: the flow will soon begin.

This is how it began for me after a long sequence of endurance tests:
- "Your backpack pocket is open, and I can see a lot of money in there. Close it, or the money will be stolen," a guy on the street saved me as I walked out of the bank after withdrawing a significant amount to pay the repairmen. And he could have remained silent.

- The strudel at my favorite café had exactly the taste that I particularly liked. That day, the cook made it mouthwatering.
- During training, I was able to complete challenging workouts on the first try. I did not even imagine that I was capable of such a thing.
- Two companies ordered my workshops at the same time, I was invited to talk on the radio to an audience of 20 million, and I received a new review of my activity on Google with the mark "Five stars".
- My hairdresser's only available appointment time was convenient for me.
- And most importantly, I was informed that my second book, "When to Say YES", had won the Best Book of Ukraine in the "Readers' Choice" category at the KBU Awards 2020, as well as the online reader vote at the "KBU Awards 2020: Best Books for Business Development and Personal Growth" contest.

When all of these events occurred on the same day, I clearly understood: the rough patch was over, and the flow had begun!

The flow begins like this:
- You arrive everywhere on time, all the right people pick up the phone immediately and are on the spot, and all the documents are issued instantly. Even the beautiful heart-melting dress in the window is your size and color, and a big discount is given on the price.
- The number of pleasant events is increasing, despite the fact that recently, worries have piled up one after another, seemingly without end.

Signs of the flow:
- You find profitable orders, are reimbursed or paid, receive a bonus, good tips, and appreciation for a job well done.
- Irritation passes. You become calmer and smile more often.
- New helpful people appear in your environment and open up new opportunities for you.
- Diseases recede, you feel and look better, and it is noticeable.
- You wake up cheerful, and you want to get down to business

as soon as possible first thing in the morning: there is confidence that everything will work out.
- You find a common language with people who you couldn't get along with. You let go of resentment. Forget about petty quarrels.
- Strangers help you. Have you had a similar experience recently?

Feel free to start something new, something you have never dared to do, take the first step in an important affair, launch marketing and advertising, remind people who owe you about money you have not yet been given or paid, express your love, and make peace.

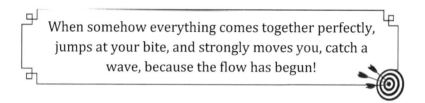

When somehow everything comes together perfectly, jumps at your bite, and strongly moves you, catch a wave, because the flow has begun!

WHEN YOUR HOLIDAY WAS RUINED

For example, a birthday. They didn't greet you at all, or didn't greet you well. No guests came. Or everyone came but him. Or he did not arrive when you expected. Or your girlfriend openly flirted with him the entire evening, knowing about your likes. And then they left together. You are sobbing in the kitchen, wanting only one thing: for this day to end fast, to forget it like a bad dream.

This is me describing a few of my birthdays. I suspect yours as well.

Never do something like that!

If it's your holiday or birthday, don't let anyone make it a bad day and steal it from you!

One of my favorite series is "Sex and the City". Those who haven't watched it, I envy you. It's a great show. Each episode is a treasure trove of quotes, life wisdom, and wit.

Here are three of my favorite episodes:
1. The main character, journalist Carrie Bradshaw, is a fan of branded clothing and shoes. A CHANEL jacket is one of her most expensive outfits. When a girl accidentally tells someone else's secret to a random boyfriend, she demands that he swear on a CHANEL jacket that he would keep her secret.
2. Carrie was entrusted to read a fairy tale to her friend Charlotte's three-year-old daughter, and she quickly adapted the story to reality: "...and Cinderella and the prince lived happily ever after... You realize that this is just a fairy tale, don't you, sweetheart? And things don't always happen like this in real life. I just think you should be aware of it now."
   That's how I, the antimother, read fairy tales to my daughter. ☺
3. The episode I quote most often is Charlotte and Harry's wedding, when everything goes wrong.
   In particular:
   • Harry saw Charlotte while she was trying on a wedding dress, which is considered a bad omen;
   • the wedding announcement in the newspaper was tainted: in the photo, there was a large smudge of printing ink right on the bride's face;
   • Charlotte spilled wine on herself during the ceremony *[translator's note: in fact, Harry spilled wine on Charlotte since he couldn't smash the glass]*, slid *[on beads]*, and would have fallen in front of everyone if Harry hadn't supported her.

A perfectly planned day was ruined. Everything happened exactly the opposite. Charlotte was crying bitterly in the dressing room, but Carrie comforted her, stating that the fact that the wedding did not go as planned was a good sign: the worse the wedding, the better the marriage. She wanted Charlotte to open her eyes since she was missing everything when she cried and complained about how bad things were. Everything! Her wedding, the fact that there was a beautiful man who loved her next to her, who would support her if she fell. Carrie didn't want Charlotte to waste such a wonderful day of her life!

Don't let bad mood, disappointment, envy, angry and indifferent people, circumstances, brawlers, or rude people steal your holiday, day, or even an hour.

Don't let yourself be robbed!

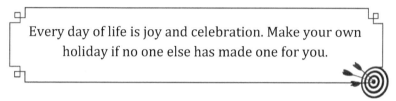

Every day of life is joy and celebration. Make your own holiday if no one else has made one for you.

Swear to me on a CHANEL jacket 😊 not to miss what is going on around you. Don't complain about how bad things are. It's just a birthday, a graduation, a day you consider unlucky.

Stop walking around in comfortable clothes (I know those comfortable clothes 😊), without makeup, and with unwashed hair. You don't need to hear yourself saying: "I'm not in the mood"! If a woman looks bad, she wants everyone to see her pain — this was written about 1000 years ago in the Indian Vedas. Stop feeling like a victim. Put on something beautiful, some makeup, head to your favorite café, and order delicious food. Don't care about calories today! If you don't have any money, just go for a walk. Do not sit alone, go to people. Count one, two, three, and step outside.

There is absolutely a place in your city or village where happy, smiling people walk. I understand that there are times when you don't want to see or talk to anyone. But you still have to go. Be amongst and with people. With those who are doing well now. Warm up from their emotions. It's easier to survive that way. Live through your grief. You will be absorbed by the energy of the field they create. It is impossible to feel unhappy while surrounded by happy people. It's hard not to smile when everyone around you is laughing. Don't be jealous. Be happy for them. Be happy for yourself that you have a holiday and that you are well.

Got it?
You feel GOOD!

WHY IS IT SO SCARY TO LIVE IN ABUNDANCE?

Do you ever buy something and immediately feel guilty? It's as if a harsh voice is saying: it's too expensive, you can do without it, you don't deserve it, you waste your money when there are so many unsolved issues. And instead of joy, you feel anxiety.

Fear of living well. But why? I discovered the reasons.

The first one is the genetic fear of our oppressed and suppressed ancestors. They were raised in a society where it was scary to live well; a society where it was dangerous to brag about achievements and accomplishments; and where all they had earned through hard work was not only taken away from them, but they could be annihilated for daring to be better!

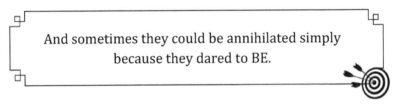

And sometimes they could be annihilated simply because they dared to BE.

Have you ever wondered why it is uncomfortable for many of us to post vacation photos on social media? Why do people hide behind closed profiles and do not write about their accomplishments, victories, and joys, or only write in their private profiles?

I am an expert in promoting and monetizing the personal brands of business owners, and actively research this topic. Most of them answer the following:

"They will hate me because everyone here works hard for pennies, people don't have enough for bread, and I only spend that kind of money on vacation. They will envy, put a jinx on me, steal, or unsubscribe."

Do you recognize yourself? I was brought up the same way. When we bought our first car (a white used "eight" for $3000 *[translator's note: an "eight" is a model of Lada, a soviet car)*), it was a big breakthrough for our family, as no one had ever owned a car before. It appeared to us to be such an extraordinary luxury that my father quite seriously advised us not to admit to the neighbors that this car was ours and say that friends had lent it to us temporarily. So that others didn't get jealous and attract thieves, who would undoubtedly rob us if they discovered our wealth.

Why? You don't have to go far, let's take a look at the stories of my relatives.

When my paternal grandfather, Kazymyr Oleksiyovych Vasyukov, an electrical network engineer, moved from Kharkiv to Lviv in 1946, he was given a choice of several service apartments with the right to buy one in the future because he was a very valuable employee. He was even offered a private house (a mansion, as they say in Lviv), furnished with antique furniture.

My friend's grandmother, a native of Lviv, worked as a cloakroom attendant at the Lviv Opera her entire life. She recalled that after the World War II, there was no one she knew, grew up with, studied with, or was friends with in her surroundings. Neither at home nor at work. It seemed as if she was in another city.

In 1946, 25,000 vacant apartments were registered in Lviv. Why were there so many empty homes? Jewish people died during the German occupation, and Poles left en masse for the West.

My grandfather Kazymyr came to such a desolate Lviv with his family. And he settled in a communal apartment: three in a passage room with one toilet for five families. As a result, my father couldn't get married until the age of 33 because there was no separate room where he could bring his wife.

For many years, I was tormented by the question: why did he choose this very modest and uncomfortable dwelling, when he could have gotten a big mansion? And it's only now that I understand his foresight and survival experience: if he lived in a spacious apartment of his own, there would always be someone who would lay eyes on it and take it away. And they wouldn't just be evicted, they could all disappear in one night, as the neighbors used to.

I have found evidence that at that time even some wealthy Lviv residents who had large houses would move into semi-basement rooms. They knew: sooner or later they would lose their property. They used to save their lives. Of course, the apartment was lost, but at least they were not repressed, as was often the case when military officials liked the apartment.

And my husband's grandfather, Ales Sinitsa? When Western Belarus, like Western Ukraine, became a part of the USSR in 1939, their family, the wealthiest owners of the village, was the first to be dispossessed.

They were lucky: they were not shot or relocated, but merely their land, livestock, and house were taken away. That is everything. They were sheltered by relatives. Of all the wealth, only jackboots remained. All village men got married wearing those jackboots: they were borrowed for weddings and put on at the threshold of the church, to which people would walk barefoot, cherishing this precious item. And when the Second World War broke out and grandfather Ales was drafted into to the Red Army, he went to war in those jackboots.

Once, bandits broke into his wife's house at night and demanded to give them those boots. They threatened to smash the newborn baby's head against the wall if she did not hand them over. In front of the icons, the grandmother swore that she didn't have jackboots, and standing on her knees pleaded not to kill the child (my husband's future mother, my mother-in-law). It was terrifying to have jackboots, and even more so to own a nice apartment or house.

The second reason is our own personal story.

Every day, people ask me on social media, in forums, and in interviews where I get my motivation and what I do when I don't have it. I answer truthfully: I don't want to return to my impoverished and hopeless past, when there was no money to buy diapers for a child or medicine for a sick mother.

One of my journalist friends says that the main motivation in his life is ceramic tiles and hot water. He didn't have that as a child. Therefore, he is prepared to do anything in order to provide for his children. How strongly it motivates and energizes!

So, it turns out that you tear every penny from your heart and think a hundred times whether it is worth spending it on something you can live without.

My friends, it is worth it!

If it pulls you down and prevents you from breathing and living.

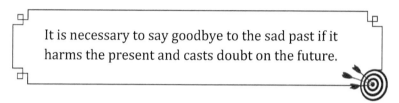

It is necessary to say goodbye to the sad past if it harms the present and casts doubt on the future.

I am desperately learning not to skimp on the things that make me happy. These are investments in our good mood, our desire to smile and like ourselves, our inner harmony, and our connection with ourselves. The most appropriate and necessary investments.

Do you want to treat yourself to something nice? Make sure to take it! You don't have to blame and convince yourself that you bought some nonsense. You are not a squanderer. You've spent money on joy: jewelry, attractions, a new blouse, expensive cosmetics, a good book, expensive cheese, travels, or a visit to your favorite café. Enjoy it! You wanted to feel happy — you succeeded.

Happy people get sick less and argue less. A happy person will easily earn more money. And if money can buy a good mood, positive emotions, and a sense of fullness of life, spend it with joy: for all ancestors who were afraid to live well, because their property would be taken away and destroyed; for yourself, who are motivated by ceramic tiles in the bathroom and hot water.

The War
After February 24, this was added to our eternal guilt over spending money and time on ourselves: can we please ourselves while so many people are in trouble, and this money is needed for our victory?

Only in the fifth month of the war did I allow myself to go to a cosmetologist. And the entire session I was tormented by a feeling of guilt for the fact that the money could have been donated. And then I realized: the fact that I looked bad wouldn't make it any easier for the boys to fight, that's for sure.

Not only would I reboot and improve my appearance (I wanted to believe that would make a difference ☺), but I would also have the resources to work harder and contribute even more.

I would boost Ukraine's economy. The money I would leave in the salon would go toward the beautician's salary, the salon's rent, and taxes. And also, toward the help on the front line.

SO THAT YOU DON'T SPEND YOUR ENTIRE LIFE NEAR THE TOILET

While Tanya was swimming, all her belongings and a sunbed were dragged to the far corner under the concrete fence near the toilet.

"You don't mind, do you?" the beach employee turned to her. "The entire company came here, they haven't seen each other in a long time, and want to stay together. And you are alone. No offense. You don't mind, do you?"
"Of course, yes. I'm comfortable here, don't worry. I'm perfectly fine. Thank you," Tanya responded automatically.

She felt so bitter in spirit! But why? She arrived at the paid beach early in the morning, chose a good spot near the water and paid for the entrance, a sunbed, and an umbrella to enjoy only three days in Odessa. She had been working so hard and saving every penny to come there. And what did she get? The company wanted to stay together, but Tanya was alone, so why not just move her? Those people needed space more than she did.

It is so selfish to protest, ruin everyone's mood, make scandals, and demand. It's ugly in certain ways. It is shameful to be offended, and it is inconvenient to stand up for yourself.

But she didn't protest.

Not annoyed and not offended. She was feeling quite comfortable, humbly sitting by the fence, listening to the noise of the street instead the roar of the surf. Was it bad there? No. The sea was nearby, she could go swimming, and the sun was shining brightly. Even ships and seagulls were visible. Sometimes. She could fantasize about things she couldn't see while sitting next to the
toilet.

How despicable it is to do this to good, humble people. Only such persons are treated that way. When the rude man opens his mouth, everyone moves fast, smiles condescendingly, and hurries around. Just to make the jerk feel comfortable.

And people like Tanya are always given spoiled fruit, expired yogurts, and stale towels. They are asked to change positions, relocate, or move over a little from their comfortable seat, pre-booked and pre-paid in advance.

And they also say it directly to your face:
"Others need it more than you do. You don't mind, do you? No offense."

> But you don't have to put up with it! And if you honestly paid for your seat, arrived first, made an agreement, or took a turn, you don't have to leave.

Yes, you have to learn it. Learn to sit according to the ticket you purchased and demand everything that is promised on the price list. No, there's no need to make a fuss, and it won't work without a lot of practice.

You must explain calmly and confidently to those who took your place that you intentionally bought a ticket near the window, on the lower shelf, in a room with a window overlooking the sea, and not with a view of the construction site. And that you ordered freshly squeezed juice for breakfast and not the juice from a box, which was brought to you at the price of freshly squeezed juice.

Otherwise, you'll spend your life next to a concrete fence and a toilet, having paid as much for it as a five-star hotel room.

The War
This is relevant even now. Always relevant.

FIVE WAYS TO SELL WITHOUT DISCOUNTS

"For a long time, I had been paying close attention to the children's books and games sold by one woman. And then I got ready for the purchase. Delivery was free for orders above 500 UAH [*translator's note: Ukrainian currency*]. I chose three books worth 420 UAH. Then I asked what games were available so that the total cost was 500 UAH, and immediately received the following answer: "With a discount, it will be 395 UAH." And I thought that there was still a long way to get to 500 UAH. Therefore, I did not select any other products. If they hadn't written about a discount (which I didn't even think about!), I would have taken their goods for 500 UAH. People simply lost 105 UAH "out of the blue". Obviously, they haven't read your books ☺" — I receive dozens of similar messages every day.

Doesn't it remind you of something?

And they also write: "Discounts attract customers and increase sales".

Right! Your constant discounts and sales are rather causing you to lose customers and your reputation. However, they attract freeloaders rather than those who truly appreciate and enjoy what you do.

So, what should you do?
- Just say "No" when asked for a discount. However, explain that you are setting a fair price from the start and what is included in it.
- Offer a cheaper alternative: a different collection, configuration, or color.
- If clients compare you with competitors that are cheaper, don't freak out; instead, tell them exactly what you will

deliver for your price. Maybe you'll provide more and of better quality. And the clients are not even aware of that. Convey it to them!

- Instead of a discount, offer a bonus: give something as a gift for a certain amount of the order or if payment is received within two hours. This significantly increases sales and loyalty: someone has asked about a discount, and you are prepared to reply and demonstrate how it can be accomplished right away.
- If you really need money or if you are asked about illiquidity, then a discount can be made. But there must be a reason behind this. A solid reason, not "just for you". Do not offer it out of the blue, as in the first example, when the customer had not even considered asking for a reduction.

OFFICIAL WARNING

This is what was written to me in a private chat. If I didn't cease inviting people to my event, I would be disgraced and kicked out of the entrepreneurial community.

I was conducting the training on their premises. Free of charge. That was going to be my first big open training session. That was in 2013. I had just completed my first business coaching course.

There were 90 seats in the hall, and there was zero PR. My future in a new profession depended on how many people would come to me, and whether they would come at all.

"The organizers don't invite people? Then I'll go and do it myself." I began a crazy activity: I began writing, calling, and inviting people. Everyone who heard about this training for the first time thanked me and registered themselves, their colleagues, and their friends right away. In two days, I recruited 120 people for 90 spots. Chairs had to be brought from all offices. That infuriated the organizers. They decided to press me.

"But who exactly does she think she is? What does she allow herself? Experienced colleagues do not do this: if there are three people in the hall, there are three, and nothing can be done. It is simply unheard of to personally invite people to your event! Selling yourself is so arrogant!"

Bullying began in the chat room. What a flurry of tomatoes the organizers and colleagues hurled at me! I couldn't sleep for a week. I kept thinking: "Maybe they're right: who am I? What am I allowing myself? How dare I impose and declare myself so loudly?"

And then I asked myself: "What is my sin? Is it the fact that I single-handedly gathered people for this business community and hosted a fun event for free? This is a plus for them because everything is under their brand. A lot of appreciation, and all of the reviews are excellent, but it irritates them even more".

Then I realized:

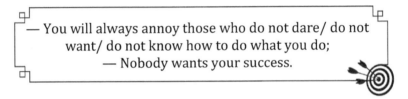

— You will always annoy those who do not dare/ do not want/ do not know how to do what you do;
— Nobody wants your success.

What should you do? Work for yourself and other people, not for haters.

10 years have passed.

What happened to that business community? The founders feuded and threw mud at each other for years, like they once did to me. Oh, the number of comments on my social media posts about them! People immediately began writing the name of the group, and it appeared that not only I, but everyone else present, was treated that way.

Where are the enraged former colleagues now? They have become irrelevant or work for food in order to stay in business.

Where are those who attended my first training? They have been my friends, partners, and clients up until now.

Where am I? In the Wikipedia, the mass media, the best forums and projects, trips to 50 countries, my own Entrepreneurs'

Club "Sales with Joy", all of my dreams have come true, and two of my books have become national bestsellers.

Sometimes I wonder: "Where would I be if I were afraid of hate, an "official warning", and didn't gather so many people for my first training on my own?"

STOP IT, IT'S DEFINITELY NOT YOURS!

Your reaction to hate is a measure of loyalty to yourself and your business. If negativity from close and distant people ("...that's not how you live, work, communicate, sell, look, or help Ukraine" and so on) forces you to stop and betray your business, it's NOT YOUR BUSINESS!

We are all reflections of others. And if someone sees something "SUCH" in these mirrors that makes them want to smash them, that does not mean that the problem is with us, but rather with them.

Hate is the problem of the person who hates. It's not about you; it's about them. This is their cry for help: "I'm so sick that I can't tell if someone is okay. And I want justice: I want others to be as bad as I am."

And if you are hated, you are not a victim. You are a savior. If they didn't write you some trash, maybe they would go somewhere and hurt or even beat someone! And that is how you saved so many people by taking on this cyber-attack.

If you only knew how many people I save every day! What messages I haven't gotten!

The War
And since February 24 [translator's note: the start of a full-scale war in Ukraine], I have been receiving "wishes" that missiles would hit my house, among other things. Why? Because I teach how to sell. How to sell without discounts. And sell during wartime.

Question: if I annoy you so much and don't share your views and values, why are you following me? Unsubscribe and block! But no! They spend their lives doing the following: they follow, enter from other accounts to read, observe, and write how horrible I am.

But I know how to work with it! I even wrote the book "When to Say "YES": How to Believe in Yourself and React to Negativity" (which was named the Best Book of Ukraine in 2020). That demonstrates how relevant the topic is to people.

For you: If a hater's comment makes you feel so bad that you want to quit and shut down, then just quit.

Stop it, it's not yours. You did not pass the strength and dedication test. It happens.

A moment of demotivation: there is no such job where everything is perfect: you have an office near your house, the salary is great, your colleagues and clients are ideal, it's interesting to work there, and you have to work only two hours a week at a time convenient for you.

Well, it doesn't happen like that. This world constantly tests our strength. And hate is one of the methods to test how ready we are for challenges. How our business is OUR business.

And how ready we are to fight for what we believe in.

A FATAL BEGINNER'S MISTAKE AND HOW TO FIX IT

How many experts (psychologists, handymen, confectioners, designers, make-up artists, and especially beauticians) write about themselves that they are just beginners!

And some even emphasize this. They say: "Look, I'm just learning (or just got certified) and now I'm just a beginner, my prices are low, so everyone please make an appointment with me."

I wrote something like that. And what happened, did the customers run to me? No. By doing this, you exhibit not merely your lack of experience.

But also, the fact that you do not have self-confidence.

Customers interpret it as follows:
— you are not confident in your skills;
— you are unsure of your price.

Will someone want to come to you and pay you money (even if it's not much yet) so that you can use them to learn and master your skills? No one.

Yes, they don't know about you yet. And you also do everything possible to undermine trust in you.

Of course, a person with self-respect, especially one who has money, will seek out an experienced specialist. Or, at the very least, someone who does not include the phrases "beginner" or "studying at..." in their profile description and every post on social media.

You yourself did everything so that a person turned to a competitor. The same one that studied with you. And he wasn't any better than you, in fact, exactly the opposite. It's just that he didn't write this "beginner" word, so he has clients, and the prices are reasonable from the start.

And you did write that you are a beginner, as if trying to be an honest person. You charge three kopecks for your work (translator's note: "kopecks" refer to the fractional currency units used in Ukraine, equivalent to "cents"). And now you're wondering why no one wants to pay you even these.

So, what should be done? How to persuade others to choose you if you're a beginner?
1. Write clearly what you are doing — the first, second, and third.
2. Who is your product aimed at (schoolchildren, mothers on maternity leave, women who want to get married, etc.)?
3. Your results over the last six months or one month of work (since you began your activity).
   For example, 300 hats were sewn and sold in five Ukrainian cities within a month of the start of the activity.
4. A beautiful story of why you decided to do this.
   For example:
   • 33 years old is the age when I returned to my childhood dream of becoming an artist;

- after giving birth, I lost 26 kg in six months and now I pass on my experience and training to others.
  Write from the heart, as though to a close friend who would ask why you decided to do what you do.
5. Stop calling yourself a beginner, writing "I'm pleasantly surprised that you decided to subscribe to my page" in thank-you messages for subscribing (That's horrible!).
6. Set appropriate prices from the start.
7. Read my books and join my online club "Sales with Joy" to learn more.

And I will become your mother, as the participants write in their reviews.

I'M A LOSER

How I wished I could just fall through the earth from that old, worn-out chair I was sitting in! Because of what, exactly? Because of my cheap tracksuit, the shabby rental flat, and the scruffy table where the woman was looking at the jewelry I was selling at the time. Suddenly, I looked at all this through her eyes, and I was overcome by such despair!

It was my first close encounter with such wealth.

The banker's wife, well-groomed and dressed in expensive branded clothes, with expensive perfume, arrived in a new Mercedes with a driver (he also arrived 20 minutes earlier because she had given him the task of making sure everything was ok, because she was going to an unfamiliar place, and there were no mobile phones yet).

How did she end up in my poor kitchen?

Her husband, the director of a well-known bank, decided to give his wife a present, but let her choose it herself. So she came to me to pick out some jewelry.

I couldn't get the words out of myself, I couldn't stop thinking what a loser I was. And when she left, I started crying hysterically. No, not because of envy. But because I realized that I would never have anything similar, no matter how hard I tried:

neither luxury items, nor a Mercedes with a driver, nor trips abroad. I would never even have my own house! Where was I supposed to get it? My husband had a salary of $45 a month *[translator's note: it was quite an average salary in Ukraine during that time]*, which had not been paid in six months, and I was walking the streets selling handcrafted jewelry.

How bitterly I cried then!

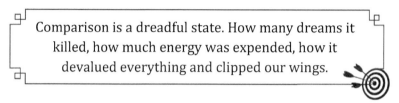

Comparison is a dreadful state. How many dreams it killed, how much energy was expended, how it devalued everything and clipped our wings.

We look at other people's happiness, success, wealth, and recognition and conclude that we are losers who will never achieve these things in our lives.

And then one time my husband Serhii came home from work and said:

"Do not compare yourself to those who have achieved more. Look at those who have much less than you. Look what a hellhole you escaped!

For a long time, we couldn't afford to rent an apartment, so we lived with our parents. I even brought bread home from work to save money. But for two months now we have been on our own: we live separately, like kings, in the warmth, right in the heart of the city.

And how many of my colleagues and your friends are suffering in cold dormitories with one toilet on the entire floor? Even with small children.

And we've made it.

The fridge is full, there is no need to bring bread from work. Oh, we even had red caviar for New Year's! It is enough to go to the movies, the theater, or simply go see our friends by taxi.

What a wonderful family we have. You have me, I have you,

we have Anya. How many lonely people exist in the world, who have no one to even argue with? And we have — we quarrel frequently.

So, you are not a loser. On the contrary, you have done quite well. You are our driving force; you never give up and you are not afraid of anything. The most hardworking and purposeful person I have ever met!

Your customers love and respect you. Otherwise, why else would that banker send his wife to you? What, there aren't any stores? More than enough! But they buy from you.

And if that millionaire decided that you were an empty place, unworthy of her attention, she would not have spent a single minute communicating with you, she would have left immediately, and definitely would not have bought from you.

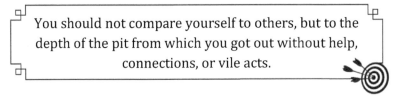

You should not compare yourself to others, but to the depth of the pit from which you got out without help, connections, or vile acts.

Look into the past. Take a look at how far you've come! Praise yourself for it. You have managed it? So, you can do even more. Set goals and move forward.

Our best days lie ahead!" Serhii promised me exactly 23 years ago.

"Our best days lie ahead!" I promised myself.

"Our best days lie ahead!" you promise yourself.

Stop and count your victories, applaud yourself, and rejoice for yourself. You already have so much that you didn't have before: experience, knowledge, self-respect, friends, and a hobby.

The War
Even if everything you worked so hard for is lost, tell yourself: "I've earned it in the past, and I'll earn it again."

And boldly move towards your dreams.

HOW TO PROPERLY UNDRESS IN FRONT OF A MAN?

- Allow the dress to fall by itself and then bend over it;
- don't take off your dress over your head, it's unsightly;
- watch your facial expression — it should be relaxed.

Do you have any idea what this is? These are instructions "How to Undress Correctly in Front of a Man", LIFE magazine, 1937.

As soon as I get into the shower, the air raid siren goes off. Sitting in the corridor between two walls, I reach for my phone and find the following in the "pre-war" notes: two ladies are undressing in the photo. One does it elegantly and professionally, while the other, like most of us, does it hastily. Especially now.

To save marriages, the "School of Undressing" advertises five classes for $5 ($30 course). 1937. The Great Depression (1929-1939) was the biggest economic crisis in the United States, with people going hungry. And they have insane bargains on undressing courses! I freaked out.

In my Instagram stories, I asked if my followers would attend such courses now. 48% of respondents answered that they would go!

The reason is "to feel alive".

And you tell me that no one needs your goods or services? Let people feel alive, worthy, and solvent. Become a resource for them, a place where they can pay for even those things they could get for free. Like coffee, hot meals, psychological help, or online English lessons. People pay for all these. So let them pay you too.

Resume work (if you haven't already), and earn for yourself and victory.

What joy it is to earn money while helping volunteers and the front!

It's over. The air raid alert has ended. I'm going to take a shower.

I will practice undressing gracefully.

THE IMPOSSIBLE DOESN'T EXIST, DOES IT?

"On the given date, there are no free seats in the system for travel between the specified stations," stubbornly displayed all railway Internet resources and offered tickets from Kyiv to Lviv in only three days.

They made me laugh! If I had believed everyone who told me there were no opportunities — no places, time, money, inspiration — or who said "I'll think about it", "It's impossible", "It won't work", "It's not yours", 'Nobody needs it", "You're doing everything wrong", and named another 101 reasons why I couldn't succeed in what I set out to do, where would I be now?

Well, if Internet resources don't help me, I should try to negotiate with living people. And so, in half an hour we're chatting with a very sexy cashier guy at the Kyiv railway station:

"Please, the nearest train to Lviv, one lower compartment seat."
"The next train to Lviv is only in three days."
"Then give me the one that's available: a first-class ticket, or in the conductor's cabin," I persist, somewhat annoying a huge queue I've just stood in.
"Girl, you probably can't hear me: there aren't any tickets to Lviv — neither "skipping along" nor "squatting" – for today and tomorrow, only in three days."

The cashier guy in front of me scores points for patience and addressing a lady well over 40, that is, me, as "girl".

I'm experienced, and I myself teach people that the first rule of a salesperson is to never give up after the first "No," and to always work out at least three refusals. I'm making a third attempt, this time using the "address the client by their name" method.

Assume you are, for example, Olya. You are walking down the street when suddenly someone shouts: "Olyaaa!" What are all the Olyas doing? That's right, they turn around. Why? A person's name instantly draws attention to the person who said it. Conclusion? Always address people by their first names to gain their favor and make significant progress toward your goals.

But how do you find out the cashier's name?
I look at his "Ukrzaliznytsya" *[Ukrainian railroad company]* badge — half dark blue, half yellow. His last name is easy to read, but his first name is not. Only the first letter is clearly visible — "A."

I have only a second to make a decision (the queue is already starting to get unruly due to the delay). Since we speak russian, I assume that the guy's name is Alexander *[Ukrainian name would be Oleksandr, starting with an "O"]*.

I lie down with my chest right on the cash register, look him straight in the eyes, and talk in a low, deep voice (I fool myself into thinking I'm sexy).

"Dear Sasha! *[Sasha is a diminutive form of Alexander]* I really need to be in Lviv tomorrow morning. Please find me a ticket! Will you find it?" — I do "the closing". Everything is the same as it is in sales. You don't just show and tell; instead, you take it and ask the client: "Are you placing an order? Shall I write a check?"
"And what makes you think I'm Sasha?" he enters the dialogue! He doesn't tell me to get lost. Cool! I build on my success.
"I saw it on your badge. I have excellent vision."

I also want to add that I am an expert in negotiations and a leading business coach in Ukraine. But I restrained myself. Modesty is my strong point.

"And I'm not Sasha," says my very sexy cashier. "I'm Arthur."

Loud laughter in the queue. Epic fail and public failure. But not mine.

"How fortunate that you are Arthur and not Sasha! Arthur suits you much better," I make one last attempt. "Please find me a ticket, I have to be in Lviv tomorrow morning!"

Impressed by my unprecedented audacity, and perhaps by my charisma and the fact that I'm a beautiful woman ☺, Sasha-Arthur writes down my name and asks me to come over in 15 minutes.

With a sense of accomplishment, I leave the cash register. And the queue, like a single organism, observes all this with curiosity and envy.
It doesn't matter if the guy finds me a ticket or not — I did everything that depended on me. Namely: I overcame refusal three times, addressed by name, and demonstrated stress resistance skills in a non-standard situation. I worked the client 100%. I mean, the cashier, Sasha-Arthur.

Well played!

But, in order to close the gestalt, as psychology teaches, and ultimately go to plan "B" (looking for an alternative way to get to Lviv urgently), I make my way through the queue in 15 minutes to ask the friendly cashier about the outcome of his search.

And here — attention! — he hands me a ticket for the train that leaves in half an hour. Seat in the lower compartment. No additional fees. No bribes. With a smile and best wishes for a pleasant journey.

I'm sitting alone in the compartment. And this is at a time when there were no free tickets at all even for money.

Here's "On the given date, there are no free seats in the system for travel between the specified stations". Here are sales skills.

The impossible does not exist. There is only the power of your conviction and your faith in yourself and others.

CHAPTER 2

A SAVING RENOVATION AND FAMILY TREASURES

When my father died, I could not stay in the apartment where he lived. It was my parents' house, where I grew up, and where my grandmother and grandfather had added another room after much labor and numerous trades.

I simply couldn't stay there. I could physically feel his pain and despair when he had been paralyzed for five years following a stroke, losing his speech and mobility. It was heartbreaking to see one of the most educated and brilliant speakers I had ever known suffering this way, and I had been fighting for him desperately.

The support of my followers and virtual friends worked wonders. Strangers shared my post with the words "Christmas miracle in Lviv" after I wrote about it on social media. This is something I wrote about in my book "Start Saying NO".

I remember how my heart broke when, in a moment of clarity, my father desperately wanted to say something to me, but he couldn't; when he crying from weakness.

Even after five years of his illness, I didn't expect to be so affected by his death. I was preparing for it by reading a lot, praying, and communicating with the right people. But when he died, especially in the first weeks, it felt as if my heart had been ripped out of my chest.

I didn't write about the fact that he was gone. I didn't tell anyone, nor did I post anything on social media. I don't even remember the day of the funeral clearly.

Only five days following his death I spoke at a large forum. I couldn't cancel my participation and let people down, since all the tickets had been sold, and people were coming from all over Ukraine. Only after my speech, did I tell the organizers about my loss. For several months, I felt as if I was living with an empty chest, devoid of feelings and emotions.

I kept my shell occupied with sports, going to the hairdresser, buying new things, and gushing on live broadcasts and at conferences, conducting training sessions, appearing in the media, managing all the projects, and politely smiling at my neighbors. It was like performing in one actor's stage, the game of someone who had nothing to complain about. But I couldn't go into my parents' apartment without feeling sick. Things couldn't go on like this forever.

Psychology describes three reactions of a living being under stress: fight, flight, and freeze.

It just doesn't work for me. I always have one reaction to stress that gets me out of hopeless situations in business and in life — action. Not even this, but more accurately: ACT!

And so I started to act, studying everything about making the home a place of happiness and strength, and put it all into action by starting a large-scale renovation.

HOW TO CLEAN AND REVITALIZE YOUR HOME

- Do you ever misplace things or documents? Can't seem to find anything in time? Do you remember where you put the charger, keys, glasses, and TV remote control; you've gone around everything five times and still can't see them, even though they lie in a prominent place?

- Are you oppressed by the atmosphere itself, do you find any reason, conscious or subconscious, not to stay at home?

- Do you lose your temper, fight over trivial things, get exhausted and tired, even though you haven't done anything in particular?

- You just cleaned and everything is dusty immediately after, the freshly washed dishes do not appear clean to the touch, an unpleasant odor haunts you no matter how much you air it out; flowers wither, pets get sick, and you can't get rid of the odors on your own?

- Do appliances suddenly stop working or frequently break down, do dishes begin to break, and do the pictures begin to fall from the walls?

If you answered "YES" to at least one of these questions, your home is sick and needs to be treated immediately.

The first thing I noticed were my parents' old possessions. The closets were filled with clothes from both my father and my mother, who died 15 years ago. She died as a result of a serious illness. Cancer.

Then there were books. A huge library. Books, covered with thick dust, were everywhere: on shelves, in cabinets, closets, on the floor, and in corridors.

So, what was I going to do with them?

And so, on one Internet resource, I read a comparison and felt as though I had been shocked.

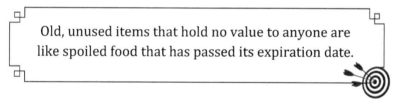

Old, unused items that hold no value to anyone are like spoiled food that has passed its expiration date.

Yes, throwing away food is a sin, but only while it is food. After all, when you throw away rotten meat, you are not throwing away food, but a dead product that is hazardous to one's health.

If you don't wear the things, if you don't read the books, they will generate negativity, the energy of stagnation and destruction. You need to get rid of them. But how? I couldn't bring myself to throw them out.

What did I come up with? With respect and affection, I spoke to each thing, to each book (it's a good thing that no one witnessed this since they would have thought I was insane. Or maybe I am ☺). I put them in boxes.

I went to the site where second-hand booksellers gathered.

There is one location in Lviv beside the Ivan Fedorov monument on Pidvalna Street. I made all the arrangements with the men. There was just one condition: I didn't need money, they could sell for as much as they wanted as long as they took everything. The men fought for me, so inspired by my offer! Everything was taken away the same day, and they thanked me profusely for contacting them. Within a week, I saw my books being actively bought by people who really needed them. One by one, the books found new homes where they were read and enjoyed.

I donated the typewriters used by my parents, who were art critics, to a book museum at one of Lviv's libraries. And children on field trips take turns having something typed on them.

And I took all of the clothing to collection points for the needy, where they also thanked me and immediately distributed it.

It was not easy. But I felt relief and joy from the recuperation of the apartment, which had been inhabited only by disease and death for so long.

And I also wrote a list of things to do to keep the house calm and cozy. So that the house takes care of you and protects you, and you protect it. It doesn't matter if it's your home or an apartment that you rent, even if only for a short time.

Use it!
1. Find your place of strength. Determine where you feel most comfortable, where you want to sit, lie down, and stand, and where you want to rest and recharge. It is the heart of your home. It should not be cluttered, and each resident should have his or her own place.
2. Don't bring problems home. Don't fight, don't curse anyone, let alone each other. Don't get angry at your loved ones if someone ruins your mood. They are your rock and support.
3. Repair or discard broken items immediately. Otherwise, they block the flow of light energy and weaken you. Make sure that all of your household items are up-to-date and that you use them regularly. Do not accumulate unnecessary things and clothing. Don't buy too much.
4. There must be guests. But not all the time. If there are too many of them, they exhaust both you and your home. Don't invite

toxic, envious, and problematic people. You don't need people who sit around for hours and complain about life, gossip, slander, and tell you how bad things are and will only get worse. But you can't do without guests. People should come and bring new energy.

Surprisingly, this is the most challenging part of the process for me. I had not invited anyone to my home for many years. I am an introvert. Moreover, I am experiencing communication overload at work. So, I made a decision: I will invite people, and I myself will finally begin visiting friends. At least I will try, what if I succeed? Spoiler alert: it didn't work 😊.

5. When you get home, change into clean and tidy home clothing. Decorate, clean, and ventilate your home. It shows respect for the space where you live. And get rid of resentment, complaints, and negative thoughts.

A HANDSOME FELLOW STUDENT, A COUNT'S HUNT, AND ANTLERS IN A DUMP

When you start doing something right, fate gives you signs of what to do next.

As I was walking down the street, I ran into a fellow student I hadn't seen in years, and the encounter immediately surprised and intrigued me. In my book "When to Say "YES," I wrote about a classmate who mismanaged all of the opportunities that fate gave him. In just a few years, the man I once knew as a lonely, lost, and unemployed drunkard, who had lost his family and job due to his addiction, had transformed into an imposing and well-groomed gentleman. As I walked down the street, he honked at me from his luxury car, and I was amazed by the positive changes in him.

Honestly, I didn't recognize him! And when I did, I canceled all my plans and eagerly accepted his invitation for coffee. I'm glad I did because our conversation not only caught me up on his incredible transformation, but it also inspired me with new ideas for my own life.

"Antlers, deer antlers! They were the reason why my grandfather and my father died at the age of 50. I know, I know, you don't believe in any kind of palmistry, but neither did I until I miraculously stopped within a hair's breadth of the abyss," Sashko told me in one of Lviv's cafés. He was speaking so emotionally and loudly that the people at the adjacent tables stopped talking and focused solely on us.

"Quieter," I asked him, "because we'll have to sell tickets for our table."

"Look who's asking me to speak more quietly! It is you who speaks so that you can be heard on the other side of Lviv. And during conferences, the electricity goes out when you pick up the microphone."

"You know it all!" I laughed and listened to him with a predatory writer's excitement: here's the story I must tell in a new book.

"Back in the day, a so-called *surreptitious placement** was used to harm someone. But now you don't even need to place anything surreptitiously. Over and over, we bring into our homes what causes conflicts, divorces, and losses. And sometimes it takes away health and even life. That's exactly what my grandfather did. In his youth, he once killed a deer while hunting. He personally cut the antlers from the deer's skull and hung them in the bedroom above the bed. Since then, all of our family's troubles began. When I accidentally came across an article about it on the Internet, I sobered up. And you know how I would drink myself to death in recent years, I lost practically everything. Antlers cut from a killed animal bring disease and trouble into the home. That's how we lived. No matter what we did, it only got worse. I took them off the wall and threw them away the same day I read that article. I said to myself: "That's it. The bad luck streak in my life is over. Evil has left the house. Nothing can stop me now." I quit drinking, found a good job, started earning money, and improved my relationship with my wife and son.

[*surreptitious placement *is when someone places a cursed object in someone else's home or near a house so that another person comes into contact with it inadvertently and becomes sick or unlucky, etc. There are cursed objects in the form of gifts. From an energetic point of view, a thrown thing affects your circle of reality, carrying negative vibrations and harming the energy of the house and its inhabitants.]

I listened attentively, ready to launch into my favorite spiel about self-hypnosis and the ineffectiveness of a curse or the evil eye on those who don't believe in them. But just as the words were about to spill out, a vivid image flashed before my eyes: the massive deer antlers that had hung in our corridor for as long as I could remember.

It made my skin crawl. On top of that, I remembered my father's story about the count, the owner of our house. He cut the antlers from the deer's skull with his own hands. It was after the hunt in 1939. Six months later, he was repressed by the soviet authorities, which had just arrived in pre-war Lviv.

And everything was taken from his wife, the countess, leaving only half of one room in the entire three-story building. There she lived into her old age — in an apartment that became a congregative housing. Her neighbors were my grandmother and grandfather, and three other families who shared one kitchen and one toilet.

In less than half an hour, I was removing big deer antlers from the wall. And within an hour they were taken away by my friend, a restoration artist, who arrived very quickly after listening to my perplexing story about a fellow student who had been an alcoholic but then transformed into a handsome man, about the hunt and a repressed count, negative energy, curse, and how I was treating my home.

CAMELS, ELEPHANTS, GLOBAL CLIMATE CHANGE, AND MOTIVATION

As I immersed myself in the renovation, I also delved into the history of the house and the street it stood on.

Lysenko Street (formerly known as Kurkowa Street) marked the beginning of the Glynianskyi tract, a road to the east that linked Lviv with Kyiv and saw the transport of goods by horses, oxen, donkeys, and even camels. These desert animals were used by Eastern merchants to bring their wares to Lviv, including spices, fabrics, carpets, weapons, and jewelry. How did they tolerate our climate? I'm talking about camels now. Easily! In the desert, where they come from, the weather is quite severe: during the day the heat is crazy, then, it's freezing cold at night. But camels don't care: their fur saves them. And there is nothing to be surprised about camels in Lviv. Elephants roamed Ukrainian cities and villages during the 18th-century Russo-Turkish wars.

Notes from Kalabukha

In the Battle of Khotyn (1621), between the combined forces of the Rzeczpospolita and Ukrainian Kozaks on the one hand, and the army of the Ottoman Empire on the other, the Turks had thousands of camel riders and four war elephants.

The goal was to demoralize and intimidate the enemy.

Elephants were carefully trained for military operations to trample the enemy with their feet, fling them with their tusks, snap with their trunks, and throw them to the ground.

Elephants were the tanks that could destroy strongholds back then. They went into battle only when irritated, so to achieve that, they were sprayed with red wine or mulberry juice.

Only the high banks of the Dniester and the deep ravines did not contribute to the combat performance of these exotics. The poor camels had nowhere to flee, so thousands of them died in the cannon rush. And no one was afraid of the elephants. They also ate a lot. When losing a battle, especially on the enemy territory, the priority was to feed yourself first.

In short, the Turk's campaign was unsuccessful, so after the peace treaty was signed, Sultan Osman II gave one of the elephants to the Polish prince Władysław (probably this was his little revenge: remember the joke about the elephant being sold?) and the rest of the elephants walked back to Turkey.

Elephants and camels as part of the combat units of the Turkish army in the 18th century roamed Ukraine already during the Russo-Turkish wars. Therefore, it is not surprising that they were depicted even on tiles in village houses.

On the slope where my house now stands, grapes were

grown in the 13th and 14th centuries. And the wine that was made from it was well-known throughout Europe. The climate in Lviv was similar to that of Transcarpathia during the time.

During my research, I came across two fascinating facts about the history of the house or street that wowed me.

Fact 1. Global climate change is commonplace for the planet

There are various factors contributing to it. These factors include:

1. Changes in the size, relief, and relative location of continents, oceans, and ocean currents.

2. Changes in the activity of the Sun, as well as parameters of the Earth's orbit and axis.

3. Volcanic activity.

4. Human activity, such as rapid global warming observed in the last 100 years, has been a significant contributor to climate change.

However, in the past, only those factors that did not depend on human activity had an impact as there were fewer people, and it was not possible for them to destroy the planet as they are doing now. Nevertheless, humans who lived in the past actively destroyed forests, which covered 99% of the Lviv Oblast's territory, by burning and uprooting them in order to have arable land and a place to build settlements.

It is fascinating to note that in the eighth century, the Black Sea froze, and sleighs traveled to Constantinople and the Caucasus. It was mentioned in Byzantine, Arab, and Western European chronicles.

Furthermore, as Europe got warmer in the 12th and 13th centuries, people began to collect more crops and eat better, which is considered to be the root cause of feudal fragmentation. As small farms could provide for themselves, they had much less reason to unite, seek protection from stronger ones, and obey them.

In contrast, the 15th century got colder, causing Tatar attacks on Lviv due to harsh winters and massive loss of livestock.

Nomads lacked food, so they went wherever they could find it.

However, the climate warmed up again until the beginning of the 19th century, when the so-called volcanic winter began.

Fact 2. A rehearsal for nuclear winter, cholera, and the birth of Vampires

In 1816, spring did not come in Europe and North America. The snow remained until June. And then it rained continuously for 130 days. After that, frost and winter returned.

People slaughtered livestock because there was no food. The sun was red and dim enough that you could look at it without averting your eyes.

The result was crop failures, famine, social unrest, and migration.

"The End of the World and God's Punishment for the Sins and Horrors of the Napoleonic Wars," was published in newspapers, announced in churches, mosques, cathedrals, and synagogues, and discussed in country inns and noble salons all over the world.

No one suspected that the cause of these climatic anomalies was the 1815 eruption of the Tambora volcano on one of Indonesia's islands, the strongest and most devastating in the history of mankind. The island of Sumbawa was buried under a thick layer of volcanic ash and became known as the Pompeii of Asia.

And the year 1816 went down in history as the "year without a summer", ushering in the 10-year Little Ice Age, which researchers in the twenty-first century referred to as a rehearsal for the nuclear winter.

Here are some of its consequences for humanity:

Cholera pandemic
While Europe and the United States were freezing, a dreadful drought in India provoked tremendous reproduction of

the cholera bacillus, resulting in the first cholera outbreak outside the peninsula, which reached Europe, Japan, and the United States in the 1830s.

Since then, millions of people around the world have been regularly mowed down. It was in Odesa in 1970 (just as my mother arrived there to rest and was quarantined), and now the Telegram channels are spreading fear with reports of cholera outbreaks in Mariupol.

The invention of the bicycle
The price of oats, which were used to feed horses, increased sevenfold due to crop failures. This prompted the inventor Karl Drais to create and patent the contemporary bicycle prototype, which was the first step toward the mechanization of personal transportation.

Mineral fertilizers
Justus von Liebig, a chemist who survived childhood poverty, devoted his life to the productivity of plants and synthesized the first mineral fertilizers in history.

The birth of vampires and Frankenstein
Lord Byron and his four friends were resting on the shores of Lake Geneva. Locked in the house by prolonged rains, they were amusing themselves by making up horror stories. This is how Byron's personal physician, Polidori, wrote the first story about vampires — immortal creatures that drink human blood. But he published it under the name of Byron, the most famous writer in Europe at that time. The book was a wild success, and Polidori's vampire launched the entire literary genre of romantic bloodsuckers. Without him, there would be no Dracula, no Twilight, and no Halloween costumes.

And 19-year-old Mary Shelley made up a story about a scientist who, with the help of galvanic electricity, revived a body composed of corpse fragments. And so the monster set out to explore the world in search of love and friendship. This is how Frankenstein was born, and with it the genres of science fiction and horror.

What were the consequences of the "year without summer"

for the future Lysenko Street? Grapes would never grow on its slopes due to chilly temperature, but active construction began. My house was supposed to be built first.

But what of cooling or warming! Every two years, there was some war — a conflict between Turks, Tatars, Swedes, Cossacks, and feudal disunities. Meanwhile, plagues and epidemics claimed the lives of up to 70% of the population!

And people continued to build, with some projects taking decades or even centuries to finish. Remarkably, many of these structures still stand without requiring renovation, despite the fact that life expectancy did not surpass 30 years for much of human history until the beginning of the 19th century. What motivated people to undertake such monumental tasks, and how did they achieve such enduring results? I believe the following factors played a role:

- faith in God;
- the understanding that every house and temple should be a fortress, capable of withstanding enemy sieges and protecting future generations.

The act of creation itself was a great resource for people. It provided a sense of accomplishment, inspiration, and even immortality, and served as a guarantee of survival. Perhaps, like myself during my greatest challenges, these builders were saved by their willingness to take action.

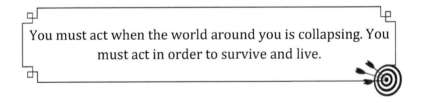

You must act when the world around you is collapsing. You must act in order to survive and live.

I felt such support and unity with these people — predecessors on this earth. Time has passed. The past and the future are cemented in the HERE and NOW. Nothing changes. We must go forward, build temples and houses, sow fields, plant gardens, and believe in our immortality, just as they sowed and planted, built and believed.

BRICKS AND HIGHLY PAID TAPPERS

In order to get rid of the odors of medicines, diseases, and troubles that had become ingrained in the walls over time, I decided to scrub everything down to the very brick. Do you know that according to the new Ukrainian orthography you shouldn't say "*штукатурені стіни*" ["*shtukatureni stiny*" — "*plastered walls*"], but "*тиньковані стіни*" ["*tynkovani stiny*" — "*drywall-covered walls*"]? Not a "*штукатур*" ["*shtukatur*" — "*plasterer*"], but a "*тинькар*" ["*tynkar*" — "*drywaller*"]? Such a colorful old word. I really like it. Now you know.

And so, I discovered new treasures in my apartment that had previously been tightly plastered over. That is, drywall-covered. And a new story.

Notes from Kalabukha
Bricks have been known to mankind for 10,000 years. It was created and used in those places where natural stone was unavailable. Do you remember the textbook on the history of the Ancient World? That's right, it was used in ancient Babylon. It was there that the term "kirpich" ["a brick"] was originally used to refer to artificial stone, which was made in the form of clay bars. This word has remained practically unchanged in the russian language.
While the Ukrainian term "tsehla" ["a brick"] is borrowed from the German word "ziegel" (a brick; a roof tile) — which comes from the Latin word "tēgula" — "to cover".

And what a rich vocabulary it has brought!
- *"tsehelnia" [a brickyard] — a place where bricks are mined or manufactured;*
- *"tsehelnyk", "tsehliar" [a bricklayer] — a specialist who makes bricks;*
- *"tsehelnykivna" — a brickmaker's daughter. (How romantic, right? Almost like a "tsarivna" [a princess]);*
- *"tsehelnychenko" — a bricklayer's son;*
- *"tsehelnychka" — a bricklayer's wife.*

I would never have guessed and would have thought that "tsehelnychka" was the name of some kind of tool like a lighter a lighter is "zapalnychka" [in Ukrainian]. Although, maybe those "tsehelnychkas" were "spitfires" and were saving their mental health. Try living with a bricklayer and a bunch of bricklayer's children. Especially at the brickyard.

The first bricks were sun-dried piles of river silt left behind after the flood. Then raw bricks appeared — they were made of mixed clay, firewood, straw, and animal manure. It is this material that is still used everywhere from Peru to Morocco.

But for complex building structures, fired bricks are needed. They have been used since ancient times. Even in each Roman legion, there was a mobile furnace for the production of bricks, from which they were building structures in the most remote corners of the empire. And how well they were built! Those structures still stand today.

How were bricks made in Galicia? Clay was mixed, poured into molds, and dried. But not in direct sunlight — in the shade, and not in a draft, since the bricks would crack. Then they were baked for several hours in special ovens, laid out so that they did not touch each other. This process resulted in the extinction of the exuberant woods and forests: everything was cut down for firewood for the production of bricks.

The quality was checked as follows: from each batch (three to four thousand pieces) 100 bricks were randomly selected and thrown from a two-meter tower onto the clay floor. If even one of them broke, the entire batch was returned. Such bricks fell sharply in price. They were used for less prestigious construction projects or pounded to make paths in parks and gardens.

In the 19th century, a construction boom began, and with it came the introduction of a conveyor belt and a new prestigious profession — a "tapper" — in brickyards. What exactly did they do? They tapped each brick with a special hammer to judge its quality based on the sound it made, checking for proper burning, cracks, and air pockets. Defective units were removed, and entire schools were dedicated to teaching this skill. It was difficult to gain entry and even more challenging to complete the training, as "tappers" needed to have perfect hearing, concentration, and quick reaction times to navigate the dangers and challenges of the production process. It was a highly-paid job that required significant qualifications.

A similar profession exists now. Do you know why railway workers knock on the wheels of trains at stations? It is not to check for a flat tire but rather to determine the state of the metal and the absence of defects based on the sound it makes. A clear sound indicates the wheel is in good condition, whereas a dull sound suggests that it has cracks and other damage.

This determination is made solely by ear!

If there are any doubts about the serviceability of the wheel, then such a car will be unfastened from the train and sent for primary diagnostics before being repaired.

We uncovered walls lined with excellent red bricks, marked with the stamp of the brickyard which began in the mid-19th century. These stamps not only served as a guarantee of quality from the manufacturer but also as an advertisement for their products.

If a defective brick was supplied for construction, it could be identified immediately.

Nowadays, every brick that bears the traces or impressions of feet, hands, or even animal tracks is a treasure sought after by collectors. These enthusiasts, called "brickophiles", are willing to pay high prices at auctions for old bricks with stamps, sometimes up to 7,000-8,000 US dollars!

As I looked at the walls, I was surrounded by living history.

The texture, quality of the masonry, and the richness of shades of red fascinated me. I imagined how each brick was sorted by a tapper, transported by horses, unloaded in the yard, and how wives and mistresses brought food to the masters. I felt like Howard Carter uncovering Tutankhamun's tomb.

Therefore, the designer, the head foreman (whom I referred to as the repair producer), and I decided not to conceal these beautiful bricks from the world, but to clean and treat them with special materials.

The result was a mega-fashionable style known as "the loft."

The renovation turned into an exciting archaeological study, bringing discoveries every other day, and the stories of the construction begged to be chronicled in a new book.

During a visit to a well-known Lviv antiquarian, I overheard something intriguing.

It was suggested that the builders who constructed my house did not drink alcohol at all.

THE BOOK OF THE SISTERHOOD OF THE GIRLS' SOBRIETY

In 1848, the Austro-Hungarian Empire, which encompassed much of Western Ukraine, abolished "panshchyna" [*"corvée"* or *"villein service"*]. Ukrainian peasants, who had previously been unable to do anything without the master's instructions or permission, were suddenly freed from serfdom and found themselves as owners of their property, land, and life. They were untrained and unprepared for this newfound freedom, and their former masters quickly figured out how to get their grubby hands on it all and turn the peasants into slaves once again: they drugged the population with alcohol as much as possible.

Pubs and taverns (establishments for the production and sale of strong alcohol) worked around the clock and served drinks on credit. Thousands of cases were documented in which people drank away not only their money, clothes, or livestock, but even their entire plots of land and farms. The Ukrainian village was rapidly sliding into the abyss of crime and degradation.

Then the Greek Catholic Metropolitan Archbishop Joseph Sembratovych created the sobriety movement. During divine services in all churches, the consumption of alcohol was condemned as one of the most serious sins. He even persuaded Pope Pius IX to bless the creation of sobriety brotherhoods so that the Austria-Hungary's power structures would have no right to interfere with their work.

Just imagine, the problem of alcoholism was so widespread

that sobriety fraternities were formed specifically for women, and the names of ladies who pledged not to drink were recorded in church books (like the one I was lucky enough to hold in my hands).

The sobriety PR campaign was so well-organized that Ukrainian peasants and townspeople willingly joined sobrieties en masse and publicly refused to drink alcohol. It became mainstream, as we say nowadays.

Sometimes, however, people would swear on the cross but whisper "Only for a year." But everyone kept the promise given to God and recorded it in The Book of Brotherhood or Sisterhood. The result was a heyday of Ukrainian communities at the beginning of the 20th century, with the construction of schools, churches, and a real revival of the peasantry. The trend for sobriety also spread to the cities.

At the beginning of the First World War, soldiers were allowed to drink alcohol at the front. Even after the war, until the start of the Second World War, it was considered bad manners to get drunk or to have many bottles on the table at weddings or christenings. Until the soviets arrived in Western Ukraine in 1939, who drank heavily from ordinary thick table glasses rather than delicate liqueur glasses, as was customary in Galicia.

When I told this story on social media, I received the following comments:
"Everything is true! Alcoholism was terrible: my great-grandfather lost his field by drinking in a tavern."
"My grandmother told me that in Poland, three liters of "horilka" ["vodka" in Ukrainian] was enough for a wedding in the village."
"The sobriety movement was so powerful that even in Central Ukraine, in particular in the Kyiv province, many rural communities refused alcohol (taverns could not be built on community land). The sobriety movement societies were very influential."
"There is still such a brotherhood in our village where they swear not to drink alcohol. Together, they pray for healing from the disease of drunkenness."

I am sure that my house was also built by Ukrainian

workers, who did an excellent job. That's why it's been standing for so long! They definitely gave up drinking alcohol and even pledged in the church not to drink, even if only for a year ☺.

CUT-OFF HOUSES OF BELARUS

"They cut it off for Varvara. And when the son got married, they cut off another part of the house. Thus, the house was divided three times and transported for the newly married couples," an old neighbor with typical Belarusian patience explained to me.

I still couldn't understand how to "cut off a house." But what could they expect from me? I was a "city girl who didn't understand anything."

In my grandfather Omelyan's homeland of Velyki Luzhki, a Belarusian village in the Mohyliv region, this is how I first heard about the strange custom of giving a part of the parental house as a dowry to the children in order to provide them with their own housing at the start.

Just imagine, wooden houses were specially built "for growth," and when the children got married one by one, they dismantled a part of the house together with the roof and foundation, transported it to another place, and reassembled it there. The newlyweds only had one wall left to build, just as the parents did in the old house after each division.

"We don't believe you!" my friends laughed. "Why bother cutting off a piece of an old house, dragging it somewhere, and reassembling it there, when Belarus is a forest country with a lot of wood?"

But it wasn't that simple. Trees for construction had to be cut down in the winter, when they had no sap, otherwise, the wood would twist and be infested with pests.

But not just any winter — only in severe frosts, on a full moon, and only on Tuesdays, Thursdays, and Saturdays. Just like in the Hutsul region *[a historical and ethnographic region located in the Carpathian Mountains of western Ukraine].* Our ancestors knew something about Feng shui and the structural performance of materials.

A forest country, you say? But how much money did they require? People still had to obtain permission! Previously, it was requested from a landowner. People have been killed for illegally picking nettles on the border with manor lands. And then permission to harvest wood had to be obtained from bribe-taking soviet bureaucrats. There, people could have been shot or evicted with the whole family for "stealing state property." There were always "good" people who used to inform the authorities if someone was doing it illegally. And how much effort did it take to cut, split, and dry wood, as well as find craftsmen who would build a house well? My ancestors were rational: they initially built everything with children in mind.

Another neighbor had a different story to tell. When the Soviet authorities came to "dekulakize" [*the policy of "dekulakization" was a brutal campaign initiated by Joseph Stalin's Soviet government in the late 1920s and early 1930s. Its primary goal was to eliminate the so-called "kulaks", who were perceived as wealthy peasants or landowners. The term "kulak" had a broad and often arbitrary definition, and many peasants were labeled as such based on criteria that included owning a bit of land or a few head of livestock*], they kicked all the residents out into the street and began dismantling the house: someone from the new government liked the decent house and wanted to move it for himself. Why build from scratch when you can take it from someone and put it where you want? Nine children were kicked out onto the street, and their father was taken away. They were saved, however, by heavy rains that lasted several weeks.

And guess what I discovered about Ukraine after becoming interested in the transportation of houses and dowries for children!

WANDERING CHURCHES AND THE POOR-RICH PRIEST'S WIFE

Story One: Churches for Sale

Another business that was quite prosperous in the village of Yablunytsya (the same one near the Bukovel resort that has been thriving thanks to skiers) in the 17th and 18th centuries was the production of wooden churches for sale. Customers were not shown scaled-down models, but could instead choose from full size real churches! The churches were displayed on a specific site. Once the price was agreed upon, they were dismantled and transported to the customer using horse-drawn carts in the summer or sleds in the winter, and then reassembled.

Historical fact: in the 16th century, salt workers from Drohobych bought a new church in Yablunytsya, paying ten cartloads of salt for it. They brough it home and placed it near the old pond. Where the church previously stood is still known as Staryi Stavok Street in Drohobych.

It also happened that the old church could no longer accommodate all of the parishioners, or they simply wanted a more modern one, therefore it was put up for sale. There were instant buyers, usually a community from a poorer village that couldn't afford a new church from the manufacturer. They had money only for an old, "used" one, but in good condition.

Story Two: A Church as a Dowry

In the same village of Yablunytsya, a wealthy landlord from Vorokhta proposed to the daughter of the local priest. Despite her youth, beauty, and hardworking nature, the girl was poor. However, she had a father who was very respected in the community. So, the villagers decided to give an old wooden church as a dowry for her. The church was dismantled and transported on numerous carts to its new location on the bank of the river, where it was reassembled. However, when the river began to flood, the church was disassembled once again and moved to a higher location on a hill. The church still stands in Vorokhta and is no longer privately owned, but the descendants of the priest's daughter's family, who told me this story, still hold the keys to the church.

CREATIVE PURSUITS AND A ROMANCE WITH A BUILDER

Those who have ever done a renovation know that it can be incredibly stressful, and it's said that a family who survives a renovation without breaking up is a strong one.

I was reminded of a story that a client told me years ago, at a particularly difficult stage of my own remodeling project, when I had fierce struggles with craftsmen and designers over my vision, as well as with various authorities and neighbors over all possible permits.

Back then, half Lviv's female population had my phone number saved as "Mila-Silver."

My client and her husband lived modestly, like most people in the late 90s, so the man moved to Moscow to earn money in construction. He worked in the apartment of a well-known psychotherapist, sending money home to his wife.

After six months, he called to say that he was divorcing his wife and marrying the psychotherapist. "Farewell," he said. "Remember me kindly."

This story astonished me at the time, but now I understand it all too well.

Do you know why? Renovating an apartment is incredibly stressful, whether you have the money or not (a harsh reality check: multiply all your estimates not by two, but by three).

And who do you communicate with the most during a renovation? The builders, of course. They're the ones who wipe your tears and redo things twenty times when you ask them to move an outlet by five centimeters to make things look better than they did before 😊. That's why the Moscow psychotherapist chose a Western Ukrainian man. She was probably tired of glamorous men whining on her couch, even if they paid her a lot for it.

Taking a father away from his child and a husband away from his wife is undoubtedly a great sin, but I understand her reasoning now after becoming very friendly with one of the construction workers on my project.

He showed incredible patience and stress resistance as he implemented all of my creative ideas, always finding the right words and arguments to comfort me and fix things when other contractors messed up.

In his free time, he read my books from the closet while standing on the ladder. Fortunately, we were both happily married people, or who knows what might have happened 😊?

As the renovation, which had not been done in over a century, continued, I felt my parents' house started to become a place of strength, inspiration, and endless gratitude to two generations of my family who lived a decent life there and were always spoken well of.

My husband and I even decided to spend the winter there, leaving our house in Vynnyky as a summer home.

The War
Who hasn't lived in our house in Vynnyky since February 24, 2022, on the way to foreign lands, driven by trouble! With children, with animals. Everyone found a kind word, a clean bed, and a cup of hot coffee. Everyone offered us money, but we, of course, turned it down. And our neighbors, who are car mechanics, repaired cars for our guests free of charge.

I created a gallery of my ancestors in the corridor according to the rules of fashionable galleries: I ordered new expensive frames for the portraits of my father and mother by a good artist. I took care of the lighting. I went through thousands of photographs before selecting 20 to decorate a whole wall with those photos with the help of a designer.

The War
And now, all of these design elements have been removed from the walls, packed into boxes, and the corridor has been transformed into our living space behind two walls. At first, we went there to sleep on a pile of bedspreads and blankets stacked on the floor (like a prince and princess on a pea) only during air raid alerts. And now we've completely settled in. I even host webinars from there.

Question: Was it necessary to do such a massive renovation of the entire flat when only the corridor was needed?

I spent half a year restoring the wooden joinery: floor-to-ceiling doors (with nearly four-meter-high ceilings) and massive three-tiered windows reminiscent of those found in a Venetian palazzo.

The neighbors had removed the windows and doors installed during the time when the count lived in the house, cutting them down and throwing them away to replace with plastic ones. This was done in a house that is protected by the state as an architectural landmark. However, enthusiastic Kalabukha preserved, restored, and fought for every inch of this historical heritage.

After completing the renovation, including purchasing new dishes, curtains, and tablecloths for everyday use and special occasions, I took down the wedding photo of my parents from the wall and, as if with an icon, went around all the corners, saying:

"My dears! Look how I've preserved everything, honoring your memory. I love you and will always remember and be grateful for everything you gave me and the way you raised me."

HOW WOULD THE WORLD CHANGE IF HE FELL THEN?

Several times a day, two cats, the seventy-year-old Mrs. Paulina (the countess's niece) and the countess Maria Jelonek herself, who was nearly ninety at the time, walked through the room where my grandmother, grandfather, and their son Oleg — my father — lived. However, this did not prevent them from becoming friends. My father quickly learned Polish and spent hours listening to stories about their former social life. He looked at the photos she kept in an old chest and helped with household chores. As a seventh-grader, he was particularly impressed by the story about the event that took place in this very apartment — an event that could change the history of not only Lviv, Ukraine, or Europe, but the entire world.

In 1911, Archduke Franz Ferdinand, the heir presumptive to the Austro-Hungarian throne, attended the consecration of St. Elizabeth Church (Elzhbeta, as Lviv locals still call it in the Polish manner). It was the same person whose death triggered the outbreak of World War I.

According to protocol, the most authoritative families of the national communities of then-Lviv were supposed to host the Archduke. After several selection rounds, numerous intrigues, and complex networks, the Jelonek family from the Polish community gained the right to receive the heir in their house on Kurkowa Street (now Lysenko Street), which is my current apartment.

This is how they arranged everything: they rented out the first and third floors. The first floor was used for offices, and the third floor was used as an apartment. The Jeloneks lived on the entire second floor in a huge apartment. A luxurious oak staircase covered with carpets led there. During the visit, Franz Ferdinand was supposed to sit in a chair that was ordered from the greatest Viennese craftsmen: a kind of mini-throne on lion's paws with the coat of arms of a distinguished guest.

Imagine a brightly lit hall, ladies in diamonds, gentlemen in formal uniforms, the aromas of perfumes, and the most exquisite dishes. The Archduke enters, accompanied by the empire's first citizens. A chair throne is solemnly presented to him, he smiles graciously and leans back. But suddenly there is a crunch: the renowned chair's leg falls off, and the Archduke falls on the floor from his own height.

Two escort officers immediately pick up the VIP. The reception is ruined, and the hosts are shamed across all of Lviv and the entire empire (there was quite a lot of press at the reception). No matter how hard they tried to hush up the scandal at the time, it became public knowledge.

An enraged count investigated the issue and found that it was the backstabbing of competitors who had been denied the opportunity to host a high-ranking guest. They bribed one of the cleaning company's employees to cut the base of one of the chair's legs. The cleaner was found and brought to the count. He initially denied everything, but eventually confessed. The count vowed to take revenge on the insolent rivals and ordered his servants to throw away the ill-fated throne.

Notes from Kalabukha

The assassination of Archduke Franz Ferdinand was the event that triggered the start of the First World War, which lasted from 1914 to 1918. Prior to the start of the Second World War, the war was referred to as the Great War.

How did it happen?

The assassination took place in the city of Sarajevo, when Serbian terrorist Gavrilo Princip shot Archduke and his wife. Austria-Hungary, offended by the assassination, declared war on Serbia. Since the Serbs are Orthodox and pro-russian, russia mobilized its army and came to Serbia's rescue.

Austria-Hungary asked the assistance of the German Kaiser, who happened to be the russian Tsar's cousin. The German Empire demanded that russia stops mobilizing, but russia refused. The cousins, who were close friends and called each other Vicky and Nicky, were outwardly similar, as if they were twins, could not reach a consensus. As a result, on August 1st, 1914, the German Empire declared war on russia, thus starting the First World War.

And so it all started!

The First World War was fought on two fronts. On one side was the Triple Entente (from the French "an agreement"), which consisted of the Great Britain, France, and russia, who had agreed to form a union. On the other side were Germany, Italy, Austria-Hungary, the Ottoman Empire, and Bulgaria.

This war was particularly tragic for Ukraine (and what war is not a tragedy?) since it pitted brothers from the East and West against each other for the illusory interests of the great powers. Ukrainians living in Eastern and Central Ukraine were mobilized for the russian army, whereas Ukrainians living in the Austro-Hungarian Empire were mobilized on the other side of the front. To fight for what? The boys taken from remote mountain villages to fight in a foreign and incomprehensible war were told they were fighting "to take revenge for the emperor's son."

The Great War involved 70 million people, 13 million of whom died and 55 million were injured.

During this war, the following were used for the first time:
- *caterpillar tracked tanks with internal combustion engines, equipped with machine guns;*
- *submarines with a combination of diesel and electric engines;*
- *cannons and mortars.*

During the First World War, the Germans deployed chemical weapons against the French for the first time. Poisonous gasses like chlorine, mustard gas, and phosgene simultaneously killed tens of thousands of people. One third died immediately, while the rest endured terrible agony over a period of one month. In response, a gas mask was created to provide protection. I once saw gas masks from that time period for horses, which were the main workhorses of armies, as well as for dogs, at an ethnographic museum in the Lviv region.

Aviation was also involved for the first time. By 1914, each side had approximately 200-250 aircraft, which were primarily used for reconnaissance. During the Great War, the concept of dropping bombs from airplanes was born. Artillery shells were launched first, followed by high-explosive, fragmentation, and incendiary rounds. The French also devised the concept of dropping fléchettes from airplanes on enemy infantry and cavalry formations. Fléchettes were small, pointed, and heavy projectiles that measured 15 centimeters or more in length. A fléchette dropped from a great height could pierce a thick board and could even go through a rider and a horse, stopping only when it hit the ground. The Germans particularly favored using fléchettes, dropping thousands of them from planes. It was a medieval weapon that caused terror and harm to those who came under its attack.

As for medieval weapons, catapults were also actively used. At first, they threw stones at the enemy. And when they adjusted their fire, they threw grenades into enemy trenches from catapults.

I also remembered the heavy armor of knights as both sides began to suffer massive losses among infantrymen. While the modern bulletproof vest is said to have been invented in the 1980s, soldiers used something similar to the heavy knightly cuirasses that could withstand even a rifle shot during the First World War. Additionally, aviators wore armored trousers that protected them against bullets shot from the ground.

At the Lviv Museum of Weapons "Arsenal" (the same one near which there are always long queues to "Rebernya" — a popular restaurant in Lviv that shares the same building), I saw several-meter-long spears that were still in use with armies at the beginning of the 20th century. Exactly the same as in medieval engravings depicting knightly tournaments. The spears were also used during the Great War of 1914-1918, when soldiers with spears held horizontally rode horses or sprinted on foot towards enemy trenches, where they were greeted by machine gun fire. Unfortunately, a similar story was repeated during the Second World War, when Soviet cavalrymen armed with sabers were sent to attack German fortifications.

By the way, the next time you want to visit the hyped-up "Rebernya", located in the basement of the museum, I recommend that you book a spot in the queue and visit the "Arsenal" to see with your own eyes how many objects there are, with which people destroyed each other for two millennia!

Before the invention of firearms, people fought primarily in close combat. One of my favorite items on the first floor of the museum is a knife that opens like a pair of scissors inside a person and cuts through all the internal organs, causing maximum pain and assuring the victim's death. It is adorned with precious stones and ivory, showcasing how people could make even the deadliest of weapons look beautiful.

You'll work up an appetite, admire the beauty, and get inspired 😊.

The First World War triggered the 1917 October Revolution, which brought the Bolsheviks to power. Consequently, millions of people died during the Red Terror, Holodomor, dekulakization, and repression. It also served as the catalyst for events that occurred throughout the 20th century in all countries, as well as the underlying reason of what is currently happening to all of us.

After the war ended, four empires ceased to exist: the russian, Austro-Hungarian, Ottoman, and German, and internecine battles for new national states erupted on their ruins. Germany, who started this war and was defeated, suffered devastating consequences. It was forced to pay enormous reparations (money for the damages caused) to the victorious countries, which exacerbated the economic crisis and contributed to Hitler's rise to power. This led to the Second World War, the Holocaust, and other horrific events that continue to have an impact on Europe and the rest of the world today.

The Spanish flu epidemic, which killed up to 100 million people globally (equivalent to 5% of the world's population at that time), was one of the consequences of that war. The Spanish flu epidemic reached pandemic proportions and killed so many people because of overcrowding, poor conditions and sanitation in the barracks, trenches, and POW camps, and, most importantly, because of the returning soldiers.

It was the first war in the history of mankind to encompass all countries and all sectors of activity. Although, at the beginning of the 20th century, futurologists (scientists who forecast the future development of humanity) assured that there would be no more wars in Europe since civilization had advanced to the point where conflicts could be resolved without the use of weapons. They believed that any clashes would only occur in the provinces or colonies, if at all.

Oh, these futurologists! Like forecasters: they are wrong once, but every day. In our time, different predictions were also made, but everything turned out the other way around.

And none of this would have happened if Archduke Franz Ferdinand had been crippled or even killed in 1911 when he fell from that throne chair in the vast space that is now my living room.

"Why didn't he fall then?" I often wonder.

A BRIBED SCRIBE, A LIFE-SAVING PHOTO, AND 60 YEARS TOGETHER

All of the photos of my grandmother, grandfather, and father are from the 50s. I selected several of them for restoration. And suddenly I discovered a small photograph, the only one from before the war: the year 1926, the wedding of my grandmother and grandfather.

Oh my goodness, how beautiful they are! My grandfather Kazymyr looks like an actor: blond hair, piercing gray eyes, wearing a fashionable suit and tie. My grandmother Mariya, dark-haired, slender, with white teeth, wearing a dark gown with a wide white collar. If you wore anything like that today, you'd be right on trend!

I remembered! I remembered what my father had told me about her. Grandmother Mariya was four years older than grandfather Kazymyr. So what did she do? She bribed the scribe, and he issued her a new passport, stating that her year of birth was not 1900, but 1904 so that they would become peers on paper.

While the passport is no longer in existence, the marriage certificate from September 4, 1926 still remains. This certificate confirms that both newlyweds were 22 years old at the time of their marriage registration.

I wonder: why did she need it? She looked fantastic. Her fiancé Kazymyr knew about her age. He had no relatives — he was an orphan. The mother-in-law would not blame her. Did she worry about what people would say? What kind of people?

And the certificate issued by the Ukrainian SSR in 1926 indicated that Kazymyr Vasyukov was Ukrainian, and Mariya (maiden name Elterman) was Jewish. This document, notably the column indicating nationality, ultimately led to her being taken to the ghetto near Kharkiv in the fall of 1941, where her entire family tragically perished. It was this ghetto that she and her nine-year-old son, who would later become my father, miraculously managed to escape.

And what about my grandfather Kazymyr? He was sent to the front from the first day of the war. For several years, he had no information about his family, who had stayed in German-occupied Kharkiv. The rumors about what was going on there were horrifying. But he always kept a small photo from their wedding close to his heart. It gave him the strength to believe that he would definitely see his Mariyka and their son alive. The photograph accompanied him through the horrors of the Second World War. Miraculously, it was not lost at the hospitals where he was lying after being gravely injured. It was this photo that we found in a drawer next to his bed, where he died in his sleep at the age of 91, having outlived his Mariyka by ten years. They have been married for 60 years.

The War
This photo, enlarged ten times, used to live on the corridor wall. But I believe the time will come when I'll unpack the boxes and hang all the photos and portraits back on the wall. Then, the corridor will once again become "the gallery of my ancestors" instead of "the place between two walls".

A STRANGER WHO RAISED ME

"People should understand why my house is a mess: I work, so I don't have time," my second grandmother used to say when people asked why she never cleaned her house.

This remark became our family joke and a powerful argument that explains a lot 😊.

I'm writing a book right now, and there's chaos around me: I returned from a business trip, left everything behind, and immediately sat down at the computer — the muse has come. Maybe I should get up from my computer and clean up? Shouldn't people understand that a working woman doesn't have time for this? I listened to my grandmother and chose a book. I'll keep writing.

I knew only one thing about my grandma Raisa Stepanchykova's (my mother's mother's) past: she was a military engineer who constantly went on long business trips. The grandfather cleaned, went grocery shopping, did laundry, ironed, walked with the children, and also worked as an engineer, exploring oil, gas, and sulfur resources throughout the former USSR. And only a month before her death at the age of 83 she told me two facts from her biography.

Her job was to design and build mines for nuclear missiles and other military facilities throughout Eastern Europe. The highest level of secrecy.

Raisa Stepanchykova's family had a tragic history. Four of her siblings perished in the 1930s Holodomor famine, which she referred to as "starvation." Her mother, my great-grandmother, a widow at that time, was half-dead from hunger when she married a man named Hryhoriy and moved to Azerbaijan with her only daughter Raisa. Hryhoriy made a vow to see Stalin's death before dying, and he kept his word by passing away in late March 1953, just as Stalin was being buried.

During the tumultuous 1990s, I was juggling the demands of work and personal life, too preoccupied to just sit down and ask about the many white areas in my grandparents' history that have left me restless:

— Why did my non-native great-grandfather, who eventually became so dear to me, vow to see Stalin's death at any cost?

— Where did he take my great-grandmother and her only daughter, and why did they end up in Azerbaijan, where my mother was born?

— How did they make their way to post-war Lviv?

— Where did my grandmother meet my Belarusian grandfather, with whom they lived for 60 years and passed away almost simultaneously?

— And why, if my grandmother had such a secret and responsible job, was the family plagued by horrible, even dire poverty and never had enough money?

Their photographs showing strong, beautiful, dear, and, surprisingly, so little-known people, are now also on the wall in my new-old apartment. On the wall in the gallery of ancestors.

The War
Were on the wall. And soon they will be again.

FIND THOSE FIVE MINUTES

What do I regret the most? Five minutes. It's so little, and yet so much. Five minutes to talk with my mother and father on the phone, or to visit my grandparents and ask them about their lives, hear about their health, have some tea, and go for a walk in the park. But there was never enough time. Or rather, there was time, but not for them. There was time for work, clients, and small talk with strangers out of courtesy or duty. But not for my family. "Later," I thought. "There are other things to worry about." I was always in a hurry, always running somewhere, always deciding something, always busy, but never with them. And it went on for years, for my whole life. Then one day, they don't need your five minutes anymore. Now you need them. I need those five minutes so badly, to a maddening degree. My family waited for me to fit them in my busy schedule.

"I cry with joy that I still have living parents" (Skryabin *[Ukrainian singer and patriot]*). How fortunate are those who have not only living parents but also grandparents! And I didn't have time. I didn't have time to do anything.

Call them, visit them, ask about their lives! Find out what gave them the strength to resist all the fate's blows, and how they managed to live in a happy marriage for 60 years despite their quite difficult behavior and such a complicated life.

Don't be late like I was!

All I have is a couple of photos and a few stories. Live, my dears, in the photographs on the wall! Live, my dears, on the pages of my books! Live!

CHAPTER 3

WHY IS CREATIVITY EVIL, AND WHAT TYPE OF ADVERTISING WILL FAIL?

CREATIVITY AND LOST LOVE

We agreed to be a couple, and I was filled with indescribable joy. I bought her the largest bouquet of flowers, spending my entire meager student savings from the 90s. Additionally, I arranged for flower delivery with a card that read "For my beloved Raisin" — that's the endearing nickname I had chosen for her.

The next day at the institute, she completely ignored me. Throughout the day she walked around as if I were a stranger, avoiding any eye contact. To my surprise, her ex-boyfriend, with whom she had broken up because of his infidelity, arrived in his car to pick her up after classes. It was as if I didn't exist, and they were getting back together despite my presence.

We graduated from the institute and went our separate ways.

I got married eventually, not because of intense love, but rather friendship. After experiencing heartbreak, I made a conscious decision to prioritize reliability and stability over passionate emotions.

And she did break up with that wealthy guy. Then she married someone else, only to be divorced again. They went through legal proceedings regarding their child. Now she is fully devoted to her career, having become a successful businesswoman and living independently for a long time.

And it wasn't until the 20th anniversary of our graduation from the institute that I mustered the courage to ask her how she changed her mind so suddenly after receiving such a grand bouquet signed with our secret word of love. No one else called her by that name. What made her decide to leave me after that?

"It was you? Why didn't you sign the card and tell me that the most beautiful flowers I'd ever seen were from you? Just like our date. A lavish, expensive bouquet with a mysterious signature. I couldn't understand how a struggling student like you could afford such luxury. So, I assumed the flowers were from him: a guilty person seeking forgiveness. I called him and told him that I had forgiven him and was willing to give our relationship another chance. But why didn't you say that the flowers were from you? Why didn't you sign your name on the card? Our entire lives could have turned out differently," she wondered.

"That's just who I am, a failed creative and a master of surprises," my old fellow student shared with me in a story once.

THE WOW EFFECT AND THE REPUTATION COLLAPSE

A phone call from an unknown number.

"Is this entrepreneur Krasko?"
"Yes, speaking."
"Are you confident in your own and your loved ones' safety? Do you sleep well at night?"

I was driving and nearly crashed into a pole. So, they tracked me down. All my sins came flooding back to me: the times I had spoken poorly of others, the times I had underpaid, the careless quarrels I had engaged in. It felt like a targeted attack. Rumor had it that the tax office's database of entrepreneurs had been stolen. It seemed that my turn had come.

Do you know what kind of call that was?

It was from a company that sells security systems! You see, they approached phone sales creatively. They had figured out how to grab attention right from the first few seconds, standing out from the countless others who were making hundreds of offers all day.

To grab attention! I nearly had an accident because of them! They certainly achieved the "wow" effect that marketers strive for. However, they failed to earn any money from me. In fact, I distinctly remember them and make a point to warn everyone not to use their services.

"Here's a story for your telephone sales training, so you can not only teach how to do things but also explain exactly how not to do them," a cautionary tale shared by a member of my online entrepreneurs' club, "Sales with Joy."

UNDUE CREATIVITY OF THE INSTAGRAM PROFILE DESCRIPTION (HEADER)

The profile description on Instagram is commonly referred to as "bio" (short for "biography"). However, it has become a custom among our people *[Ukrainians]* to call it a "header."

99% of Instagram pages have improperly written profile descriptions, significantly increasing the cost of acquiring new followers and greatly reducing sales potential.

One of the reasons for this is the influence of popular courses that encourage people to be creative, unique, and unlike others. I can already see you puffing up your chest, preparing to engage in a debate with me.

But let's discuss this further.

Meanwhile, here are four common mistakes found in profile descriptions, along with real-life examples.

1. **Suspense**
   Eyebrow Master:
   - "I won't let you go until your eyebrows are perfect";
   - "I will free you from the captivity of tweezers at home".
   Manicure:
   - "I'll break your bonds with burrs";
   - "I'll provide an aesthetic orgasm for your fingers";
   - "I paint happiness on your nails".
   Sugaring:
   - "I'll get the cactus out of your underpants";
   - "Queen of bald pussies";

- "Mistress of sugar and smoothness".
  Handmade:
- "I knit love and warmth";
- "I'll bring joy to your loved ones";
- "Inspiration, femininity, rhythm".
  Tutor:
- "I will run English through your veins";
- "I'm the dark side of your English";
- "Children will start using their brains".

There is one main rule: write the profile description for new followers! It should not include inside jokes that only long-time followers will understand.

2. "AWWW"
If you are not a mom blogger, avoid writing that you are a "happy wife and mother of three children" in your profile description. Also, avoid claiming that you live between Berdychiv and New York, dance in your stories, and including the birth dates of your "angels/dragons."

People looking for a copywriter are primarily interested in your skills and experience, not personal information such as how many kids you have, your cooking preferences, or your weight loss journey (which is sometimes mentioned in expert profile descriptions!). To attract potential clients, focus on highlighting your skills and professional background.

If you are an eyebrow master, you don't need to include additional clarifications such as "an eyebrow master and chef with dark humor" or "I post recipes for delicious dishes and make chic eyebrows." Potential clients who are specifically seeking eyebrow services aren't interested in your cooking skills, and those looking for recipes will seek out a cook. To attract the right audience, focus on highlighting your skills as an eyebrow specialist.

It is better to describe clearly what services you offer: first, second, third, and to explain why customers should choose you and how to make a purchase: click here, message here, or call here.

3. "Milk-and-Water"
- Personal touch

- We will make all your dreams come true
- High quality
- Fast delivery
- Affordable prices
- Graduated specialist
- Certified master

4. The profile description is left blank!

Absolutely nothing is written there. And then people message me every day, complaining about the lack of sales.

So, what should you do?

Your profile description should clearly state what you are selling. Keep it simple, so that even someone who doesn't know you, can peek at your profile while commuting or waiting at a traffic light and easily understand what you offer. You only have three seconds to grab their attention and convince them to stay on your page or move on.

People will leave your page quickly if it's not clear why they were directed there.

You should write:
- "Manicure" and specify the types of manicure you offer, instead of "I paint dreams on your nails";
- "Custom-made knitted hats" instead of "In captivity of knitting needles and yarn".

Here are some more masterpieces of profile descriptions that need improvement: "I will help you cure your wallet's dystrophy"; "I will help you build strong muscles by carrying suitcases"; "Dr. Doolittle of your soul".

And "the icing on the cake": "I will eliminate parasites from your life," a psychologist wrote in his profile description. He probably meant inner demons. Or not. Maybe he was a multidisciplinary specialist who also exorcised demons. Total disinfection of the entire body!

Don't write like that. It's important to be clear and avoid ambiguous statements.

ANTIQUE CREATIVITY AND ADVERTISING THAT WORKS

The first advertisement was discovered among the ruins of the ancient Egyptian city of Memphis:

"Residing here is Minos, hailing from the island of Crete, blessed by the gods with the gift of dream interpretation, offered for a reasonable fee."

Short and clear: what they sell and at what prices. This is a perfect example of a well-crafted profile header description.

Additionally, the marketing strategies employed by brothels in Ancient Rome have always held a prominent place in my personal ranking of the greatest. It is evident that people had a strong inclination towards advertising even back then!

1. Follow Me
In Ancient Rome prostitutes reportedly wore shoes with a special inscription on the sole. When I asked my Instagram followers what they thought was written there, they came up with some intriguing suggestions:
- The name of the brothel.
- The address of the brothel.
- "I put out for money."
- "To know the price, write in Direct."
- "The Highway to Heaven."
- One sandal bears the prostitute's name, while the other bears her patronymic.

And, in fact, the girls left behind a trail with the inscription "Follow me." They not only catered to the explicit desires of their customers but also actively influenced and shaped them.

I recently came across an advertisement for a company that offers custom printing on the soles of rubber slippers. Interestingly, one of the most popular requests and orders is the iconic phrase used by ancient Roman prostitutes: "Follow me."

2. Young She-Wolves
Prostitutes were called "lupas" because they howled and moaned very loudly during the performance of their official duties,

while houses of debauchery were called "lupanarias". "Lupa" means "she-wolf" in Latin.

I wonder whether Oleh Vynnyk is aware of this fact? ☺
[Oleh Vynnyk is a popular Ukrainian singer with a hit song "She-Wolf"]

3. Infographics with Prices
There were people in the Roman Empire who were not fluent in Latin. What did the clever lupanarias marketers do? In order to cater to a diverse clientele, they utilized visual communication by creating boards with pictorial representations of the brothel services. These boards would also display the corresponding prices next to each service, allowing potential clients to understand and make informed choices.

I constantly emphasize that it is important to clearly display prices in social media posts and on websites for the convenience of clients. Similarly, in Ancient Rome, brothels implemented a system that aimed to simplify the process for customers. This allowed customers to easily understand the options available, choose what they desired, and indicate their selection by pointing at the corresponding picture.

By the way, here's a life hack on how to increase reach and sales on your social media pages: share stories of how people have historically sold similar products or services in different times and countries. This kind of content is intriguing and captures people's interest. Utilize your experience and unique perspective to showcase these historical selling techniques, providing your audience with valuable insights. There is a wealth of information available through a simple Google search, so leverage it to create engaging and informative content.

My marketing research, interactive content, and historical quests receive a significant amount of engagement and views.

And in the subsequent stories, transition immediately into selling. People will keep reading out of curiosity about how ancient Romans or other cultures approached similar practices, and that's when you can introduce your products or services.

"RAMSES' PASSPORT"

In 1974, Egypt issued a passport to Pharaoh Ramses II, who was born in 1303 BC. When I asked in my Instagram stories, "Why do you think it was necessary?" my friends suggested several versions:

- to legitimize the tomb;
- to ride minibuses for free with a pension card;
- to prove his Egyptian citizenship;
- as proof of the pharaoh's existence;
- to take loans in his name;
- to be recognized in the afterlife;
- to register the mummy brand;
- to legalize pyramid trading;
- to be reunited with his body.

You may find it amusing, but Ramses needed a passport to travel abroad. His mummy was experiencing significant deterioration and needed to be restored in France. However, according to French law, any person, living or dead, can only enter the country with a passport. In 1974, Ramses was issued a passport and granted a five-year visa, which stated the following information that was known at the time:

Full Name: RAMESSES
Date Of Birth: --/--/1303 BC
Place Of Birth: ---
Nationality: EGYPTIAN
Sex: M
Profession: King (deceased)

So join in! If you come across anything interesting, such as historical facts or funny commercials, feel free to send them my way. I would appreciate your contributions. You can find me on Instagram, where I'll be eagerly waiting for your messages:

kalabukha.l

SOME STRANGE ADVICE FROM DR. SPOCK

"When buying a bicycle for your child, consider buying two at the same time. Why? So that your child can rent the bicycle to other children in the neighborhood for a fee. By involving your children in entrepreneurial activities from an early age, you can teach them about earning money and developing business skills."

I came across such advice from Dr. Spock in a book that was considered the ultimate guide to parenting when my daughter Anya was little. Ha ha! Back then, mom bloggers didn't exist 😊.

I remember thinking, "Is this some kind of heresy?"

If I follow this advice, no one will want to play with my child in the yard. I'll end up spending more money on child psychologists than my daughter, Anya, would earn from renting out the second bicycle.

Back in the tumultuous 90s, I came to the realization that Dr. Spock's advice in his book "Baby and Childcare" (1946), which became the largest bestseller in the history of the United States, wasn't suitable for our situation. Neither the American nor the russian sales methods worked for us. We have a different market, a different mentality, and a different historical and social background.

What I have found to work perfectly for us is what I have gathered and tested on people both offline and online over the course of my 28 years in sales. It's all compiled here, as well as in my other books.

As for the advice about the second bicycle from the parenting guru's book, perhaps I have been too judgmental. Maybe that's indeed the way it should be done 😊.

WHAT SHOULD YOU DO WITH CREATIVITY IN BUSINESS AND LIFE?

How to avoid losing money, reputation, and love?

1. In both life and sales, when faced with a choice between creativity and simplicity, always opt for simplicity, clarity, and comprehensibility. Right from the beginning, from the very first line and sentence of your profile description and photo on your social media pages, it should be clear who you are, what you sell, what experience you have, how to contact you, and why clients should take immediate action.

2. Don't leave any room for uncertainty.

Take a moment to call or text your loved ones, parents, and children right now and express your love for them. There's no need to wait for the perfect moment until grievances subside, or for everyone to reach a certain level of maturity, realize their mistakes, and come to you with apologies and regret.

Do you value these people? Take the initiative and explain the situation without delay. There's no need to constantly check your phone, waiting for them to call or message you.

Instead, be proactive and call or email your clients today to discuss any payment and cooperation issues. You can approach the conversation in the following manner:
- Are our terms suitable for you?
- Are you interested in collaborating?
- Are you ready to place an order?
- Should I proceed with packing and sending your package?

By taking these proactive steps, you'll be amazed at how much more joy, love, and accomplished tasks will fill your life. And, of course, it will also bring financial rewards.

CHAPTER 4

HOW TO BECOME AN ARTIST, LIVE AS AN ARTIST, AND SELL ART IN UKRAINE

YEVHEN LAVRENCHUK'S STORIES

STORY ONE:
How a hooligan from Lviv received world recognition

In 1998, during my tenth grade at an eleven-year school, I was expelled because of my poor behavior.

Starting from sixth grade, there were repeated conversation about my expulsion, but I managed to avoid it by organizing and participating in school plays that consistently won district and regional competitions. However, it wasn't until my avant-garde performance titled "Vasyl Stus — How Wonderful It Is That I Am Not Afraid of Death" was videotaped and viewed by a wide audience, including headmasters from neighboring schools and even the cleaning staff, that I gained real fame.

Fame caused a division among the teaching staff, with one group adoring and supporting me, considering me a genius, while the other group despised and bullied me, seeing me as a low-achiever and adversary.

And they had good reasons to despise me ☺. I behaved so badly that I'm embarrassed to talk about it. Now I'm ashamed of those actions, and I despise myself for disrupting lessons, arguing with teachers, and causing them distress and tears. However, I felt like a noble rebel at the time, viewing it as my protest against a system that, in my perception, oppressed individuality.

I was outraged by everything! I couldn't stand the fact that in our Polish school (which was always considered exemplary and strict), there was an atmosphere of constant politeness and obedience. I couldn't accept the ban on running and shouting in the corridors, even during breaks. It bothered me that we, as free individuals (meaning us, the students), were constantly commanded to "Open your notebooks and write." What frustrated me the most was that no one seemed to care about our opinions or whether we agreed with these rules or not.

Here is one of the most innocent pranks I pulled off.

Before class, I would hide in the large closet where we kept our belongings and shoes. Then, after roll call, when the teacher sighed with relief and said, "Thank goodness, Lavrenchuk is absent, it will finally be quiet," I would theatrically emerge from the closet and announce, "And here I am!"

That allowed me to avoid studying and answering questions during lessons without being punished. Why? Here's the hooligan's life hack: the checkmark cell in the attendance sheet was already marked with the letter "N" *[which means "absent" in Ukrainian schools]*, thus there was no room left for another negative mark.

How did my family react to my misbehavior?

My parents tried to explain things to me and actively attempted to calm me down, saying, "Well, if you don't enjoy chemistry/physics/mathematics, then sit quietly and reflect on yourself." However, I couldn't comply. I physically sensed that my time was being wasted on unnecessary tasks that didn't contribute to my ultimate goal of being on the big stage.

But the one who was always on my side was my beloved grandmother, Tamara, with whom I lived. I affectionately called her "My Cherepashka" *[which means "My Turtle" in English]*.

She was my first acting student, and it was often her who was summoned to school because of my mischievous behavior. How fiercely she defended me!

For example, when the teacher told her, "Your grandson doesn't study chemistry," she boldly responded, "He is a humanitarian and a future genius!" Her words led to a meeting with the class teacher, who then referred her to the headmaster. In that meeting, my dear Cherepashka fearlessly expressed her thoughts about stifling educational methods, the damaging categorization of children as polite or disobedient, and her critique of the education system as a whole.

It never ended well! On the contrary, her visit only fueled the fire of conflict, intensifying it with tremendous force, as my grandmother fought fiercely and passionately for my cause.

I understood that and suggested, "Cherepashka, when you come to school, start crying and complaining about what a difficult grandson you have. Then everyone will sympathize with you, and no one will argue with you." So I taught her to cry on demand. At the first request, I would say. I showed her how to "open and close vocal cords," and she managed to do it right away! As soon as she arrived at school, she'd burst into tears. And when the teachers exclaimed, "Look at what you've done to your grandmother," I'd skillfully burst into tears as well. That's how she and I misbehaved together ☺.

I still consider the death of my beloved grandmother Cherepashka the greatest loss of my life.

But by the 10th grade, everyone had reached their limit, and I was expelled. This experience motivated me to prove to the world how valuable I was. I was certain I would make it as a director. My idol was the renowned Roman Viktyuk from Lviv. I resolved to find a way to learn from him at any cost. At that time, Viktyuk was teaching directing at the russian Institute of Theater Arts GITIS.

At that time, GITIS was one of the most prestigious theater universities not only in the former USSR, but also in the world. It was extremely challenging to gain admission to the institute.

Everything was further complicated by the fact that Viktyuk was already teaching his second-year students. This meant that I would have to wait five years before getting the opportunity to join his course. However, I was not willing to wait. I took decisive action and made my way to moscow.

The first exam was the director's explication, which involved describing the future performance. I had to articulate my vision for the characters, set design, costumes, props, and creative elements such as lighting, technology, and music that I intended to use.

I went with Pushkin's "A Feast in Time of Plague." The play is set in 17th-century England during a plague epidemic. It depicts a group of people who, tired of hiding and living in fear, gather in the street, set up a table, and hold a feast, defiantly enjoying themselves despite the presence of death all around them.

How I envisioned the production:

- The stage is set as an empty space with chairs dangling chaotically from the ceiling. All of the characters are dressed in black stretch sweaters and brown corduroy pants;
- the Plague is portrayed as an attractive woman in a beautiful dress who takes turns cutting the ropes. The falling and breaking chairs symbolize people dying one by one from the disease;
- in the finale, I planned for a wagon filled with dead bodies to drive onto the stage, with broken chairs strewn about to represent the aftermath.

And the examiners liked it! They approved my vision for the play. However, that's when the real challenges started: I had to write an essay in russian.

I read a lot in russian, but I had never written anything. The permissible number of errors for an applicant was four. Those who made more mistakes were not allowed to proceed further. My odds of passing that exam with a passing grade appeared to be nil. So here's what I did: I included a note with my work, stating that I had never formally studied the russian language in my life.

The number of my mistakes was difficult to count. However, the writing was so fresh and witty that it impressed the examiners. As a result, I was enrolled in the program of studies!

So, at the age of 16, with no money, influential connections, in a foreign country, and no knowledge of written russian, not even a high school diploma, I successfully passed a highly competitive examination with an acceptance rate of 200 applicants per spot and gained admission to the directing faculty of one of the world's most prestigious theater universities. Riding the wave of success, I swiftly completed the entire first-year program and found myself in the second-year course under the guidance of the maestro I admired so much.

If you were to share this story, it would be hard for anyone to believe: while being a second-year student at GITIS in moscow, I was also studying extramurally in the 11th grade in Lviv. As a result, I obtained both secondary and higher education at the same time. At the age of 19 and a half, I achieved the distinction of being the youngest graduate of GITIS' directing faculty in its 122-year history. This remarkable feat took place in the year 2000.

Now, at the age of 41, I have been teaching for a long time. My perspective has shifted dramatically, and I am sincerely grateful to my school teachers for their immense patience and unwavering dedication in their daily endeavors.

Yevhen Lavrenchuk is an opera director and a laureate of numerous Ukrainian and international competitions and festivals. He is actively engaged in performances and educational activities across Ukraine, Poland, Germany, Lithuania, and Israel.

He is the creator of a unique seven-level method for teaching acting and directing. Yevhen Lavrenchuk speaks russian, English, French, Hebrew, and Polish fluently. In addition, he is the Rector of the First Ukrainian Theater and Cinema School.

STORY TWO:
How an artist should promote their projects and survive job loss, harassment, breakup, betrayal, or divorce

Yevhen and I did a series of live broadcasts for my Instagram blog, and the wisdom he shared during those sessions continues to be quoted by my followers.

Here's the valuable advice from this maestro of world opera directing:

- **How to overcome the fear of performing on stage, on camera, in live broadcasts, or in public speaking?**
  The key is not to engage in a fight against your fears.

Struggle only leads to conflict and destruction. Instead, embrace and acknowledge your anxieties, especially our universal national fear of "What will people say?"

Avoid lying, being shy, or pretending to be someone you're not. Instead, be honest about your anxiety and accept your weaknesses. They are simply extensions of your strengths.

For instance, if you have difficulty pronouncing a particular letter or your eye twitches from excitement, don't hesitate to share it during a talk, presentation, or live broadcast.

Say something along these lines:
"Friends, I have a hard time pronouncing the 31st letter of the alphabet, and my eye twitches when I'm excited. That's who I am! Accept and embrace me, and let this become our unique feature. And if you notice this happening, please let me know in the comments."

What will happen if you do this? Because of your sincerity, the audience will connect with you. They see you as imperfect, just like themselves. This vulnerability creates a sense of authenticity and relatability, and fosters a deeper connection with the audience.

- **How can we deal with people who undermine our self-confidence and act as haters?**
Approach them with love and gratitude. See them as valuable assets rather than sources of offense. Their reviews and comments can actually work in your favor by increasing your popularity, and the best part is that it's free. Instead of getting offended, embrace them with joy and encourage their engagement as much as possible. Be grateful for their presence because, without haters, genuine recognition is hard to come by.

- **What steps may artists take to effectively market their works?**
One of the most common mistakes artists make is believing that their masterpieces will automatically sell themselves. If you aspire to gain popularity and financial success, simply producing exceptional work is not enough.

As an artist, it is crucial to shift your mindset away from

viewing your creations as your own children. Disassociate yourself from this viewpoint and let go of it. By doing so, you will avoid feeling resentful towards the world for not instantly admiring and appreciating the part of your soul you've poured into your works.

Instead, try to see yourself from an external perspective. Approach your art as a product that someone else has created. Take on the role of a skilled salesperson and manager who must effectively market and sell the product. Your goal is to generate revenue. After all, money matters.

By adopting this perspective, you will be less likely to take offense when potential buyers compare your work to other offerings on the market, inquire about pricing, negotiate, or take their time making a decision.

Yevhen Lavrenchuk's advice to artists:

1. Embrace your imperfections and be proud of them.
2. Acknowledge that haters can contribute to your popularity. Their absence indicates that you are not making an impact.
3. Shift your mindset from being offended by criticism to becoming a successful manager of your projects.

- **What should you do when everything you believed in and worked for is taken away?**
Always invest in yourself. Focus on personal growth and development. Improve your skills and competences. This is what will protect you in situations where you face a job loss, business setbacks, or the loss of assets due to changes in your life, country, or the world.

No one can take away your talents, skills, and experience. They are priceless and cannot be diminished or stolen. You are the greatest treasure and wealth that you possess.

Regardless, approach your work with passion, strive to become the best, and forge ahead, surpassing others and conquering new heights.

If you feel undervalued in your current environment, have the courage to leave and seek a place where your worth will be recognized and where you can experience rapid personal growth.

- **How long does it take to recover from life's setbacks?**

Recovery time can vary, but it generally takes at least two months. During this time, you may notice that things you built or worked on are falling into the hands of others who have taken over your business or project. However, after these two months, despite any initial pain, you will find a renewed energy and reach a new level in both your business endeavors and self-understanding.

- **Where can you find the resources to weather life's storms?**

The key is to transform negative situations and mistakes into valuable experiences. Humans tend to be lazy and weak by nature. Without a significant push we may be unwilling to leave our comfort zones or make necessary changes. However, it is through setbacks and failures that new opportunities and avenues for personal growth are revealed. Embrace these challenges as catalysts for ambition and advancement. Throughout my own journey, I have found that such experiences have provided me with encouragement and motivation.

STORY THREE:
Italian prison, mafia, Papal patronage, four releases, and protest across Europe

In early 2022, numerous media outlets around the world reported that "the Ukrainian opera director Yevhen Lavrenchuk had been detained by Interpol in Naples on an extradition request. He was charged with a crime and is currently being held in solitary confinement".

As the story spread through the global art community, Yevhen found himself in an Italian prison, anxiously anticipating each time he was escorted out of his cell, unsure of his fate and facing extradition to russia for a crime he strongly denied committing.

Yevhen Lavrenchuk recounts his experience in his own words:

After graduating in 2003, I decided to stay in russia and establish a private Polish theater in moscow, despite the lack of state funding. For a decade, I dedicated myself to running this theater. However, following the annexation of Crimea, I made the decision to decline any further offers to work in russia. Instead, I returned to Ukraine, where I engaged in several projects.

Eight years later, while in Naples, I was approached by Interpol agents who presented me with a document claiming that the Tagansky District Court in moscow had charged me with fraud and financial misconduct. The court had purportedly sentenced me to ten years in prison. Astonishingly, they even claimed that I had embezzled 4 million rubles (equivalent to 45 thousand Euros at the time) from the russian federation.

Exchange fund

I must admit that I was very anxious while waiting for the documents from russia. Having been responsible for the organization for many years and possessing the authority to sign financial documents, I acknowledged the possibility that I may have made some mistakes. However, I had no idea what exactly those errors could have been. Nevertheless, when I reviewed the fabricated documents, which contradicted one another, I found solace.

It didn't take long for Interpol to realize that this was a clear example of political persecution. Consequently, they rejected the russian federation's extradition request on the grounds of insufficient evidence to prove my guilt.

But I was already under arrest, confined to the same cells as thieves and serial killers while my case was being investigated by the prosecutor's office.

The question arises: Why? It has now been revealed that I was being exploited as part of a scheme to create an exchange fund comprised of Ukrainian citizens who had previously worked in russia. The intention was to exchange this group for important russian individuals such as hackers, high-ranking officials, or military men. These individuals would be detained in Ukraine or captured after February 24, 2022. I had unwittingly become a pawn in this exchange and manipulation.

The night arrest
On December 17, 2021, I was supposed to fly from Naples to Lviv. However, at three o'clock in the morning, there was a sudden knock on the door of my hotel room. I opened the door, only to find myself being arrested, handcuffed, and taken away in a police car to the detention center. As I was being transported, I couldn't help but wonder whether it was all just a dream or if it was actually happening. It felt as though I had stepped into a computer game or a movie.

My experience during the two and a half months in Italian prisons can only be described as a combination of thriller, horror, musical, and melodrama. During this time, I was released four times.

Pre-trial detention center
My confinement at the detention center lasted three days.

During that time, I shared the facility with seven other individuals:
1. There was a nerdy guy who, driven by jealousy, sent threatening messages to his girlfriend. Unfortunately, she reported him to the police, and that's how he ended up there. It was a stark reminder of the reality of such situations in Europe.
2. There were also a few guys who had been involved in robberies at gas stations and stores using toy guns. I never imagined such incidents could occur in real life, yet they did. They seemed resigned to the consequences and had a philosophical outlook on their impending imprisonment.
3. There was one man I nicknamed the "Professor." He was knowledgeable about legal matters and provided interpretations of everyone's documents. Fluent in Italian and English, he offered advice on what to expect and how to navigate the situation. When I inquired about his own

circumstances, he simply replied, "I will be here for a long time."

My time in the pre-trial detention center proved to be interesting, as I developed good relationships with the other inmates.

The trial eventually took place, and Interpol removed the Red Notice against me. This meant that they no longer had grounds to detain me for the purpose of extradition.

Notes from Kalabukha

The primary goal of Interpol (International Criminal Police Organization, ICPO) is to facilitate international cooperation in combating crime. Headquartered in Lyon, France, Interpol operates by uniting the efforts of various countries in the fight against crime. Interpol was founded in 1914 during the first International Criminal Police Congress. It was established in 1923. Its current constitution was adopted in 1956.

Within the Interpol database, different types of "notices" are used to provide information about wanted individuals or objects:

- *"Yellow Notice" is used to find missing people or identify individuals who are unable to identify themselves.*
- *"Blue Notice" is issued to locate, identify, or gather information about a person of interest in a criminal investigation.*
- *"Black Notice" is used to seek information on unidentified bodies.*
- *"Green Notice" is issued to warn about a person's criminal activities if they are considered a potential threat to public safety.*
- *"Orange Notice" is utilized to alert authorities about an event, person, object, or process that poses an imminent threat and danger to individuals or property.*
- *"Purple Notice" provides information on the modus operandi, procedures, objects, devices, or hiding places used by criminals.*

The most common type of notice is the "Red Notice," which is issued to seek the location and arrest of a person wanted by a judicial authority or international tribunal with the intention of extradition.

In Yevhen's case, he was initially arrested based on a Red Notice, but later the charges were dropped.

The second cell and eight hardened prisoners

I was released on the fourth day following my arrest after Interpol recognized russia's demand for my extradition as political persecution. However, I had already fallen under the jurisdiction of the prosecutor's office and remained physically incarcerated. Only the authorities who had imprisoned me had the power to release me, and the process was lengthy and continuous.

During this time, I was transferred from the pre-trial detention center to Poggioreale, one of the most notorious prisons in Italy. I was put in a real cell alongside thieves, rapists, and even a convicted serial killer.

What did the cell look like? It had three-tiered bunk beds, accommodating a total of nine people. Fortunately, there was a separate room with a shower and toilet, which was a relief. Unlike some prisons where a shared toilet is located in a corner. When I entered the cell, there were vacant beds on the "third floor" of the bunk beds, so I quickly claimed one for myself. Being unfamiliar with prison etiquette, I entered the cell as if I were entering a compartment where people were already traveling. I greeted everyone with a "Hello" and introduced myself as Eugenio. Some greeted me kindly, some frowned, and some didn't react at all.

As for clothing, prison uniforms such as gray striped outfits seen in concentration camps or orange overalls depicted in American films were not supplied. Everyone wore their own civilian clothing. Among my neighbors, I was the most elegantly dressed ☺.

Many people ask why I didn't protest when I was placed in prison with hardened criminals. My response is that I tried to accept the circumstances I found myself in and avoid exploiting my status as a renowned director.

In general, I received respectful treatment from both fellow inmates and the prison staff, particularly after they learned about my identity following the first court hearing. The staff expressed apologies for having to use handcuffs on me.

Violence and service personnel

In Italian prisons, there are no "rogue" elements among the inmates or the staff. Two years ago, during the COVID-19 pandemic and the resulting quarantine restrictions, riots erupted prompting reforms. As a result, if any violence or fights occur in a cell, the entire shift of guards is immediately dismissed.

I can't speak for how things used to be, but the prison staff today is more akin to hotel staff than harsh guards. They can be called upon to bring food, medicine, and escort prisoners to see a psychologist. When I requested books, they brought me everything they could find, although there was no library available. The selection mostly consisted of ladies' novels and detective stories, genres I had never read before. Nonetheless, I ended up rereading them four times and even memorized some passages.

A language barrier

Language became a significant issue. Neither the prisoners nor my cellmates spoke English or, surprisingly, even Italian! In fact, they couldn't read, write, or understand Italian at all. Instead, they spoke a distinct Neapolitan dialect.

As a result, I primarily communicated with only two people: a German who knew English and a Romanian who had a basic understanding of Polish. However, I tried to limit my interactions with them to a minimum.

Food

The food was surprisingly good. It felt like I was in a nice hotel. Seriously! We would be escorted to the canteen, but meals were also delivered to the cell, and the prisoners' dietary needs were accommodated. We had unlimited access to various types of cheese, prosciutto, pesto, marmalade, vegetables, and fruits. As a vegetarian, I received special meals tailored to my dietary preferences.

There was even a shop where you could order whatever you wanted, but delivery took five to six days. However, it required cash, and since I had all my money on my bank card, I couldn't take advantage of this convenience. I hadn't anticipated the need for cash in an Italian prison.

I spent two weeks there until bureaucratic procedures

finally led to my transfer to a cell with intellectuals and drug dealers. It was in that cell that I learned about the beginning of the war in Ukraine.

The third prison cell, drug dealers, and the war in Ukraine

One of my new cellmates didn't speak a word of Italian. The other had a limited grasp of the language and could only catch a few words, mostly from TV newscasts.

Oh! Television was my greatest source of distress, and there was no escaping it. I normally live without a TV, as I am particularly sensitive to loud sounds and modern music. It's a professional quirk of mine — outside of work I require complete silence. Despite having brought earplugs with me, they provided little relief.

It was a true endurance test. The television was constantly blaring at full volume in all three cells where I was being held. My cellmates spent their time engrossed in shows, movies, and commercials.

Yes, there were opportunities to work in the kitchen or help with cleaning the facility, and they even paid a salary for those tasks, which would be issued after completing the sentence. However, participation in such work was voluntary. No one was coerced into forced labor. This is not the USSR, it's Europe, where human rights are fully respected. Nonetheless, none of my fellow inmates, including myself, opted to work and had no intention of doing so.

Italian Yanukovych

My arrest coincided with the presidential elections, which witnessed a fierce battle between the incumbent president, Sergio Mattarella, and the former Prime Minister (who had served three terms!), Silvio Berlusconi, who was known for his pro-putin stance and his government's alignment with russia.

The balance of power between the candidates was evenly distributed, with a 50-50 split. Whether or not I would be extradited to russia depended heavily on whether Mattarella would secure re-election as president or if Berlusconi would stage a comeback, employing his notorious political maneuvers similar to

Yanukovych.

An Italian lawyer, who discreetly shared information with me, revealed this political backdrop. Despite being an accomplished legal professional renowned for handling international extradition requests, he had recently lost a case involving a russian extradition request during Berlusconi's tenure as Prime Minister.

When the news on a forever-on TV finally broke that Berlusconi had withdrawn his candidacy and Sergio Mattarella remained as the president of Italy, I felt a slight sense of relief. The likelihood of my release increased significantly.

There is a stereotype that Italians are pro-russian, but in reality, it's not the case. Italians hold deep disdain for Berlusconi and his corrupt government, much like our disdain for Yanukovych *[pro-russian Ukrainian former president who fled to russia]*. Italy is not pro-russian; rather, it is plagued by an alarming level of criminal activity. The mafia's influence permeates throughout society and remains an enduring force.

The mafia is immortal.

Notes from Kalabukha

For centuries, Italy was under foreign rule. Because of exploitation and repressions, Italians were forced to somehow defend their rights and lives. That's why noble robbers began to emerge in all regions, robbing wealthy foreigners, sometimes (a key word here ☺) sharing the loot with fellow villagers, resolving minor conflicts, and providing loans.

They protected people as best they could when there was no one else to protect them. This is how the mafia ("courage" in the Sicilian dialect) was formed, a criminal organization with its own rules, spheres of influence, and jargon.

The mafia is composed of "families" ("famiglia" in Italian). The "family" itself has a strong hierarchical structure, subordinate to the so-called "godfather", and controls a certain territory ranging from a few streets to entire provinces.

The most famous Italian organized crime groups are Cosa

Nostra (Sicily) and Camorra (Naples).

The term "godfather" gained worldwide popularity through Mario Puzo's novel "The Godfather" and the subsequent movie based on his book.

Even before my arrest, I was deeply disturbed by Naples with its slums, street thefts, and criminal conflicts involving shootings, reminiscent of the 80s movies about Police Commissioner Cattani. Nothing has changed since then: the city remains dirty, frightening, gray, and depressing. There are some streets that you simply cannot enter without risking your life.

Half of the parliament is made up of official mafia representatives. They can be found both among the convicts and the police force. This topic is so dangerous and taboo that it is never openly discussed, although everyone is aware of where each group's godfather resides, who their deputy is, the names and phone numbers of their members, and the legal and illegal businesses they are involved in. They are the ones who effectively govern Italy and hold true power over what matters to Italians.

Regarding the political awareness of the prisoners, they simply don't have it. Due to their lack of education, they have no knowledge of countries like Ukraine and russia, nor do they have any desire to learn about them.

Sports in prison
No, there were no weight rooms or gyms in Poggioreale prison. It is an ancient fortress with 5-meter-high walls and several old, abandoned courtyards with wilted grass growing between the concrete.

Each prison block had its own yard for recreation. During my time there, I was housed with drug dealers, who were considered elite prisoners. When we were taken out for recreation in the first cell I was in, there were over 100 people. It was a crowded environment. In comparison, now there were usually around a dozen people in the new block I was transferred to during recreation time. People would smoke, drink coffee, and engage in conversations on their walks.

Asking others about the reason for their imprisonment is considered impolite. If someone wishes to share, they do so voluntarily. However, it seemed that everyone, except for me, was there on drug-related charges.

This is how it works for them there: if they are caught with a small amount of drugs for the first time (typically for street-level sales), they are let go on the first offense. The same is true for the second, third, and so on, up to a total of nine times. When they attempt this for the tenth time, they are well aware that they have already been flagged in all the databases and they know the consequences awaiting them. Therefore, everyone I encountered in the prison yard had been there before, not for the first time, and most likely not for the last. They were simply waiting for their release to resume their activities.

These individuals do not have the desire or the ability to learn, and they are unfamiliar with the Italian language. Surprisingly, they show no desire to grow or make positive changes in their lives. Their conversations consist of simple comments about what they see: "here's a fork" and "here is a spoon"; "turn on the light because it's dark"; "oh, the light is turned on" and "now it's off because we have to sleep"; "let's sleep."

I pondered extensively on the circumstances surrounding these people's time in prison. It is not an institution that can rehabilitate them. Instead, it appears to have a degrading effect, leaving individuals broken and even more bitter when they are released.

The War
It was while watching the Italian news on TV in a cell with drug dealers that I learned about the war that had begun in Ukraine. From that point on, it became the leading news story in every broadcast. I was deeply concerned for the safety of my family and friends. Unfortunately, I was unable to make a phone call or go online, even though others were permitted to call once a week. It wasn't that my right was being denied, rather the process for obtaining international authorization was lengthy and bureaucratic. By the time the authorization would have been granted, I had already been released.

How did I stay connected with the outside world? Through Ukrainian and Italian lawyers. Initially, they visited me once every ten days, and a day later they would bring me the news. It was through them that I discovered the tremendous support I had from around the world.

A wave of rallies with the slogan "Freedom for Lavrenchuk" swept through dozens of cities in Italy and Ukraine. People gathered outside the consulates of Italy, russia, and Ukraine, and congregated near theaters such as La Scala in Milan. Fellow artists, politicians, ministers, diplomats, cultural and human rights organizations, my friends, and even strangers came to my defense! Proactive individuals created the Facebook community "Free Yevhen Lavrenchuk!" and launched a petition to the Italian government. The Italian Minister of Justice personally intervened on my behalf. Even Pope Francis demanded my immediate release from the Italian prosecutor's office, arguing that Italy should not be perceived by the global community as a country that supports the political persecution of the putin regime. Therefore, at that moment, I was aware of the significant support I had received and felt reassured that everything would turn out well.

The third discharge and farewell, as if in the musical
It was evening, around 8 p.m. Every day I hoped that someone would come and say, "You are being released." But no one came. And that day was no different. That's why I felt sad.

Then the guard on duty turned to me in the corridor and gestured with his fingers for me to gather my belongings and leave. He didn't speak Italian. I asked him twice if I was being released, and he confirmed with a repeated "Yes!" My cellmates started to greet me, and the news quickly spread throughout the floor. Everyone started singing, shouting, and pounding their plates on the floor. There was no jealousy or cursing aimed at me. They bid farewell as if in a musical. By that time, I had already gotten to know everyone, so I entered their cells to say goodbye and exchange hugs. It was a very touching moment. As I was leaving, it was announced that I wasn't being fully released, but rather placed under house arrest.

House arrest
When the court received the appeal from the Pope and the

Minister of Justice, they were immediately prepared to grant me house arrest. The issue, however, was that I am not an Italian citizen and don't have a personal residence, family, or a residence permit.

They had to find an apartment for me and assign it to someone. They also had to approve two Ukrainian women who would come to assist me with household chores. All of these arrangements required extensive checks, coordination, and preparation, which took a considerable amount of time. Meanwhile, I remained behind bars, as I had been throughout this entire process.

The apartment was provided to me by an employee of the Ukrainian consulate in Naples, who was in Ukraine at the time. They trusted me, so I wasn't required to wear any cinematic wristbands that would explode if I stepped out of bounds ☺.

In reality, the bracelet functions as follows: when you go beyond the designated perimeter, a special chip sends a signal to the nearest police station, and the officers respond promptly.

That's why I didn't even step outside the door to water the flowers in the stairwell. I gave my honest word and honored it: I couldn't disappoint the people who had supported me, believed in me, and provided me with this apartment.

The police would come twice a day, once during the day and once at night, to check if I was abiding by the rules ☺. It was particularly stressful during the night checks, which occurred at two o'clock, three o'clock, and even four o'clock in the morning. And this happened every day. They would ring the doorbell, and I would open the door and let them in. So I was expecting someone to arrive all the time.

Refusal of the third release and house arrest all over again

When I received the document regarding my release, I decided to fight it in court. What was the issue? The reason for my release was not my innocence, but rather the ongoing war between russia and Ukraine. Even if I were guilty of fraud, murder, or rape, I would not be extradited because of the war.

It didn't satisfy me. My reputation was on the line. I insisted that the document state that I was released because I am innocent, not because of the war.

I won the trial, and although the new document was being processed, I remained in detention for another three weeks. Finally, all charges against me were dropped.

FREE!

On March 25, 2022, I wrote on my Facebook page:

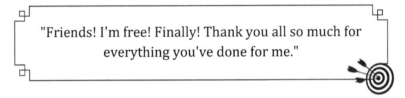

"Friends! I'm free! Finally! Thank you all so much for everything you've done for me."

The feeling when you step out for the first time in three months as a free person is strange. It's like waking up after sleeping for two days straight, your head feels dizzy and foggy.

I kept looking around for police cars. I am afraid of them now, just as I am afraid of sharp sounds at night. I still live with the constant fear that they might come and take me away in the middle of the night without any explanation, reminiscent of the times under stalin's rule. Recently, a police car pulled up to my house in Warsaw at three o'clock in the morning, and I immediately jolted awake, grabbed my glasses, and anxiously watched to see where they were headed.

I went on living in an apartment in a small town near Naples. When I stepped outside, I was greeted by the sight of Ukrainian flags everywhere. It was a powerful demonstration of support from our people, many of whom had already gathered there. I was fortunate to have the assistance of two wonderful volunteers from Ukraine, Mrs. Nadiya and Romania. Despite being under house arrest, I kept up with the news and continued to send humanitarian aid and medicine to Ukraine. I also worked on numerous projects with Italian activists.

After leaving Italy, I promptly traveled to Poland where I have various contractual commitments. I hold a residency at the Polish National Opera in Warsaw and the Zbigniew Raszewski Theatre Institute. I am a permanent member of the Grand Theatre in Poznań and have also received numerous offers from Germany.

I became actively involved in the Ukrainian volunteer movement in Poland right away. My activist friends Yevgeny Klimakin and Natalka Panchenko and I orchestrated a highly visible act of protest by pouring red syrup on the russian federation ambassador on May 9, as he prepared to lay flowers at the memorial to the Unknown Soldier. We also raise funds for the acquisition of Bayraktar drones and organize rallies to support the cause.

"The last victim of russian exploitation of Interpol"
This is how I was officially recognized by The Guardian, one of the most reputable publications in Great Britain, published since 1821.

According to a report completed by my lawyers, russia makes 40% of all requests to Interpol from around the world, and the organization is used for political persecution. This is a clear violation of Interpol's statute. Based on this information, Interpol has initiated the procedure to suspend russia from the system, as the Deputy Secretary General of Interpol informed me over the phone. In the near future, russia may be labeled as a terrorist state. If russia is expelled from the UN, it will automatically be expelled from Interpol as well. Consequently, russia will no longer be able to make arrests through Interpol, despite continuous incoming requests.

As I analyze the entirety of this story, I often ponder whether my time in prison, the global media coverage of my wrongful arrest, and the spotlight that was placed on me have actually put an end to a series of abuses and crimes committed by russia via Interpol. Could it be that this has always been my mission?

HOW TO GET A JOB WHEN THERE ARE 1000 PEOPLE PER PLACE

I hadn't seen so many good-looking men in a long time. They were tall, broad-shouldered, with blond, brunette, and red hair, and there was even one Afro-Ukrainian (perhaps that's how we should refer to our black-skinned Ukrainian citizens). They formed a long line that moved slowly, and every minute, new beauties joined the queue. Twenty years ago, I witnessed a competition for a drama artist position in one of the Lviv theaters. Candidates came from all over Ukraine, hoping to become the new sex symbol and romantic hero of local productions, with highly desirable pay at the time.

It was at that moment that I encountered an old acquaintance of my parents — the spouse of the theater's main director. She had stepped out for a break after several hours of listening to monologues, poems, and fables presented by the finest representatives of Ukraine's gene pool.

"And whom will you hire?" I asked. "Have you discovered a talent yet? Honestly, I can't imagine how you can pick just one from all of them!"

"None of them," she replied.

"What do you mean, none?"

"That's right. We published the job opening announcement in the newspaper just as a formality. None of the people we listened to, including those still in line, will be chosen for the position. We had already promised it to one actor a long time ago. And you know who it is."

Notes from Kalabukha

In 2004, the Faculty of Culture and Arts was established at the Ivan Franko National University of Lviv, where dozens of young talents are admitted each year through fierce competition. Many students enrolled as fee-paying students. Both prospective and current students were impressed by the employment opportunities available to graduates specializing in "Acting Art of Theater and Cinema," including professional theater groups, cinema, television, and radio.

The reality, however, was different. As my friend, who is

knowledgeable about the industry, pointed out, "Not so many actors die yearly to replace them with the new ones in our theatres." Furthermore, we can count the number of university graduates working in their specified field of study on one hand. Therefore, the chances of finding employment in the theater or cinema during those times without Instagram and TikTok were practically zero.

Graduates quickly removed their rose-colored glasses to face the harsh reality. The majority of them ended up changing professions and finding "regular" jobs that could at least provide them with a living. Only a select few were fortunate enough to secure employment in related artistic ventures. It was often referred to as an "expensive hobby" that was supported by completely unrelated work.

But there was also a long and energy-consuming way, used by one person. Let's refer to him as Roman. Even when he was still a student, Roman devoted his days and nights to one of the theaters in Lviv. He took on various roles, serving as a stagehand — a "cable master" as they called it in the theater — assisting costume designers, working with lighting, and even serving as a porter. Gradually, he became involved in productions. He started out as an extra, and subsequently he was entrusted with small roles. Remarkably, Roman carried out all of these responsibilities without receiving any compensation. He dedicated himself to the theater from morning till night, working tirelessly for three consecutive years without a day off.

One young actress, who had recently gone through a divorce, took notice of him and started advocating for his interests. The theater staff grew fond of him, and when a vacancy for a drama artist became available, the management made a unanimous decision to hire him.

"Is he a genius?" I asked. "Is he better than all these young actors, including the Afro-Ukrainian who auditioned for the lead role in a theater that predominantly performs Ukrainian classics? Isn't there a new Bohdan Stupka *[Ukrainian famous actor]* among them? Why are you hiring him?"

"No, he's not a genius at all. There are incredibly talented individuals among them that leave us speechless, but we choose him."

"But why?"

"He is a responsible person. During the three years that he worked for us without pay, he never complained about anything, never drank alcohol, and never acted like a "star" with demands or preferences that "he will do that" and "he won't do that". He was always the first to arrive at rehearsals and the last to leave. He never had any issues, and if he did, he kept them to himself. He rarely took sick days, never had conflicts with anyone, and never spoke ill of others. In fact, he started a family with one of our actresses, and her children from a previous marriage adore him. Yes, he is not a genius. Do you know what some of these geniuses do? They drink excessively. Imagine the following scenario: a sold-out show, the theater packed with people who came to see him play, and he shows up drunk, barely conscious. What are we supposed to do then? Refund everyone's tickets? Or imagine this: we have a tour planned abroad, involving significant efforts to secure his visa for the United States, and he suddenly has a creative crisis, declaring himself worthless and unable to perform on stage again. What are we supposed to do when all the arrangements, tickets, and performances with him are canceled? We also need to consider how these new so-called geniuses would behave in terms of discipline and responsibility, as well as how they would fit into the team. It's a pity, of course, for those guys who waited in line for three days in the scorching sun and spent money on tickets and accommodations. We will continue casting until the end and listen to everyone. However, we won't be hiring any of them."

I was quite impressed. I spent several days reflecting on everything I had witnessed and heard. People often ask me why I don't write fiction. But why should I? The truth itself is captivating enough to be a blockbuster. That's why I write, to share the truth.

P.S. Information for those who are concerned about the Ukrainian theater.

This individual was indeed hired at that time. However, he struggled with the role of a leading actor in a renowned theater. He couldn't embody the image of a sex symbol or a captivating hero in both modern and classical productions. Even his comedic characters lacked humor, and his portrayal of tragic roles was unconvincing.

And three years after his dismissal, the residents and

visitors of Lviv witnessed once again a line-up of male contestants, resembling a television show, in front of the theater.

Conclusion: Being responsible, reliable, and a good person is not enough to become an exceptional actor who is adored by the public. Talent is also a crucial factor.

"I DON'T KNOW HOW TO SELL AND WON'T LEARN"

This is what one artist wrote to me the other day. He wrote with pride as if showcasing his superiority. However, in the following sentence, he expressed despair, claiming that he had no money to support himself because no one was buying his paintings.
He has the freedom to think and live as he pleases. However, there is nothing to be proud of if you lack knowledge and refuse to learn.

We live in a multitasking world. It is not enough to excel at something, even surpassing others. Nowadays, the most crucial skill is the ability to sell an idea, product, or service, to generate interest in your business, and to captivate people to the extent that they want to be a part of it and invest their time and money. This skill must be mastered. There's no need to hide behind the mask of "I'm an artist—poor, but proud."

I can teach it. I teach everyone.

First, it requires stepping out of the comfort zone. Not everything will work out immediately. But then everything starts to progress and develop. I'm so proud of the results! It's such an exhilarating experience!

I am a woman of action. He approached me with a problem — I offered a solution. I shared feedback from some artists, who are also my clients, and who are now selling like gods, and then invited him to join my "Sales with Joy" Club.

He wrote that he was not someone who would impose himself and that only a poor artist or product relied on advertising. According to him, having lost their taste and failed to recognize true value, people ended up buying promoted junk. In general, he believed that a time would come when cockroaches would feed on rats, but he saw himself as someone who would endure. However, I didn't quite grasp my position in his worldview — was I a cockroach or a rat?

How easy it is to make everyone bad and guilty.

In general, taking on a role of a victim is quite convenient. It's also a choice. However, why invest so much energy in insults and proving oneself right when you can simply learn to sell in order to live and work joyfully for yourself and others?

SALES DESPITE "I CAN'T", NEW PRICES, AND TEARS IN ZOOM

"I won't be able to do this!" The artist, let's call her Olha, told me for the fifth time and started crying during the Zoom call.

"You will be," I reassured her. But deep down, my heart sank. I understood the delicate mental disposition of an artist, coming from a family of artists myself. I used to be an artist before I became an entrepreneur. To resist being affected by her tears, I imagined myself as a doctor causing temporary pain to a patient for the sake of their ultimate well-being. "Say: "250 euros". Just say it with conviction and confidence, so that I believe you."

This is how I consulted an incredible artist who, prior to our meeting, had not sold any of her paintings. And it wasn't because few people knew about her or because her works lacked talent. No! On the contrary, she had already held 15 solo exhibitions in 10 countries around the world!

"How can this be?" I asked during the consultation. "You're in the spotlight, surrounded by cameras and people who want to buy your paintings. What happens next?"

"They ask about the price."

"And what do you say?"

"I tell them I don't know."

"What do you mean you don't know? You don't know the value of your own work? Don't you have prices for your paintings?"

"No, I don't have any."

116

"And what do people do?"

"They turn away and leave. And I cry because I feel like a lousy artist whose paintings nobody wants to buy. I attend new workshops, learn new techniques, invest in more expensive materials, and the cycle continues. They don't buy it."

"You're not a bad artist. You're a bad seller. But don't worry, I'll teach you. Do you know why people turn around and leave? It's because they don't want to set their own prices for your work. If they offer too little, they might think they're taking advantage of you. If they pay too much, they might feel like they've been foolishly overcharged. It is easier for them not to buy anything rather than go through all that trouble. I dedicated an entire chapter in my book "When to Say YES" to comments like "How much are you willing to offer?", "Let's come to an agreement," and "We'll work something out." You should read it! Show me your paintings, and we'll set the prices for them together."

That's how I transitioned from being a business consultant to an art dealer. And Olha, who resided in Poland, had an exhibition opening in Kyiv the very next day. The prices for her artwork needed to be determined right away.

"Let's set the price for this one at 180 euros, and for that one at 250. Does that sound reasonable to you?" I proposed during a Zoom call, taking into consideration factors such as size, technique, and framing.

"Yes, but isn't that expensive?" she asked.

"It's actually still quite cheap! You have to start somewhere. And now the most challenging part is confidently announcing your price to people."

This is precisely what we grappled with for a long time. I played both a good cop and a bad cop. I even found an affirmation for her on the Internet (keep it for yourself, you might need it): "My work is valuable, and I have the right to receive fair compensation for my efforts."

"I don't believe it. I don't believe you. Until you confidently state the price, until you believe it yourself, no one else will believe you. Tell me in a way that leaves no room for doubt that this painting is worth 250 euros."

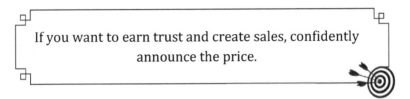

If you want to earn trust and create sales, confidently announce the price.

And that is precisely the problem we face! Do you know what I constantly observe when I'm preparing for training or when I'm interacting with managers as part of the "Mystery Shopper" promotion? When asked "How much does it cost?" most people mumble something in a shaky voice. What do customers think? They perceive it as expensive. The price seems so high that even the seller doesn't believe in it and is afraid to say it out loud. And if it's not worth that much, why should they overpay or buy it at all? The client concludes, "I don't believe you," and tells you, "Thank you, I'll think about it." So, who is causing these doubts? Who is to blame for the emergence of this objection? It's the seller who is uncertain about the price.

Remember, or rather, write down great wisdom from Kalabukha:

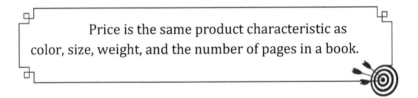

Price is the same product characteristic as color, size, weight, and the number of pages in a book.

There's no need to step back when it comes to announcing the price. Repeat it 20 times until it becomes second nature. This is especially important when you're raising prices. And if you find it difficult to say it out loud (because I didn't spend an hour on Zoom with you practicing telling the price 😊), write it down. Write the new price with a firm hand and send it immediately before your courage wanes.

That's how Olha and I practiced communicating with potential customers ten times. We attached price tags to all her works and began to eagerly await the opening of the exhibition.

Late at night, she called me in tears. She was crying so

intensely that she could barely speak coherently. My heart sank and I thought to myself, "Perhaps my methods are too harsh for creative individuals. Have I really caused such distress to someone's nervous system? What should I do now to help?"

And here's what happened: for the first time in her life, my incredible Olha sold her artworks for 1500 euros. This goes to show that a talented person has talent in every aspect. She did it! She was able to do it! She confidently and firmly announced the price, and everything worked out. People bought her artwork for themselves or as gifts to express their appreciation. Not a single person even tried to negotiate the price!

"Let's not get complacent, this is just the beginning," I said firmly, putting a stop to the flow of happy tears in Kalabukha style. "If you did such an excellent job and the market accepted the price, we can raise it. Add 100 euros to each painting. Attach new price tags. So now everything that was 250 euros will be 350. Knock it out of the park!"

And my clever Olga calmly and confidently stated the prices for all the artworks; the new prices, which were 100 euros higher than yesterday and were initially challenging for her to accept.

Eh, why can't I mention the real name of my talented artist ☺? Why can't I share a link to her social networks? I gave her my word.

I gave her my word to tell everything as it happened, only without using her real name. And it's the right thing to do because there's a 100% chance that her clients are reading this.

What happened next? Olha sold the entire exhibition completely. It was the first time in her life that she had done so. She mastered my techniques so well that she now sells paintings for up to four thousand euros per month solely through her personal Facebook page without spending a penny on advertising. She organizes auctions, sales, promotions, and contests. She even reaches out to potential clients with her proposals and has implemented a 100% advance payment policy for her work.

And they say that artists cannot sell. But they absolutely

can! They just need to be taught, just like anyone else. That's precisely why I teach.

CHAPTER 5

HOW THE MONA LISA BECAME THE MOST EXPENSIVE PAINTING IN THE WORLD, AND OLEH VASIUKOV'S SENSATIONAL STUDY

PART ONE: SCANDAL IS THE BEST PR

The most scandalous robbery turned the painting, previously known only to a small circle of researchers, into the world's main artistic masterpiece. And this is how it happened.

On August 22, 1911, a craftsman working in the Louvre installing glass entered the hall where Leonardo da Vinci's "Mona Lisa" (also known as "Gioconda" after the likely patron of the portrait) was displayed. He carefully removed the painting from its frame, concealed it under his cloak, and successfully smuggled it out of the museum.

The absence of the painting was discovered only two days later when the Louvre was undergoing technical work. Initially, everyone assumed that the painting had been temporarily removed for cleaning purposes.

The only clue was the presence of clear fingerprints on the newly installed protective glass and frame, which were found on the Louvre steps. However, at that time, the head of the French police did not believe in the emerging practice of fingerprinting, which was gaining recognition worldwide. As a result, he neglected to cross-reference the fingerprints with the existing police database.

Do you know why he didn't do it? Because he extensively promoted his own method of finding criminals, which never gained widespread acceptance due to its imperfections. He flatly refused to employ any other methods of investigation that he hadn't devised himself.

As later recounted by researchers, the search for the renowned portrait lasted two years and they may have continued to this day due to the detective's arrogance. The search would have taken as little as two hours if the detective had been instructed to check the fingerprint database. It is quite astonishing, considering that the Italian glass worker had already left his fingerprints, which the French police had on file.

> Within a day, the portrait of the smiling Italian woman went viral: her image graced the covers of all major media publications around the world.

And so Giocondomania swept the world: in Parisian cabarets, women danced wearing masks depicting Mona Lisa's enigmatic smile, popular singers of the time gained fame through songs dedicated to the painting, and ordinary people like housewives, laundresses, and cooks adorned their kitchen cabinets with reproductions of the masterpiece. The Louvre experienced a surge in visitors, with long queues stretching into the museum just for a glimpse at the empty space where the painting once hung.

There was also a heated debate about whether the woman depicted in this portrait could be considered beautiful. I, too, have pondered this question on several occasions until I stumbled upon information about the standards of beauty during the time the painting was created.

Notes from Kalabukha
I am convinced that 16th century people would not consider modern-day recognized beauties to be beautiful in any way.

What was the standard of beauty back then? Thin lips and a small mouth were considered desirable. Round and large eyes were also favored. And as for eyebrows and eyelashes? They had to be plucked! Completely plucked. That's how girls "shaped their eyebrows". Just like how we currently desperately remove hair from all parts of the body where it naturally grows. Although, even in the early 20th century, having unshaven armpits was not considered a crime against humanity.

That was until 1915, when Gillette marketers invented a

problem that most women didn't even know existed: the idea that being hairy was indecent. They actively started to address and eliminate this problem, although, in reality, they were promoting their new product to the market.

Interestingly, this fashion did not immediately catch on everywhere. Even in the 1950s, prominent actresses in open-shouldered dresses on calendars and movie postcards showcased an abundance of unshaven hair. This was the case in Europe, the United States, and even the Soviet Union, and it didn't cause any big uproar. It was a sort of body positivity movement of the mid-20th century. But it wasn't just the brows and eyelashes that were subject to grooming. Hair was mercilessly plucked all the way up to the nape of the neck. Why? To visually elongate the face's oval shape; a swan-like neck was considered fashionable.

Traces of this 15th-century fashion can be seen in the eyebrowless and artificially raised hairline of the Mona Lisa (1503-1505). The lady was truly fashionable and embodied the beauty standards of that era.

When it came to makeup, the beauties of that time were not far behind. Some particularly daring individuals even invited artists to events who would "paint" their faces using brushes and oil paints. Powdered marble, pearls, and even wolf skulls were used to whiten teeth. Crushed eggshells could serve as tooth powder, assuming all the local wolves had been hunted down.

Journalists made this story the main event of the year. The director of the Louvre, who liked to boast that it was easier to steal Notre Dame from France than something from the Louvre, resigned with great fanfare.

Only the "Titanic" disaster temporarily pushed "Gioconda" to the second page of newspapers. Although the investigation of the theft became a national case for the French police, it yielded no results. However, in December 1913, the painting was unexpectedly found. An antique dealer in Florence received a letter offering to buy the artwork and invited the director of the Uffizi Gallery to the meeting. They could hardly believe their eyes when they saw the original painting by Leonardo da Vinci, which had been hunted by police all over the world. The "Mona Lisa" was discovered hidden under the bed of the same glass worker, where it had been kept for two years.

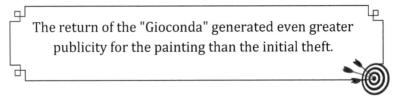

> The return of the "Gioconda" generated even greater publicity for the painting than the initial theft.

At the trial, the thief, Vincenzo Peruggia from Italy, accused the French of stealing Italian cultural heritage and presented himself as a champion of justice whose mission was to return masterpieces to his homeland. He was unfazed by the fact that Leonardo da Vinci had willingly brought the painting to France when invited by King Francis I, who had purchased the "Mona Lisa" from one of da Vinci's students (as evidenced by documents). Peruggia's eloquent and persuasive arguments about his "patriotic act" won sympathy from the court. He was sentenced to one year in prison but was released after only a few months.

After being exhibited in various cities in Italy in January 1914, the painting returned to Paris. Over time, the Mona Lisa continued to grace the covers of newspapers and magazines around the world. It was featured on stamps and postcards, and it's no wonder that the woman in the painting became an object of adoration, surpassing the popularity of movie actresses and opera divas. Special evening excursions to the Louvre were organized for factory workers, who had just one desire — to see the Mona Lisa and nothing else.

I have to remind you:

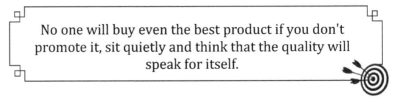

> No one will buy even the best product if you don't promote it, sit quietly and think that the quality will speak for itself.

Even a masterpiece created by Leonardo da Vinci's brush needed publicity to increase its value to 3 billion US dollars (the amount for which the Louvre insured it) and achieve such widespread popularity and global recognition.

PART TWO:
WHO IS REALLY THE WOMAN IN THE PORTRAIT? THE RESEARCH OF MY FATHER OLEH VASIUKOV

My father, Oleh Vasyukov, a philosophy professor, poet, journalist, and one of the founders of Lviv Television, sparked a true revolution in Leonardo studies with his book "The Passionate Secret of Gioconda." *[Oleh Vasiukov. Zhahucha taina Dzhokondy. Lviv: Liha-Pres, 2012. 264 p.]*

For over 500 years, researchers have been haunted by the following questions:
- Who is the enigmatic woman who smiles at us from the world's most famous painting?
- Why does this painting have multiple names, and where did they originate from? After all, Leonardo da Vinci never signed his works.
- Why is the woman, believed to be the contented wife of a wealthy Florentine man for whom this portrait was intended as a gift, depicted wearing a mourning widow's veil and devoid of any jewelry?
- Why did the commissioned portrait remain in the possession of the artist rather than being delivered to the patron, and eventually end up in the possession of the French King Francis I?

My father dedicated his entire life to researching this fascinating story.

I remember how passionately he recounted the cunning and untamed customs of the era, which brought forth an abundance of the greatest geniuses in the entire history of European civilization. He delved into the countless wars and epidemics that plagued those times, the inventive ways in which people inflicted suffering and destruction upon each other, and the betrayals, broken promises, and deceptions that permeated every aspect of business, love, and life. Yet, despite it all, those times would be hailed as magnificent and bestowed with the resounding name — the Renaissance era.

We had a large reproduction of this painting for as long as I can remember. During interviews, my father always made it clear that he cherished three women in his life: his wife (my mother), his daughter (me), and Gioconda. However, when my daughter Anya was born, she became an additional beloved woman in my father's family, pushing Gioconda to fourth position. From that moment on, he had four cherished women in his life.

To give you an idea of how captivated my parents were by this subject, they went to great lengths to visit moscow in 1974 to see the legendary painting with their own eyes. They did everything within their power to make that trip a reality.

After its theft in 1911, the "Gioconda" left the Louvre twice: in 1963, it visited the United States, and in 1974, it visited Japan. When it was announced that the "Gioconda" was being sent to Tokyo, the director of The Pushkin State Museum of Fine Arts, along with the current USSR Minister of Culture, ensured that the famous artwork would also visit moscow upon its return from Japan.

The conditions for the Mona Lisa's exhibition included a bulletproof transparent capsule, specially manufactured by a defense enterprise, and an unprecedented foreign currency insurance coverage of $100 million. The "feat" of the Italian patriot Peruggia in 1911, who stole the painting, as well as the damaging attempts in 1953 when one person splashed acid on the painting and another threw a stone, prompted these measures.

For 45 days, soviet citizens stood in line for seven to eight hours just to catch a glimpse of the mysterious smile of the "Gioconda" for 10-15 seconds. It was during this time that my pregnant mother immersed me in this incredible story.

"Mona Lisa" (or "Gioconda") was painted by Leonardo da Vinci between 1503 and 1505. It is believed to portray a noblewoman named Lisa (or Mona Lisa, as women were commonly referred to at the time), the wife of a silk merchant from Florence.

A woman by the name of Lisa did indeed live in Florence during the 16th century. Her portrait is housed in the Hermitage Museum in St. Petersburg and is titled "Portrait of a Woman as Flora" or "La Columbina". In the painting, she is depicted wearing an elaborate dress and a ruby brooch on her chest *[the original text says "ruby ornament on her neck", which is incorrect - the brooch is on her chest]*. The attributed author of the painting is Francesco Melzi, a student of Leonardo da Vinci. Melzi is known to have completed several of his teacher's works, which is why researchers often associate them with him.

And according to my father, Oleh Vasiukov, the real Gioconda, the one smiling at us from the painting in the Louvre, is the beloved of the Italian aristocrat Giuliano de Medici.

Her real name is Pacifica Brandano. Due to her cheerful and sharp-tongued nature, she was given the nickname "Gioconda" (pronounced exactly that way), which means "smiling" or "playful" in Italian. She met Giuliano when she was already a widow of a Spanish nobleman. She captured Giuliano's heart but tragically unraveled her own life. Pacifica became Giuliano de Medici's secret lover and gave birth to a son named Ippolito.

What always strikes me as particularly moving in these medieval stories is the fact that all children, regardless of whether they were born to an aristocratic mistress or a peasant servant, were acknowledged and provided for. They were welcomed into castles and palaces, where boys received an education and girls received dowries.

In our civilized times, irresponsible "fathers" often abandon their own legitimate children and fail to participate in their lives. They do not consider it necessary to fulfill their parental responsibilities. However, in the past, fathers regarded their children as sacred, irrespective of whether they were born within a marriage or not. They took their roles as fathers seriously and actively participated in their children's lives.

That is how black aristocrats emerged in Europe: children who were born to slave women were recognized by their fathers, raised alongside legitimate children, provided for, and given opportunities for successful careers. Their fathers ensured that they received the same level of support and opportunities as their legitimate siblings.

Giuliano de' Medici acknowledged his beloved's son, gave him his surname, and brought him to the palace. During the early stages of their romance, a wealthy patron commissioned a portrait of his woman. And not just from anyone, but from Leonardo da Vinci himself! The artist worked on the portrait for two years, and he continued to work on it throughout his life. But why? Because the patron never collected the finished painting. Giuliano eventually married someone else, not because he had fallen out of love with Pacifica, but due to dynastic considerations. His older brother, Pope Leo X, chose a different bride whom he believed would strengthen the Medici family's wealth and influence in the political arena of that time.

Giuliano's wife was not just any wealthy woman, but Philiberta of Savoy, a relative of the French king. As you may know, conflicting with kings can be quite risky, even resulting in losing one's head. Hence, Pacifica was expelled from the Medici Palace, and instead, Leonardo da Vinci received an invitation to the House of Savoy to paint a wedding portrait. However, over the years, the artist developed a close friendship with Pacifica and became so enamored by her intelligence and charm that he refused to paint a picture of the wedding. Pacifica's destiny reminded Leonardo of his own mother's fate as an illegitimate wife. During their painting sessions, which lasted for hours each day, Leonardo made sure she didn't grow tired. He would read her poems, invite musicians, and do everything possible to keep the captivating smile on her lips, which later became the subject of poems worldwide.

The Medici did not forgive the artist for his refusal to paint the wedding portrait and subsequently withdrew their patronage and commissions from him. Such is the price one pays for genuine friendship and personal convictions when serving the powerful of this world. "The Medici both created and destroyed me," Leonardo wrote in his journal.

Giuliano did not live long with his lawful wife, and there is speculation of poisoning surrounding his death. This is not surprising considering his position as the commander of the papal troops, which likely made him a target for many individuals with malicious intentions.

History does not provide information about the duration or intensity of his wife's mourning, especially considering the advancements in chemistry at the time *[According to Encyclopedia.com, Giuliano's death at the age of 37 was sincerely* mourned by Philiberta and the people of Florence. However, it is worth noting that Philiberta herself passed away at the young age of 26 in 1524.]

Notes from Kalabukha

During that time, poisoning one's relatives, particularly in Italy and France, became a widespread practice, almost like a national endeavor. People were investing heavily in "chemical startups" as a means to carry out such acts.

Unfaithful wives and husbands were often poisoned, as were those who became boring in a relationship. Enemies and competitors who posed a threat were also poisoned. Even friends who were envied or resented could fall victim to poisoning, as the saying goes: "No person, no problem." In such a toxic environment, anyone who happened to be in the wrong place at the wrong time could be poisoned, including accidental incidents where poisoners themselves consumed from the wrong glass or plate.

But the death of a loved one, even a traitor, was a devastating blow for Pacifica, who referred to herself as "twice a widow" ever since. She maintained her connection with Leonardo, and he continued to paint her. As her life changed, so did her image. This is evident in the nearly completed portrait in Leonardo's studio, where a dark widow's cape adorns her head, and all jewelry has disappeared from her neck and fingers (modern studies have revealed their presence in earlier versions).

Leonardo and his student left Rome, where he had been painting the captivating Pacifica. They took several paintings with them, including the one that would later be housed in the Hermitage under the name "Portrait of a Woman as Flora" or "La Columbina" — a portrait of Mona Lisa, the wife of a Florentine merchant — as well as "Gioconda" — a portrait of Pacifica. None of these paintings were claimed by their intended patrons.

Question: When it comes to Giuliano Medici, everything is clear, but why didn't the Florentine merchant accept the commissioned portrait? It was because Leonardo da Vinci painted one of his wife's breasts being revealed (you can search for it online and appreciate its artistic beauty). According to legend, the customer did not want such a "shameful" painting to hang in the house of an honorable man and entrepreneur. When the artist refused to cover up the "shame," the customer left with threats to leave negative reviews everywhere, loudly slamming the door.

Surprised? Such things happened to Leonardo da Vinci as well, not just to you.

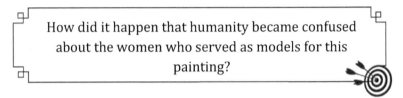

How did it happen that humanity became confused about the women who served as models for this painting?

One of the culprits, according to my father, was the Italian art critic Giorgio Vasari, whose work "The Lives of the Most Excellent Painters, Sculptors, and Architects" was published in the mid-16th century, 50 years after Leonardo's death. The book was written with skill and vigor. However, the author frequently mixed up names, dates, and facts. He would sometimes combine two artists into one, a mistake that researchers, including his contemporaries, have pointed out throughout history. When confronted about these inaccuracies, Vasari would respond, "I am an artist, and this is how I see it. I write what I want. It's my opinion. If you don't like it, don't read it." Interestingly, Vasari never saw any of the portraits or the women themselves, yet he combined them into one woman and one portrait. This error has persisted in the art world for over five centuries.

What happened to the key figures in this story, and how did their destinies unfold? Unaware of the significance of the rejection of his wife's portrait and the ensuing scandal, the Florentine merchant could never have imagined that his name would become associated with the woman in the legendary canvas for the next 500 years. Unfortunately, little is known about his subsequent whereabouts, and his trail has been lost to history.

The son of beautiful Pacifica, Ippolito Medici, received a superb education, eventually becoming a cardinal and gaining significant influence with the Pope himself. However, his promising life was tragically cut short when he was poisoned at a young age by his cousin, Alessandro Medici, who was also a bastard (an illegitimate child) and harbored intense jealousy towards him.

What else interests us about Ippolito? For me, it is noteworthy that he was in love with the young Catherine de Medici, who would later become the queen of France and the mother of three kings. However, back then marriages were based on political considerations rather than love. In those times, princesses and princes were often used as pawns in the political maneuvers of their families. Thus, Catherine was compelled to end her relationship with her lover and marry a French prince whom she despised. Despite this, she went on to bear him ten children, even though he continued his affair with a mistress who was 20 years his senior. It is believed that Catherine de Medici was the mastermind behind the infamous Massacre of St. Bartholomew's Day, seeking revenge on those around her for her own unhappy life. However, that is a completely different story altogether.

But what became of Pacifica? She didn't poison anyone, nor was she involved in scandals or politics. Overwhelmed by the grief of losing Giuliano and later her son, she quietly faded away, living out her days as a twice-widowed woman. Despite the challenges she faced, Pacifica left behind a legacy as one of the most intelligent and elegant women of her time. She was known for her sharp wit, cheerful demeanor, and captivating charm, earning her the nickname "Gioconda," which means "smiling" or "playful" in Italian. According to the research of my father, Oleh Vasiukov, it was her portrait that found its place in the Louvre and became one of the most valuable and renowned paintings in the modern world.

If my father were to discover how I portrayed the outcome of his research, I am certain he would laugh!

Because every line in his book, every thesis, date, and name is supported by dozens of references to the most reliable sources. The book is filled with numerous illustrations of all the individuals involved and reproductions of paintings. It is a substantial scientific work that has made waves in the field of Leonardo studies. And it was written by my father, Oleh Vasiukov from Lviv.

These were the bedtime stories I grew up with, written with such vividness and attention to detail as if he had lived alongside these people his entire life. I want you, my friends, to be the ones to learn about the culmination of my father's life's work, not just the scientists in their scholarly offices!

As I write this, it feels as if my father is sitting right beside me, recounting once more the tales of Leonardo, the enchanting Pacifica, the treacherous Medici, and the tumultuous lives of kings and queens. He reads me his poems, comforting me in times of sorrow and celebrating my triumphs with joy.

As I write this, I can vividly picture my parents, young and deeply in love, holding hands as they patiently wait in the long line at the Pushkin Museum in moscow. They excitedly await the brief moments they will spend gazing into the eyes of the enigmatic woman portrayed in the painting, safe behind the bulletproof glass. I imagine my mother gently caressing her rounded belly, sharing what she perceives in the essence of Gioconda with the future child within her. And I, nestled in her womb, am part of that moment in the year 1974.

I imagine how 35 years later my parents, now recognized and renowned art critics, will stand hand in hand before the same portrait at the Louvre. They will find it hard to believe that they have made it here to encounter a woman with an enchanting smile.

And now I'm certain they are young once again, filled with love and happiness, holding hands, looking down at me from heaven. Somewhere close by, Leonardo is engrossed in his creations, inventing devices that are centuries ahead of their time, while she, the Italian woman from the renowned portrait, continues to wear her enigmatic smile. She possesses a knowledge that we, the people of the 21st century with all our advancements in technology, have yet to comprehend.

CHAPTER 6

TURKISH-STYLE BUSINESS: HOW TO SELL A LOT, EXPENSIVELY, AND WITHOUT EXCEPTIONS

GOD-STRUCK; SEX AND MONEY: REGULARLY

"I am captivated by your beauty and eloquence; tonight, I will dream of you," said a Turkish man in clear russian, with a captivating appearance reminiscent of a movie star and a name that sounded like "God-Struck." Well, not exactly "God-Struck," but something close, like "Estrakh." I formed associations to aid my memory. His gaze was remarkably sincere, profound, and honest, much like that of all mischievous individuals 😊.

And when God-Struck (or whatever his name was) took our group to various factories, it seemed like every other person was buying furs, diamonds, and carpets worth thousands of euros (for those who claim people don't have money, this would have been an eye-opener!). I thoroughly enjoyed observing the Turkish sellers at work.

What do they do? They shower us with compliments!

"Goddess, queen! How perfectly it complements your eyes! You are a lovely fairy-tale princess! Take both white and blue to captivate everyone with your beauty and taste."

And they also assist in trying on clothes, helping to put them on, fasten them, and take them off. They express admiration with their entire demeanor. How can one not surrender to their charm? I mean, how can you not buy something from them (a Freudian slip 😊)? Our ladies are simply enthralled when they hear Oleh Vynnyk's songs (that's how you should know your Target Audience), accompanied by champagne, gallantly served, and they emotionally spend extravagant amounts of money on it all.

Do not envy, do not sulk, but learn from Turkish sellers. If not their oriental skill and eloquence, then at least acquire basic abilities to compliment and say pleasant things to people.

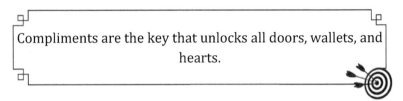

Compliments are the key that unlocks all doors, wallets, and hearts.

Why is it so challenging for us? Why do we find it difficult to simply say a heartfelt "thank you" and express kind words to others? The answer lies in our rigid upbringing and our experiences in a society where people are often disliked and underappreciated. We haven't received much praise ourselves, and we haven't been taught how to give it. Even leaving a simple like or comment on someone's social media post can be a struggle.

I recall giving a speech at a conference for restaurateurs and hoteliers. The topic was mail-order commerce. The room was filled with attentive listeners jotting down notes as I spoke. Then, all of a sudden, a hush fell over the crowd. It was evident that people were not prepared to embrace the recommendations I was offering.

Do you know what exactly I suggested? We analyzed 20 different approaches to ensure that the client follows through with payment. A common scenario is when you address an objection (rather than just saying "Have a good day! Let me know when you're ready"), the client appears to agree with everything, promises to make the payment, and then suddenly disappears.

What happens next:
1. You don't remind them about yourself or the payment. But why? Isn't that pressuring the person? How can you impose yourself on them? They might think that you're just after their money. Excuse me, but why do you go to work or start a business in the first place? Is it to bring balance to the universe? Do you, your children and elderly parents survive on dew and pollen? What a load of nonsense! You're here to make money, and they should pay you for your work.
2. You notice that your message was read, but customers remain silent. You wait and hope that they will eventually make the payment as they promised. Some even dare to initiate a dialogue with messages like "Hello!", "Liudmyla, are you there?" or simply "???". Sometimes a voice message

is sent. And what happens as a result? Do they make the payment? No. Instead, they block you. Mercilessly and irreversibly.

The first piece of advice I shared on that forum, and the advice I give everywhere, is to do some preparatory work before reaching out to someone. Specifically, I recommend liking and commenting on the person's last three social media posts. Just give a like (or as it's trendy to say now, a thumbs up) and write a few kind words under what they have shared on their pages.

What kind of posts do people typically share on their personal pages?

- They go fishing, to the beach, to barbecues, to restaurants, to concerts, and to the movies. We can write something like: "Oh, I'd love to experience that too! It looks like you're having a wonderful and enjoyable time!"
- Happy parents often share the news of their child's achievements, such as starting school, reaching a milestone, or winning a competition. We can respond by writing: "Congratulations from the bottom of my heart! Well done, you must be proud of their accomplishments."
- Someone shares their opinion or quotes someone else's with supposedly deep meaning. We can respond by writing: "How apt and heartfelt. It resonates with me."

It doesn't take any money, time, or any extraordinary skills. In this day and age, when everyone is vying for your attention, it piques your interest to know who wrote something to you. In all my books, webinars, and workshops, I emphasize: likes and comments are the currency of social networks. They are a free and highly effective tool for capturing attention and fostering customer loyalty.

But it was the suggestion to write a sincere comment that truly provoked a reaction from the audience in the hall. Here and there, islands of strong disagreement started to emerge.

"Well, we're willing to go as far as giving a like. But writing a comment is definitely not our cup of tea."

"Of course," I replied. "It's far better to invest another few thousand dollars in advertising, hoping that this time it will attract people who won't 'hesitate,' 'remain silent,' or 'disappear.' That way, we won't have to resort to methods that contradict our moral principles just to push them to book, purchase, and pay. But writing kind words in the comments to someone who shares their joy on social network is simply unheard of. It's not our style; we won't be able to remind, capture attention, and distinguish ourselves from the faceless competitors who don't engage in such practices. We are above that and refuse to be sycophants."

Then we all laughed with the hoteliers and restaurateurs because I had articulated exactly what they were thinking. During my master class's break, participants started sharing screenshots of payments they had received from clients. They said it felt like magic. After just a few kind comments, people responded with messages like, "It's so nice that you're following me and supporting me. I lost track of our conversation, but I'm glad you remembered. I'm ready to pay now!"

> Stop withholding a smile or a kind word — it's a lingering effect of childhood traumas inflicted by our soviet parents, who themselves were scarred by their experiences.

Think of yourself when you used to get "excellent" or top grades. What did you hear?
— As if you were going to fail! So much was invested in you!
— I didn't expect you would get a lower score; that's how it should be, there's no other way!
— Why not 200 points? Lilya Petrivna's daughter attended a regular school, not a specialized one like yours, and scored 198 points! And you only scored 197!

That's not normal. In a healthy society of well-adjusted individuals, it is natural and appropriate to praise our children, friends, loved ones, clients, colleagues, or even strangers who look good, have accomplished something, or have helped us in some way. It's important to acknowledge those who genuinely align with what we offer and who deserve recognition.

Then people will naturally be inclined to purchase from us and will find the means to pay for our products or services rather than relying on clever Turkish (or any other) sellers. And we will have everything we want: happiness, sex, and money. Regularly.

"ANYONE WHO OFFENDS A CAT WILL GO TO HELL"

This is exactly what the Prophet Muhammad commanded. And he had good reason for it. When a snake crawled into his robe sleeve, it was the cat who saved him. In return, he granted her nine lives. He respected her so much that he changed his clothes so as not to wake the cat when she fell asleep on his robe. He even preached with a cat on his lap on several occasions. As a result, cats became sacred animals in Islam, and the inhabitants of Istanbul became faithful servants of cats. Residents of the city feed, care for, and treat the furry ones. They even build special dwellings for them so that they have a place to hide from the elements. And they also believe that cats go to Paradise and can tell Allah about the good people who helped them.

And it works! I have never seen such beautiful cats anywhere else. What brought them to Istanbul? For centuries, ships from all over the world have been arriving in the port city, bringing with them cats that were brought aboard to catch ship rats. The present-day cats are descendants of those traveling cats. There's such a mix of breeds here! They are gentle, purring, and well-groomed — and they are welcome guests in all shops, institutions, high-end hotels, and even mosques.

The dogs, on the other hand, are not so fortunate. They are considered unclean animals.

20 years ago, I was surprised by my Polish business partners. When I asked if I may call early on Sunday or if they would be in church (Poles are considered the most devout Catholics in Europe), I was told: "We are not practicing Catholics."

And in Turkey, only non-religious Turks keep dogs at home. Those who "aren't practicing." And they are usually very wealthy. Owning dogs is considered an expensive luxury.

And Istanbul's street animals have their own "Ambulance" — a service that helps the city improve. If you encounter an animal that is in distress, you can call 153. They will come and pick it up, provide medical treatment, and return it to the spot where it was found. All these services are provided free of charge. They also carry out sterilization of stray animals.

The love for cats is so profound that even during the initial, strict months of quarantine (when people in Turkey were only allowed to go out for groceries twice a week), individuals risked fines of 180 euros to feed the cats.

Some cats even have their own Instagram profiles, like Gli, the cat who lived in Hagia Sophia. She boasts 120,000 followers and posts photos alongside presidents and movie stars.

In Turkish, cats are called "pissy-pissy-pissy," not "keets-keets-keets" like in our country [Ukraine]. By the way, I have compiled a list of how you can call cats in different countries around the world. Here are some examples: Tunisia: "besh-besh-besh"; Latvia: "minka-minka"; Lithuania: "kats-kats-kats"; Czech Republic: "chh-chh-chh"; Hungary: "tsits-tsits-tsits"; Japan: "shoo-shoo-shoo"; Italy: "micio-micio-micio"; United Kingdom: "pussy-pussy"; United States: "kitty-kitty-kitty"; Georgia: "pees-pees-pees"; China: "mi-mi-mi"; Azerbaijan: "pish-pish-pish"; Bulgaria: "mats-mats-mats"; Germany: "mitz-mitz-mitz"; Netherlands: "push-push-push"; France: "minou-minou-minou" (with emphasis on the last syllable — mi-NOO, otherwise French cats will not understand you if you call them incorrectly).

I have gained so much wisdom now, but in the past, I used to say "keets-keets-keets" to cats in the 50 countries I visited. All I got were their dismissive glances. Cats know their worth, and so should we!

In short, cats in Istanbul live a good life. I would often encounter them during my walks and would take photographs of them. I must admit, I even felt a twinge of jealousy towards them - they are loved, nourished, and well taken care of.

What can we do to live like Istanbul cats? How can we treat each other the way Istanbul locals treat their street furry friends?

When you're there, start calling them "pissy-pissy-pissy" right away. Now, you've read this book for at least one good reason 🙂.

I'M GREAT, COOL, OR SIMPLY GOOD IF...

And then there's a whole list of requirements that I must meet in order to consider myself as such. If I lose weight, get married, have a child (or second, or third), defend my thesis, learn another language, take another course, stay at that cool hotel by the sea, or buy a new iPhone/car/apartment. This list is constantly being updated, and it feels like real life will only begin "if".

I evaluate myself based on achievements (both material and social status), just like I do other people: are they the same as me, better, or worse?

"It appears to me that I work and achieve far too little; there is room for more. Others accomplish more. They have more. So, I need to push myself once again, take a leap forward, raise the bar higher, and when I finally reach that desired peak, I realize it's merely the foothill of a new mountain that needs to be conquered," the clients remarked again during the consultation.

Did that strike a chord with you? That's how we live, enslaved by the trend of "success at all costs" and perpetual debts to everyone, debts that we'll never be able to repay. But in Istanbul, everyone I observed, from the cleaner to the top manager, lives differently!

Do you know how? "I'm great, cool, or just good by default." Perhaps this is influenced by the mild Mediterranean climate. Maybe it's the influence of religion, which teaches that only God Almighty is perfect and that humans are inherently prone to making mistakes. That's why we are human beings! And perfectionism we often boast of is nothing but pride, and pride is considered a sin. As a result, people have a fundamental trust in both the world (believing that everything is in the hands of God, "Inshallah") and in themselves ("I'm fine the way I am").

So let's learn from the Turks what we, Ukrainians, often lack: self-satisfaction and gratitude for what we have and who we are. Let's stop demanding perfection from ourselves, comparing ourselves to others, and categorizing people as either "worse" or "better" than us.

And starting today, let our mantra be: "My self-esteem does not depend on others' opinions of me. Someone else's success does not diminish my own. I am already great and worthy, without any conditions or doubts."

LOVE, MONEY, AND A COFFIN FILLED WITH HONEY

Three million gold coins were offered as a bounty for the man's head, which was displayed on a stake in Istanbul. The Turkish Sultan made this demand, and it was paid. The reason behind this payment was love. Regina Żółkiewska loved her husband, Stanisław Żółkiewski, who held the positions of the crown hetman and chancellor (equivalent to the roles of minister of defense and foreign affairs) with infinite devotion.

He dedicated his entire life to battles and campaigns, defending the borders of the Polish-Lithuanian Commonwealth against the Tatars and Turks, opposing the Swedes, defeating the Muscovites, and even residing as a ruler in the moscow kremlin for half a year. He consistently emphasized army discipline and firmly believed in honoring one's word, even when dealing with the enemy. However, despite his extensive experience as a great commander, it proved insufficient when facing a formidable force of 130,000 Turks and Tatars against his 12,000-strong army.

There was also an ill omen — an ominous sign. A comet appeared in the sky as the fighting began. Even if they had chosen to wait and postpone the military campaign for a few days or weeks, it would have made no difference. The very intent was destined for failure, and her husband was doomed to meet his demise.

But she would never have dared to dissuade her husband, a great warrior and commander, from going to war. It wasn't the first time he'd gone to battle, and she remained behind to oversee their brainchild, their ideal city of Zhovkva, which had no parallels in Europe.

How did this city come to be? Their brother-in-law lost a considerable sum of money in a card game. Left with no means to repay his debts, he had only one asset remaining: a plot of land. However, even that land had already been mortgaged and re-mortgaged. He approached his relatives in tears and asked them to buy off his gambling debts, offering them vast estates in return. And so, the magnificent city of Zhovkva in the Lviv region emerged on the banks of the Svynia River (a name that would later amuse descendants and spark debate among historians).

A unique private city in which all residents, whether they were Poles, Catholics, Orthodox Ruthenians, or Jews, enjoyed equal rights and could live together, conduct business, and establish churches, chapels, or synagogues. Remarkably, the Jewish community even had their own cemetery, an unprecedented arrangement at a time when their counterparts throughout the Polish-Lithuanian Commonwealth would bring their deceased to Lviv for burial.

During the Battle of Cecora, Regina's husband, Crown Hetman and Chancellor Stanisław Żółkiewski, tragically passed away on the night of October 6-7, 1620 AD, at the age of 73. Despite being attired as a common soldier, his body was eventually discovered and recognized.

He was beheaded, his body was taken to Istanbul, paraded through the city streets, and exhibited at the gate of the Sultan's palace. While the Turks reveled in their triumph, they pondered, "Why not profit from this? The family is not impoverished; perhaps they will pay."

And a messenger delivered a letter to Regina, a grieving widow, with a stark demand: "Do you desire the return of your husband's body? 3 million gold coins must be paid. In cash."

An unprecedented sum. Regina did not hesitate for a moment.

"I will pay," the letter was sent back to the Turkish Sultan. Another letter was also sent to the King, stating, "Please grant me permission to establish a private mint in Zhovkva for the purpose of minting coins to purchase my husband's body for burial."

The King granted permission, marking an unprecedented case in European history. And she began her endeavor. She melted gold and silver plates, candlesticks, and jewelry. She painstakingly unraveled gold threads from the brocade. She sold several villages and towns. She spared no expense or effort. She struck deals with everyone she could. And she accumulated them. She amassed 3 million gold coins.

The money was transported to Istanbul in chests on carts with strong security. Meanwhile, her beloved's body was being transported to meet them. How was it carried? In a coffin filled with honey, the primary preservative of that time.

Historians are still divided on how long it took to transport the body to Istanbul, send messengers to Regina, return to the Sultan, then to the King, and back again.

And to collect, mint, and import the money? And, finally, to receive the body (which had to be identifiable, for how else would they know that the deceased they paid for had been brought to them)?

Can you imagine it took two years? It's not like sending an SMS or a direct message, or flying to the other side of the globe in 12 hours (oh, how long that feels!)

By the way, there's another story that struck me about the preservatives used to transport the bodies of important deceased individuals.

Horror from Kalabukha

In 1805, the Battle of Trafalgar took place off the coast of Spain — a naval battle in which the British fleet, commanded by Vice-Admiral Horatio Nelson, defeated Napoleon's fleet. This proved to be Nelson's final battle as he lost his life in the process.

How were deceased sailors buried back then? They were simply thrown overboard. However, it was decided to transport the body of the legendary commander Nelson to London. But how could this be done in a warm climate without refrigerators, formalin, and vacuum packaging?

There was no honey on ships at that time either. They did, however, have alcohol. A strong, inexpensive drink called rum, which was a South American moonshine made from cane sugar. It was used for a practical purpose — to disinfect water that spoiled during the voyage.

So, in order to prevent Nelson's body from degrading, the assistant captain ordered that he be immersed in a barrel of rum and instructed the crew to refrain from consuming rum during the voyage. However, upon the ship's arrival in London, it was discovered that the vice admiral was lying in an almost empty barrel: the sailors had drilled a hole and consumed all of the rum, referring to it as "Nelson's blood" among themselves.

That's why rum has been associated with that story ever since! It is often referenced with playful labels, and the Internet is filled with recipes for cocktails named "Nelson's Blood".

In Istanbul, I stood in front of magnificent mosques, libraries, hammams, and madrasahs (educational complexes), marveling at the wonders of architecture and the sophistication of the culture of the Ottoman Empire, the most powerful worldwide empire of its time.

Money, all this required lots of money. This is how it was obtained. This is how everything we now admire so much was financed.

And I remembered the great love story of Regina and Stanisław Żółkiewski, mature people who had been married for many years. A love that was stronger than death. Love that was stronger than money.

CHAPTER 7

LIFE, DEATH, GASTRONOMIC HORRORS AND THE DECOLUMBIZATION OF MEXICO

THE ROAD TO A DREAM AND A MEXICAN-STYLE QUARANTINE

Back in 2019, we purchased tickets with plans to travel in April, but as fate would have it, 2020 was downloaded with an error — the quarantine. I wonder what we will have to say about 2022.

So read it and reminisce with nostalgia about those times that seemed incredibly challenging to us. And not just about the quarantine, but also the Mexican lockdown, with the taste of tequila on our lips and the crunch of dried crickets between our teeth.

After extensive negotiations and numerous ticket exchanges, we found ourselves on the other side of the world. What was the journey like? Empty train stations and airports, vacant tourist facilities that were once bustling with visitors, and deserted planes. We became the first tour group in seven months, and the locals couldn't have been happier. We witnessed firsthand their expressions of gratitude as they fervently offered prayers to the Virgin Mary and their Native American Indian gods simultaneously.

People residing in perpetually warm climates tend to be relaxed and easy-going, and often pay less attention to prohibitions and sanctions. Despite our different climates, Mexicans and Ukrainians share this characteristic.

What do we particularly remember about the realities of quarantine?
1. **Mask mode.** Initially, Mexicans largely ignored all government decisions. However, when fines were introduced — $150 for going outside without a mask—it disciplined them significantly. After that, everyone, including teenagers and elderly people, walked the streets wearing masks.
2. **Disinfection.** I haven't seen such discipline regarding disinfection anywhere in Ukraine. At the entrance to any

cafe, shop, and especially a museum, hotel, or tourist attraction, there were strong men who not only took your temperature but also sprayed disinfectant on your palm (I tried to refuse several times, but it didn't work). In some public places, we were sprayed from head to toe on both sides. And in the hotels, our suitcases were carefully treated, and our bus was disinfected and ventilated twice a day (morning and evening).

3. **Social distancing.** Every ten meters in the museums, there were vigilant women who would ensure that you, God forbid, did not lower your mask to take a photo or come closer than one and a half meters to someone else. I, being a bit naughty, even had an armed guard called on me at the Frida Kahlo Museum for my several attempts to stick my nose out for a quick photo. There were floor markings everywhere, even in the elevators, indicating where you could stand and where you couldn't. And whenever our tourist group, brimming with impressions and tequila, attempted to storm the reception of a hotel, store, or, based on old habits, cram into the elevator, the staff members immediately materialized and, with great politeness but firmness, pushed us to maintain a distance of one and a half meters from each other.

Churches were closed for six months, which was a significant blow to Mexicans. Out of the 130 million population, 90% are deeply religious Catholics, for whom attending church on Sundays and numerous holidays is mandatory.

The children immediately switched to remote learning and did not attend school. This posed a significant problem for the country, as 40% of the population did not have access to the Internet. Unlike Germany, for instance, where the state provided children with electronic devices, Mexico faced challenges in ensuring universal access.

There were many illiterate people who could neither read nor write and would use their thumbprint as a signature (the passport, in addition to the photo, includes a thumbprint). Additionally, there are pictures next to the station names in the Mexico City metro to assist those who cannot read.

THE DESTROYED STEREOTYPES

In 2017, we visited the legendary Lake Titicaca in Peru, which borders Colombia, an epicenter of drug trafficking. The city itself resembled a Hollywood set: crumbling houses, a lack of trees, roads in complete disrepair, yellow dust covering everything, and numerous small tornadoes of garbage on deserted streets.

We were warned that in this God-forsaken place the whole population is somehow involved in drug trafficking and always carries weapons. I've never experienced such a sense of hopelessness and danger as I did there. Additionally, my friend witnessed an elderly woman crossing the road while dragging a coffin along the asphalt with a rope.

Do you know the name of this city? It's Juliaca! *[in Ukrainian the name sounds a little vulgar and funny, so it may become the subject of jokes]* You can Google it, and you'll see that it's really called that! To our surprise, there is an airport there from where we continued our journey. We even joked that pilots land planes in Juliaca with their eyes closed just to avoid seeing the horrors of the city. They also take off quickly in order to leave this place as soon as possible.

Well, I was under the impression that Mexico is similar to Juliaca! But I was surprised to learn that it's actually a very optimistic country with a low unemployment rate of 3.7%, comparable to prosperous Austria. Everyone has a job there. The issue lies in the fact that wages are very low. People simply earn very little. Additionally, families tend to be large, with many children. This is why the poorest segments of the population are so eager to migrate to the United States, where they can earn significantly more for the same work.

KIDNAPPING

"He was taken to a basement, where he was held for two weeks until his parents in Ukraine managed to collect a $20,000 ransom. That's what happened when the guy called a wrong taxi in

Mexico," shared with me a travel blogger, recounting the horrifying story.

If previously kidnappings were meticulously planned and targeted wealthy and prominent families, demanding millions in ransom, now the scheme has simplified — they are even targeting modest families and returning the victims for a smaller sum of money.

Do you know who is being kidnapped? Children. If a man's wife or vice versa, parents, or siblings are kidnapped, it is not certain that everyone will immediately start collecting money and buying them out at any price. But when it comes to children, they are willing to give everything.

Our guide told us the story of her Spanish teacher's son being kidnapped. The teacher and her husband, who was a priest, came from a very poor family. They managed to secure their son's release a week later by paying a $1,500 ransom.

That is why in Mexico, you will rarely encounter a child wandering alone on the streets. Those who approach and sell items to tourists are left untouched, as there is little that can be done for them. Not all children attend school regularly, as not all parents have the resources to do so. However, parents or their representatives are responsible for taking children to school or clubs and picking them up afterward.

Honestly, after these conversations, we were quite concerned. We started taking extra precautions for our own safety. Even though we are not children, one can never predict what might happen.

INSECTS AND DOG MEAT: WHAT DID THEY AND WE EAT BEFORE THE DISCOVERY OF AMERICA?

Before Columbus' expeditions, potatoes, pumpkins, squash, cocoa, tomatoes, beans, corn, sweet and bitter peppers, and sunflowers were not present in Europe.

Questions: What did our ancestors eat before "our" Ukrainian products arrived to our land in the 18th century? And what did the indigenous people across the ocean eat until ships with adventurers brought diseases, alcohol, and dietary habits that had deadly consequences and continue to affect the indigenous populations?

Before Europeans arrived on the American continent, Native American domestic animals included turkeys (which were also brought to our land from there), guinea pigs, and dogs. Yes, that's right! Hairless dogs Xoloitzcuintle are known as the oldest breed on Earth. They were not only regarded as mythical guides of souls to the Realm of the Dead, but were also raised and fattened, similar to pigs, for consumption during major festivities and as sacrificial offerings to the gods. The Spaniards, too, quickly recognized their taste, as documented in the chronicles.

Due to the scarcity of meat and eggs as the indigenous people did not know about dairy products at all, they relied on a diet that included a wide variety of insects, fish, and seafood.

Mexican cuisine left the most vivid impression on our trip, and it is no surprise that UNESCO has recognized it as an intangible heritage of humanity (just like our borscht!). Mexican cuisine has managed to preserve and continue preparing dishes and drinks from pre-Hispanic times. We made sure to explore and indulge in a wide range of street food and visit some fantastic restaurants to taste everything we could find.

TOP-5 OF OUR GASTRONOMY EXPERIENCE:
- Escamol (Ant's larvae) — These delicate larvae are hand-collected in the wild, carefully washed in a large amount of water, and delivered to fine dining restaurants. They must be consumed within 72 hours after removal from the anthill. They have a unique taste reminiscent of butter with a hint of nuts.
- Chapulines — grasshoppers flavored with lemon, chili, and garlic. Their flour received funding in the US at a startup competition as a highly nutritious product. They taste like delicious crispy chips.
- Huitlacoche is a delicacy made from blackened corn that

has been intentionally infected with a certain type of truffle-flavored fungus.
- Grilled and marinated caterpillars.
- Cacti, prepared in various ways: fried, stewed, raw, with meat or fish. They can also be found in the form of juices, desserts, honey, and jam.

We also discovered and became fans of dozens of different types of tequila and mezcal (agave-based alcoholic beverage).

COCA-COLA ADDICTION IN THE EPICENTER OF DRUG TRAFFICKING

Despite being known as the epicenter of drug trafficking, Mexico has relatively fewer drug addicts, smokers, and alcoholics compared to other countries. The biggest societal issue, however, is obesity, with Mexico continuously ranking among the top five countries worldwide and, unfortunately, holding the first place in childhood obesity. It is astonishing how, despite having a rich and diverse cuisine suitable for any budget, a significant portion of the population still relies heavily on over-fried fast-food options.

The second unfortunate first place in the world goes to Coca-Cola consumption, not drugs usage, and in this regard, Mexico has even surpassed the United States. Just a few years ago, a bottle of Coca-Cola was cheaper than a bottle of water in Mexico. However, after a significant struggle with American lobbyists, changes were made to both the pricing and policies surrounding soda consumption. Now, social advertising campaigns are primarily focused on combating excessive Coca-Cola consumption, particularly among children.

When Coca-Cola first made its way into remote mountain areas a few decades ago, the inexperienced indigenous people were amazed and declared it a sacred drink. During our visit to a Christian church, we observed a unique practice where the locals incorporated Coca-Cola into their religious rituals. Alongside their prayers to the ancient gods of America and chicken sacrifices, they also drank Coca-Cola as if it were holy water. The community members would pass around a plastic cup, allowing everyone to take a sip and even feed little infants. They believed that belching from the bubbles in the soda would expel evil spirits and cleanse them of their sins, serving as a form of spiritual purification.

While cigarette packs in our country bear the message that smoking kills, accompanied by frightening images, Mexico takes a similar approach with Coca-Cola, spreading booklets with photos depicting the organs that can be damaged by this drink, as well as detailed explanations of the irreversible harm it can cause to one's health and life.

MEXICAN FEMINISM

"If a man comes up to you in the subway and starts groping your ass or squeezing you, immediately blow this whistle! Then three women will come to your aid and beat up the offender. A woman is no worse, even better than a man. Therefore, do not obey the will of your father, husband, or manager, whether at work or in the family. Don't settle for something you don't want to do," reads a bright pink pamphlet distributed by feminists in the Mexico City metro. It comes with a pink whistle that should be used in case of sexual harassment by passionate machos.

A feminist rally had just ended a few hours before our arrival to this city of 25 million. Following impassioned speeches about gender equality, they gathered in the square and set fire to symbols of women's oppression: bras and kitchen utensils.

If you want to go on strike and rally, go ahead, just make sure not to engage in any destruction. And the Mexicans are indeed rallying, but in a polite manner, without resorting to violence. It's a democracy but with a Mexican touch. While only two of the 32 states allow abortions, same-sex marriages have long been legal.

During rush hour, the first two subway cars are designated for women only, ensuring that a man's hand does not slip under someone's skirt. Men are aware that if they try to do anything like that, they will face consequences. Additionally, the last car during this time is reserved for members of the LGBT community, providing them with a safe and comfortable space where the rights of gays and lesbians are respected and upheld.

Regarding the effectiveness of the pink whistle, our guide carried it with her for a year, and she didn't encounter any instances of harassment from machos. Everyone was polite.

In general, matriarchy is prevalent in Mexico, where the oldest woman in the family takes charge. Men genuinely fear their mothers and wives, although it doesn't stop them from having two families — an official one and one for the soul and body. Perhaps this is why feminists symbolically burn bras and pans in the squares; the scheme works. Women in Mexico truly realize their value and worth. Wish we would do the same!

MERRY DEAD WITH MARIGOLDS AND PROMOTIONAL CEMETERY PLOTS

Why not title the essay "How We Spent the Day of the Dead 2020"? "Flowers of the Dead" – that's what our marigolds, which come from Mexico, are called there. It is believed that the souls of the dead follow the path of their petals to find their way back to the world of the living.

The ancient tradition of the American Indians was combined with the Christian All Saints' Day, transforming a cozy family holiday into a vibrant festival. At every turn, one could find an "ofrenda", an altar adorned with photographs of deceased managers, colleagues, relatives, and famous people.

In one of the hotels, an "ofrenda" was dedicated to Princess Diana. Amongst the marigolds, candles, and colorful skulls, there were offerings of beer, tequila, cornbread, and local fruits, all meant to treat her soul.

In the Frida Kahlo Museum, there is a table set with signed cards not only for the hostess and her contemporaries, but also for Molière, Cervantes, and a dozen other artists from all times and nations.

Here, they sincerely believe in the afterlife, which resembles our world, complete with restaurants and shops. Once a year, the dead return from there, following a path of marigold petals, to feast on their favorite dishes and visit those who remember them.

Anyone who wants to immerse themselves in the mythology of the Mexican holiday should watch the 2017 animated film "Coco," which deservedly received numerous awards. Watch it with your children and parents for an hour and a half of laughter, tears, and a new perspective on many things.

On November 1-2, you can see mariachi musicians singing and playing near graves as relatives pay for this service as a way to honor the deceased. Additionally, you can also meet sellers of a comfortable transition to the next world who offer three meters of land for the price of two, burial clothing, and a memorial banquet at a promotional price. These sellers understand their target audience and know how to make an offer to buy right now and from no one else but them.

The food from the altars is consumed after the holiday. It is believed that the soul of the dead had eaten it because the food has lost its flavor.

Colorful skulls, elegant skeletons in evening gowns and hats, makeup resembling the deceased, folk celebrations, and even car and motorcycle parades despite quarantine restrictions — these all represent the intriguing and unique philosophy of Mexicans who embrace death, inviting it to visit and organizing joyful festivities in its honor.

DECOLUMBIANIZATION AND THE SEARCH FOR THE INDIGENOUS SOUL

While statues commemorating Columbus as a prominent historical figure can be found throughout Europe, and even a street in Lviv is named in his honor, Mexico is currently undergoing a process of de-Columbianization, similar to the decommunization efforts in our state *[Ukraine]*.

Historians have reviewed Columbus's role, and the majority of them agree that his impact was predominantly negative. The arrival of the Spaniards in the New World led to the annihilation of approximately 80% of the indigenous population, largely due to the introduction of diseases brought by the Europeans and the inhumane treatment of the native people. The indigenous population was dehumanized and subjected to brutal violence.

With their superior weaponry and the introduction of novel animals such as horses, the Europeans had a significant advantage, which demoralized the indigenous communities and suppressed even the smallest forms of resistance.

Then, a Dominican monk who happened to be the son of one of Columbus' expedition members was deeply disturbed by the atrocities committed by his compatriots in the New World, prompting him to advocate for the rights of the indigenous people. This led to the initiation of a groundbreaking human rights court process, marking the first instance of such a proceeding in Western civilization's history. The central question was whether the indigenous people, the Indians, possessed souls and thus deserved to be recognized as humans rather than mere animals. The dispute between scholars unfolded in the Spanish city of Valladolid and lasted for an entire year in the mid-16th century.

The underlying motivation for the court process was primarily economic. If the indigenous people were acknowledged as human beings, they would be entitled to payment for their labor instead of being treated as mere commodities forced into harsh mining conditions. This is why protest rallies take place in Latin America on the anniversary of Columbus' arrival, often involving the defacement and destruction of his monuments. In Mexico City, the bronze statue of Columbus was discreetly removed for an extensive restoration, leaving behind only the pedestal.

HOW DID 600 SPANIARDS CONQUER THE AZTEC EMPIRE OF 15 MILLION?

Prophecies
The Spaniards, led by Cortés, appeared to the indigenous people as fair-skinned deities. They came from the east with powerful weapons unknown to the natives, such as rifles and cannons. Consequently, the indigenous population approached them with offerings and eagerly opened the gates to their cities.

Horses
The Spaniards brought 20 horses, which were completely new to the Americas, further accentuating the divine nature of the

foreigners. The horses played a significant role in shaping the perception of the Spanish conquerors. It is believed that the horses seen in movies ridden by Native Americans are descendants of those initial 20 horses. Over time, some of them escaped and formed wild herds, giving rise to the iconic mustangs that were later heroically tamed by cowboys.

Principles

Aztec cities lacked fortress walls and defense mechanisms because they had never experienced sudden attacks. The Aztecs believed that everything was determined by the will of the gods, and it would be sacrilegious to interfere with their plans. Moreover, they avoided engaging in conflicts during the night, as it was believed that the gods battled each other at that time. The Aztecs followed these beliefs faithfully, fearing divine punishment. Unfortunately, the Spaniards took advantage of these beliefs. They falsely portrayed themselves as gods and, in their pursuit of wealth, mercilessly beat the Aztec king to death when he refused to reveal the location of the empire's gold and treasures, which, incidentally, have yet to be discovered.

Traitor

The Aztecs offered Cortés a gift of 20 women, including Malinche, who later became his concubine, translator, and chief adviser. Malinche possessed extensive knowledge of the empire, including its languages, political alliances, and secret routes. Historians argue that her role played a significant part in the downfall of the Aztec empire.

Diseases

The indigenous population was severely affected by diseases introduced by Europeans to which they had no immunity. Within a span of 100 years, approximately 90% of the population perished. The scale of devastation is truly staggering. It was during this time that the term "biological invasion" emerged to describe the devastating impact of such diseases on native communities.

We were standing at the foot of the great pyramids, amazed, and were once again convinced:
- you should listen to your heart and common sense, rather than believe prophecies and even authoritative recommendations;

- there is always a traitor: be careful with important information and passwords. So that it doesn't happen like in one of the most famous medical institutions in Lviv: the fired marketer changed all passwords overnight and blackmailed her former employer for half a year until they were bought back from her;
- no matter how noble your principles and stupendous achievements are, they will never be respected by strangers who come to your house with weapons.

BUSINESS PLAN FOR SECRETS

Even the most famous pyramids have only been excavated to a maximum of 10%. And every year they have to be reclaimed from the jungle, which mercilessly captures everything in its path.

Therefore, if a group of enthusiasts wishes to undertake the excavation of some "symmetrical mountain," they must develop a comprehensive business plan that must be presented and approved at the state level. The business plan should estimate expedition costs, the excavation process, the establishment of tourist facilities, marketing and promotion strategies, as well as projections for reaching the break-even point, cost-effectiveness, and potential profits.

Is it not possible for someone like Elon Musk to invest money in the study of potential alien civilizations on Earth rather than focusing solely on Mars? Easily!

However, there have been few individuals who could effectively pitch such ideas to him and other investors. Due to the lack of business acumen and profit-oriented mindset among passionate researchers, humanity is left waiting for funding to unravel the mysteries surrounding ancient structures that defy scientific explanation. The question remains: were they constructed by mysterious deities, advanced civilizations predating our own, or even extraterrestrial beings?

In addition, Mexico does not heavily promote itself as a tourist destination. It shares the widespread belief that a good product does not require extensive advertising. This contrasts with

Italy, which consistently occupies the top spot in global tourism due to its substantial investments in advertising and promotion.

Temazcal

"This is a magical place where wishes always come true," said the shaman. "However, not for oneself. Often, a person doesn't truly know what they need. But for others, yes. Only then will the soul of the Universe hear you and begin to assist people on whose behalf you are making the request."

"For someone else? Not for myself? How does that work? Everyone advises making a wish for oneself," I wondered.

And then, in the dim light, amidst the rumbling of hot volcanic stones and the thick steam in the adobe Indian bathhouse, I whispered, "I wish for all the good and hardworking people to receive support and assistance. May they always believe in themselves and may their dreams come true."

Today, as I glanced at a photo from Mexico on my phone, I saw pyramids, waterfalls, cacti, pirate fortresses, and the vast ocean. I closed my eyes tightly, transporting myself back to the starry sky above the Mexican forest. In my mind, I blew the trumpet made of big seashells, resonating its sound to every corner of the world. I gently touched the earth with my hands, seeking permission to return to its nurturing embrace — the "house of burning stones," the ancient Indian bath known as temazcal. It is a place where dreams are realized and wishes come true.

My main lesson from Mexico is this: when the world around you seems to crumble, when the ground beneath your feet feels unsteady, dare to make a wish. But let it not be solely for yourself. Instead, direct your intentions toward others in need. I implore the Universe to extend its helping hand to those who need it more urgently than I do.

CHAPTER 8

HOW TO GET WHAT YOU WANT

"I COULDN'T DO IT"

I have known Vika for over 30 years. We first met during our student days, and despite the fact that she did not live in Lviv, we made every effort to meet whenever possible. Our conversations were endless, and we couldn't help but engage in deep discussions whenever we were together.

What is my Vika like? She is a smiling, friendly, intelligent, beautiful, and aristocratic woman — someone you aspire to be like. She is the type of person you are proud to call your friend. She genuinely rejoices in my successes, and before her eyes, I have become an entrepreneur, a business coach, a media expert, and a writer.

An economist by education, Vika dedicated many years of her career to working in a private clinic, pouring her heart, professionalism, and passion into her work. From a humble office, the company transformed into a prominent symbol of the city and became one of the most well-known brands. She played a crucial role in assisting the owner in creating a successful franchise that has been successfully sold both in Ukraine and abroad. Multiple establishments have already opened under this brand.

Vika was the mastermind behind the concept of exemplary service, outlining and standardizing business processes. She took the lead in training her own team and then extended her expertise to the clinic teams operating under the franchise. As word of her success spread, administrators from numerous private clinics in the region sought her out for training and guidance.

She came to my training sessions, and I provided her with guidance and assistance. I also used her as an expert in several of my projects.

But then I learned that her son had been in a car accident and suffered severe injuries. Vika was now fighting tirelessly for his recovery. I couldn't help but wonder how she managed to continue conducting two or three two-day training sessions per month, visiting clinics, consulting franchisees in the midst of such a personal tragedy. Despite it all, she maintained a flawless appearance and radiated success and positivity (how can you continue to believe social media after that?).

I'll never forget that rainy day in Lviv when she called me. What she told me both infuriated and deeply moved me. It turns out that Vika works tirelessly from morning till night, traveling all over the country to consult with clinics affiliated the brand and even conducting several two-day training sessions. And all of this for a wage that is only half of the market rate!

She asked me to assist her in negotiating with the management, specifically the owner of the company to which she had dedicated more than 15 years of her life. The reason was her desperate need for financial support. At that point, she had accumulated $20,000 in debt from multiple surgeries that, unfortunately, did not yield the expected results. Her son required treatment abroad, along with incredibly expensive rehabilitation. Her current pay was simply insufficient to meet her needs. Despite her hard work, the owner showed no inclination to increase her compensation, offer a bonus, or provide any financial assistance.

As for her husband, he declined the option of seeking financial support through illicit means. He expressed that he was exhausted from living in a negative environment, witnessing his wife's unhappiness and constant distress. The hospitals and continuous problems had taken a toll on his mental well-being, leading to depression.

He began to distance himself at first, living as a separate lodger. He stopped visiting his son in the hospital. Eventually, he expressed that he was not willing to sacrifice his own life and give everything up only because his son had made the reckless decision to not wear a seatbelt on the slippery road, which led to the unfortunate accident.

He pathetically declared that he had always been honest with Vika and would remain so. He revealed that he had met another woman who understood him and brought joy and ease to his life. As a result, he expressed his intention to divorce Vika and marry the other woman. Furthermore, they were expecting a child together, and he had exhausted all his resources, both material and emotional, in caring for their sick and troubled child. He asserted that he deserved to live a happy life and believed he had the right to do so, leading him to make the difficult decision to leave Vika and their son.

This was the situation Vika found herself in when she sought my professional help as a business consultant: she needed guidance on how to negotiate a raise with management.

Of course, I adamantly refused to accept any payment from her and eagerly rushed to help her with all my heart.

The goal was to increase her salary by 50%, despite the fact that rival institutions bombarded her with offers that provided far better conditions and significantly higher salaries than the market average. So why didn't she consider those offers? It was because she remained loyal to the company and its management, who had believed in her from the beginning. Vika had made a personal commitment to dedicate her life to repaying that intangible debt she had created for herself, even though she had already repaid it with interest a long time ago.

This is how we worked:
—   wrote down all possible negotiation scenarios (minimum, optimal, and maximum result);
—   clearly defined which activities, achievements, and projects she was related to and why she wanted a salary increase;
—   worked out in detail all possible scenarios for the development of events in business games (I played either the male or the female owner).

We identified the most opportune moment to approach the management. Finally, the day arrived when Vika had to showcase everything we had worked on together over the past week. It was a crucial moment, and I felt proud of my job as a coach, confident in the value I could provide.

A day, two days, and three days passed, and I did not hear a squeak from Vika. She remained deafeningly silent. She didn't write or call. When I eventually reached out to her, she spoke with sadness in her voice: "You know, I couldn't do it. I just couldn't. How could I come and boldly demand more money? I work so hard, I put so much effort into the company. I believe that when the owners have the means, they will recognize my dedication and raise my pay. Then I'll be able to pay off my bills." In the meantime, she had borrowed another $10,000 for her child's medical treatment.

I found myself in a state of rare speechlessness. A deep sense of apathy overwhelmed me, rendering me unable to work for two days. There was only one question echoing in my mind: why, oh why did she make that decision? Why didn't she at least make an attempt to bring about change? I even began to doubt my own abilities as a coach.

Here's a comment from my daughter Anya: "This is a terrible selfish act! If she can't do it for herself, she should do it for her son's sake. Conducting such negotiations asking for a salary increase is the right thing to do."

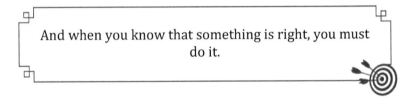

And when you know that something is right, you must do it.

"Of course, she should have approached the management and presented her case when she had such strong arguments. There was no need for her to be confrontational, boastful, or resort to threats or blackmail. On the contrary, she had everything to clearly articulate the reasons why she deserved a higher salary for the amount of work she was putting in," Anya continued, adding:

"Don't blame yourself, Mom, for not being able to make it happen. It's not your fault. You genuinely wanted to help with all your might. But if she doesn't want to help herself, there's nothing anyone can do. It's her life and her choice. You did everything right by giving your best to support your friend when she asked for your help. The question remains as to why she didn't approach those who truly owed her money."

It has been a few years since something happened between

us. She stopped writing to me, and I stopped writing to her as well. I regularly see updates on social media about the new projects she manages in the same clinic. In the photos, she always appears smiling and happy.

I'd like to think that the owners have learnt to properly appreciate a dedicated employee, or that she herself had the courage to carry out those well-prepared negotiations. But that may not be the case. It's also a choice, her choice, despite my wishes for it to be different.

"I WAS UNCOMFORTABLE "

My father-in-law spent many years working in the North. During the soviet era, people had the opportunity to buy a communal apartment with just one season's earnings on the outskirts of the vast USSR. It was available to everyone who went to work there, including artists and teachers. The oil workers, in particular, earned tremendous amounts of money. My future father-in-law went there in search of such substantial and easily earned income.

He worked in the North for ten years, spending only two weeks a year at home before returning. Interestingly, he never sent a single penny back home and never brought any money with him when he visited. As for my mother-in-law, she saved up throughout the year to prepare a lavish feast for her husband's arrival, despite the fact that the cleaning lady managed to support two children on her salary. However, when he fell seriously ill, he came to her to spend his final days, without any financial means. The family was living in such poverty that they couldn't afford to buy a coffin, and they considered burying him in a plastic bag until kind-hearted people offered to help. This happened in the 1990s.

When I asked my mother-in-law why she didn't demand money to support the family and where the millions he earned there went, she replied:
"Well, I was feeling uncomfortable. I kept waiting for him to send or bring something."

She didn't say anything. She remained silent, even after

discovering a photo of her husband hugging another woman in his jacket. And you know what she did? She silently washed and ironed his clothes, then quietly placed the picture back where she found it.

"Why, why didn't you tell him anything?" I asked.
"Still, he was coming for at least two weeks..."
"Without a single penny!"
"Yes, without a penny, but everyone could see that I had a husband. And if I confronted him about the woman in the photo, he might not have even come back. And what would people say? That my husband has abandoned me? I let it be, whatever happens, happens."
"And I understand why he didn't send or bring you any money, mother. For what? The wife is waiting, content with everything, always smiling, and the table is filled with abundant food. The children are like blossoming flowers, well cared for, well-fed, and well-behaved. If everything is like this, there must be money somewhere. And if the wife doesn't ask for anything, it must mean that she doesn't need anything."

And when I asked why she didn't inquire about the money he had earned in the North over the course of ten years, especially since he arrived penniless and, on his deathbed, my husband's mother simply waved her hands and said, "Well, in such a difficult situation and with him being sick, how could I possibly upset him? If he had the money, he would have given it himself."

When I was writing this book, I asked my husband if I could share this story without revealing who it is about. I'd refer to her as "my friend's mother" in the book.

But he said, "Write the truth, write it as it is. This story represents not just one woman, but a whole generation of mothers from the soviet past. Don't alter anything."

The mother-in-law also agreed to the publication, saying, "Write in a way that resonates with readers and helps them understand the importance of doing things differently."

"PROVE THAT YOU ARE WORTH YOUR SALARY"

Tania worked as a marketer in a large medical company. The management had either recently undergone some training or had simply decided to restrain everyone. They sent her a letter, instructing her to clearly document her responsibilities, accomplishments, and the value she had brought to the company. For what purpose? The goal was for her to gather arguments to sell her case (that's exactly what they wrote!) and demonstrate her worth to justify her current salary.

Tania sat down to compile a list of the projects she was in charge of. As she wrote, she realized that her current salary did not reflect the extent and impact of her work. Rather than sending this report to management as intended, she decided to put it, along with her resume, on a job search website.

Within 30 minutes, a competitor company contacted her and promptly called her, offering her a job at a significantly higher salary, performing similar tasks. Tania accepted the offer and honestly communicated her reasons for leaving to her former management.

What did the leaders do? They accused her of betrayal. They made no effort to retain such a valuable employee. And after she left, they ended up hiring three workers to replace what Tania used to handle on her own. They did, however, struggle to keep up. Tania occasionally comes across job advertisements on various platforms that offer multiple positions with a list of tasks that she alone used to handle.

I SENT A DIRECT MESSAGE AND RECEIVED 200,000

Just that much my friend Julia was lacking to open her own language school (to complete the renovation and get started). So, she took the initiative and sent 20 direct messages to wealthy people in Lutsk, asking them to purchase her services in advance. She didn't want to borrow or take a loan. She knew how to present her proposal in such a way that would convince them to agree.

Twelve of them did not respond. Two declined, and six

immediately agreed to pre-purchase her language learning services for themselves and their teams.

Just imagine! Twenty direct messages, and six strangers agreed to provide funding. Two hundred thousand hryvnias, all at once.

Julia Yakovlyuk, a student and friend from Lutsk, is my pride. You may have read her fascinating story "Pampered Halya and the Dutch Millionaire" in my second book, "When to Say YES". If you haven't read it yet, I recommend starting with that story to dispel illusions and boost your self-esteem.

And if you think that you won't be able to do it (Who? You? Haven't even dared to ask for a deposit yet!), I guarantee you will be able to! You just need to know who to approach, how to contact them, and what to write.

SLEEPING MY WAY TO THE TOP: HOW I BECAME A MEDIA STAR

Do not believe those who claim that their success is solely based on doing their job well, showcasing their life, or simply looking beautiful, which leads to media invites or cool projects! They don't want to reveal the blood, sweat, and tears it took them to get there. "Instant success" is in vogue. But let me tell you the truth. Everything is achieved through sleeping your way up.

"I constantly listen to this cool radio station in the car, and today one of your colleagues was speaking, but I bet you speak better!" my husband told me in bed.

I immediately asked that colleague (who was not a rival) if he could give me the journalist's contact. He flatly refused. Then, immediately from bed (well, I like to work from bed), I searched for the host of this great show on social media and messaged her, expressing my interest in appearing on her program.

Can you imagine how many messages like mine she receives every day? However, she responded and provided me with the contacts of the guest editors, who are the ones deciding whether to invite someone on air or not. I reached out to them as well. Additionally, I contacted the Kyiv studio, aiming for my message to reach their 10 million-strong target audience not just through audio, but also visually on their popular YouTube channel. Since that time, for two years now, every week I've been giving pearls of wisdom about sales over the phone from Lviv.

Similarly, I managed to secure participation in other projects and established myself as an expert at prestigious conferences and forums. How did I do it? I took the initiative and personally reached out to nearly all of them! And I continue doing so. I craft my messages in a way that prompts them to respond, invite me, and even pay me for my participation. I can teach you how to do the same.

Yes, indeed, I will teach you how to do it! Simply contact me and we can discuss the format that suits you best. There's no need to go anywhere since everything can be done online. Your success stories will even be featured in my upcoming books.

FIND YOUR "PERSON OF THE YEAR"

Find your driving force, or better yet, become one for yourself and others.

When asked how she could marry Aristotle Onassis, an older, less attractive, and shorter billionaire, following the death of her husband, President John F. Kennedy (who was handsome!), Jacqueline Kennedy said: "When Onassis stands on his wallet, he looks much taller."

She answered honestly. She spoke the truth. However, times have changed, and each of us now has the opportunity to earn money for ourselves. We have the ability to stand on our own wallets and even support others. Even if everyone around us (particularly ourselves) tries to convince us otherwise, it is not true.

Here's a valuable life hack: identify and connect with influential people in your personal life, business, and career. In my book "When to Say NO," I dedicated an entire chapter to networking, a pearl of wisdom passed down from my grandfather

Omelian. Over the years, his "33 generals" technique has consistently worked for me, and it can do the same for you. If you haven't read it yet, I highly recommend it. No matter how skilled we are, we all need someone to assist us. These people can introduce us to important contacts, offer valuable advice, and provide support during challenging times.

Think about your most significant accomplishment of the year: a successful sale, a significant deal, a publication or media feature, a pivotal introduction, or an award. Take the time to analyze the various factors that contributed to your success. Who played a crucial role in recommending or supporting you throughout the process? By understanding the key components that led to your achievement, you can replicate and expand on them in the future.

Here's an exercise from Kalabukha "How did I end up here?"

1. Analyze your most recent personal and professional triumph: who played a significant role in propelling you forward? Take a moment to mentally retrace, or better yet, document the series of actions and events that brought you to this accomplishment.
2. Write or call to thank everyone who contributed to your success. Even if you've already thanked them, do it again. It will undoubtedly benefit you in the future.
3. Create your own "Person of the Year" list. Every year since 2015, when I started focusing on my personal development, I have been identifying individuals who have had a significant impact on my life. Analyze the circumstances in which you encountered these people so that you might reproduce them, establish a system, and expedite your journey toward your desired destination.

Do you want love, friends, a career, money, and recognition? Merely dreaming about them will not suffice. Building valuable connections and surrounding yourself with the right people won't happen on its own. It requires effort on your part. Write, reach out, inquire, and negotiate for yourself. Take the initiative to bring about changes in your life. By doing so, you ensure a 100% chance of success.

Sometimes you may face being ignored, receiving no response, getting blocked, being told to get lost, or even being scolded for daring to approach busy and influential people. It can be demotivating and exhausting. However, this is not the end, but merely the beginning of taking the necessary steps to promote your product, project, or idea to the world.

Yes, some (and perhaps many) will refuse. However, there will also be those who will accept and provide support. And when you achieve a result that surpasses all your previous unsuccessful attempts, it will make all the difference.

Just like my friend, who was determined to publish her collection of children's fairy tales. She sent 108 letters to various companies, 105 of which went unanswered. However, the 106th, 107th, and 108th letters received responses offering funding that was sufficient for two print runs instead of just one.

> Do not expect that someone will hand you things in life just because you exist or because you really need them. Take matters into your own hands. Make money. Promote yourself.

Then others will pay you money, seek your friendship, write about you, and use you as an example, asking you to affirm that they are cool, as you confidently "stand on your wallet".

CHAPTER 9

HOW TO CERTAINLY LOSE RESPECT, FRIENDSHIP, AND REPUTATION

THE INTELLECTUAL AND €50

He adeptly quoted "Faust" both in translation and in German, allowing us to savor the essence of Goethe's poetry. He spoke so captivatingly about his experiences and encounters in all 50 countries he had visited. His conversations were so thought-provoking that we listened with admiration, realizing we were fortunate to have such an intelligent and profound companion on our journey through Switzerland. What a luck!

Until on the third day of the trip he asked to borrow 50 euros from me. He didn't have enough money to pay at the restaurant. I myself offered to lend him the money. How could I let such a cultured person feel uncomfortable? He promised to give it back at the next bus stop where there was an ATM nearby.

What happened next?

Throughout the entire ten-day tour, I made numerous attempts to get my money back, despite facing various excuses. It was frustrating to see him withdrawing money from the ATM multiple times, and the amounts clearly exceeded 50 euros.

My respect for him had been completely shattered. His intellectual conversations, artistic knowledge of European history, proficiency in three languages, and quotes from Goethe and Nietzsche were insufficient to revive my respect. He valued his reputation at a mere 50 euros. And buried it. For the sake of 50 euros.

P.S. I wheedled my money out of him on the last day of the trip ☺. Everything worked out fine.

A MEDICINE PROFESSOR, A RING, AND A BLIND MASSAGE THERAPIST

"Bring your jewelry tomorrow. My wife is coming, and I want to give her a silver ring," said the massage therapist I saw for back pain.

After dragging a ten-kilogram suitcase behind you for ten hours a day, your entire body aches. It was the 90s: we didn't have cell phones or social networks, and the internet had just recently been invented somewhere on the other side of the world. That's why I walked the streets of Lviv, dragging my "boutique in a suitcase" with me.

To be honest, I find it amusing when people tell me how difficult it is to sell on the Internet! You didn't experience business in the 90s. You didn't drag bags on trains while hiding money for goods in your underwear. You didn't have two additional "waist wallets" with specifically allocated sums of money: one for ransom from bandits who attacked such "businessmen," and the other for "representatives of authorities" who engaged in similar practices.

You weren't escorted out of offices by armed guards or kicked out while being cursed in the crudest possible language by outraged citizens who disliked frequent visits from "door-to-door sellers." But I didn't give up. After experiencing thousands of failures, tears, and tough luck, I finally started earning. And it felt like I was making a lot of money at the time! I had enough income to not only meet the basic needs of my family, but even to afford treatments for my back at a private clinic owned by one of my clients, who happened to be a medical professor.

Both the massage therapist and his wife were blind. I made thorough preparations for our encounter. I described each ring in detail, guided her fingers along the patterns on the jewelry, and assisted her in trying on and taking off the rings.

I had close interactions with blind people for the first time, and I was amazed by the range of emotions on their faces: their happiness, attentive listening, and the many genuine shades of mood I observed. It was at that moment that I realized I wasn't merely a wage earner, sacrificing my health for a living. I discovered I had a mission: to work with human joy and bring happiness to people! I felt needed and useful. I realized that I could make the world a better place.

Not only did I choose the best ring for my lovely clients (ensuring that it wouldn't snag on anything, had a clear gemstone, and a beautiful floral design), but I also decided to give one to their child as a gift.

The next day, inspired and moved, I met a professor of medicine, the clinic's owner, in the corridor. And she said:

"Well, what a fool this masseur Volodya is! Why did he buy a ring for his wife? They will never see it anyway — neither he nor she! And who is she going to show off to? She stays at home, doesn't go anywhere — is she going to wear it while taking out the trash in front of homeless people near the garbage can? Its' just a waste of money."

I was numb. I felt disgusted. It became scary. And all the respect I had for this highly esteemed medical worker, whose office was adorned with diplomas, including foreign ones, vanished in an instant. Although more than twenty years have passed since then, I still feel a burning resentment towards her.

A FAMILY OF MARKETERS AND A DECEIVED REALTOR

"Congratulations to me! I am now the proud owner of my dream apartment, which I have been searching for for a year. Oh my goodness, the countless meetings I had with those realtors! Remember how everyone said I wouldn't find a place that meets my requirements, claiming it didn't exist? Well, the one I found not only meets but exceeds all of my expectations! I'm starting the renovation on Monday."

We met at a business conference where we were both speakers. She had a solid reputation and a track record of successful client cases in her professional field. Her husband was also a marketer working for a large company. They were well-traveled, experienced, and knowledgeable individuals. We connected not only on a professional level but also as friends, involving our families in our interactions. Despite the fact that our busy schedules only allowed us to meet occasionally, we kept each other updated on our business and personal endeavors.

After exchanging greetings, I was presented with a detailed description of the apartment, including the cost breakdown of various elements such as the property itself, notary services, and other associated expenses.

"And what was the percentage for the realtor who tirelessly supported you throughout the process and eventually found you your dream home?" I asked.

"We decided not to pay him anything. It was already expensive for us without his services," she continued, without changing her triumphant tone.

"Do you mean you didn't pay for the realtor's services? But what about the work these people did for you? How long did they spent searching for a suitable place and finding something even better than what you wanted! How could you possibly not pay them?"

"Yeah, can you imagine? We got lucky! When we found the apartment, my husband used his connections to reach out to the owner, negotiated directly with him, and we didn't have to pay any real estate fees. Why pay when you can avoid it!" The excitement about their own cleverness was simply off the charts.

What was I thinking as I listened to that? Thank goodness I didn't do business with them. Thank goodness I didn't let these people into my heart and my business. They even visited my house and ate at my table.

Not only did they take advantage of those who did their work properly and honestly, but she didn't even think it was wrong. She even boasted about it! And they are not poor people. They are well-known in the city and even in the country. God forbid I have such clients. And as professionals, I will never recommend them to anyone. It is unclear how they will treat their customers.

That day, they were added to my personal blacklist of people I would NEVER do business with. And later on, I discovered that I was not the only one who had taken that stance.

They saved money. They made money. And yeah, they put the finishing touches.

CHAPTER 10

NATALIYA SPIZHENKO'S STORIES

PART ONE:
THE ANTICIPATORY WILL; SEX, TRACTORS, AND A LINEAR ACCELERATOR

The Anticipatory Will

"You have one to three months left with a kidney tumor of this kind," the Poltava entrepreneur was told after being diagnosed simultaneously in two clinics.

"That's it," he decided. He settled all his affairs. He transferred his property, as if in a fairy tale, to his three sons: one received an apartment, the second a business, and the third a country house and a car. And he came to us with no expectations, other than simply to await his death.

But he had chosen the wrong place to die. It was not easy to pass away in the Spizhenko Oncology Clinic.

What was the result of the treatment?

The illness subsided. He left the hospital on his own two feet. And he started thinking about what to do with his unexpected new life: no property, no business. Taking away from his sons wouldn't be right.

He developed a new business from the ground up, and it began to grow rapidly! He also found new love, got married, and had a child.

And for 11 years, he has been bringing us moonshine, lard, and wonderful news about his health. The doctors and I laugh and cry when we remember those times.

Odessa. The summer of 2020. An exclusive forum for businesswomen. I overheard someone passionately sharing this story on the backstage (well, she was talking just like me!). How could I resist approaching? Goosebumps covered my entire body.

That's how I became friends with Natalka Spizhenko. And now for a moment of pathos: we both won the TOP-100 Outstanding People and Brands award, which modern Ukraine takes pride in.

At first, there was cooperation — I advised Natalia on social media and reports for forums. Then we had long, heartfelt conversations and made trips to Kyiv to visit her and to Lviv to visit me. She shared true stories about how business is done in Ukraine, stories that are not often shared at pompous conferences or written about in Forbes.

Stories meant only for close acquaintances, but I convinced Natalya that everyone is close to me. And close people should know these stories.

Sex, Tractors, and Linear Accelerator
"In 2012, we were the first in Ukraine to install the Elekta Synergy linear accelerator, manufactured in the United Kingdom. It is a radiotherapy complex used for irradiating malignant neoplasms with the ability to precisely dose radiation at the center of a malignant tumor."

"How much is it worth, can we write it?"

"Over a million euros. I took out a separate loan for it. I told the manufacturers, "We will arrange transportation through my friends—I have been working with the same company for a long time. They are reliable and will offer a more affordable price." However, the manufacturers did not agree to this. The equipment from the London plant is issued strictly according to the protocol, with their designated carrier and no other options.

Well, if there's no other option, then there's no other option. We loaded our linear accelerator onto a ten-ton truck and placed a beacon on it to track the cargo. And then we began to wait.

In the clinic, I constructed a dedicated bunker for its installation in a remarkable four months and 15 days (typically, such a process takes a year) so that surgeries could begin immediately. I had to start repaying the loan.

And so, we began to track the shipment's progress. The

vehicle had already crossed the Polish border and suddenly vanished. The truck simply failed to appear. We initially comforted ourselves with the possibility that perhaps the driver took a wrong turn or encountered signal problems in that area. However, after the signal was missing for an entire day, we started contemplating the worst-case scenario: that the shipment had been stolen by bandits. What else could explain its disappearance? What may have happened to it?

I mobilized all my contacts, and a specialized team was dispatched to search for the missing cargo."

"And what's next? Did you find it?"

"Yes, we located the truck. It turned out that the driver had deviated from his route to visit his mistress in a village. He ended up spending the night with her. While maneuvering the large truck on country roads, the beacon got caught on something, flew into a puddle, and stopped working as a result."

"Did this driver know that he was carrying a cargo worth a million euros?"

"Yes, he knew. When he was located, a group of eight masked individuals simultaneously entered through the windows and doors. At that moment, he was having sex with his mistress. He was taken aback when they apprehended him. He kept insisting, "What's the matter? Everything is still intact; I didn't steal anything!"

"Thank God!"

"But the story does not yet have a happy ending. This heroic lover parked the car on the lakeshore, and as a heavy downpour started, the ten-ton truck began to slide into the lake."

"What did you do then?"

"We managed to find a tractor in that village, but it couldn't move the truck. The tracks on the tractor were simply collapsing, and our accelerator was slowly falling into the water.

I was watching all of this unfold from afar and understood that the situation was catastrophic. If the truck had slipped into the water, I would have lost much more than a million euros. Even if I took out another loan, I wouldn't be able to buy and transport a new accelerator right away. This is not a product that is readily available for purchase. The manufacturing time alone is nine months, assuming the next customers would allow me to skip the line. And during all this time, I would have to repay two loans and wouldn't earn a single penny from using the accelerator.

We immediately started looking for other tractors. We went to every house, gathering everyone who had a large vehicle that could help. We explained the situation: it was expensive medical equipment that needed to be urgently saved. It required a strong pulling force, but also careful handling to ensure the settings didn't get disrupted and the truck didn't overturn. We promised a comprehensive examination in our clinic to anyone who would help us.

Even though it was a day off, we managed to find three more tractors, and together they successfully pulled the truck back from the edge of the lake, saving our accelerator."

"And all this headache and damages occurred because of one man who couldn't resist his urge for sex during an important work assignment? What action did you take against him?"

"Nothing at all."

"Nothing at all?! Why?"

"I was so overwhelmed with stress — first from the beacon's disappearance, then from the truck almost sinking — that I simply didn't have the energy to focus my emotions on anything else. I had invested all my savings into this accelerator and took out a substantial loan. That's why I was relieved that the device was safe and ready to use right away. I let that man go without taking further action. He expressed remorse for another week and swore he wouldn't even think about sex for six months."

"And what about the people from that village who helped pull out the truck? Did they come to you for an examination?"

"Yes, we examined ten people. I am still grateful to them. People came out on their day off, offered their vehicles, and towed the truck. They were a tremendous help!

Now a large photo of this epic rescue hangs in our clinic as a reminder of how we pulled the hero-lover away from the bed with the help of special forces and retrieved the truck from the lake with three tractors."

Nataliya Spizhenko is the founder of the first oncology and radiosurgery center in Eastern Europe, the "Spizhenko Clinic." She holds a candidate degree in medical sciences and has received several prestigious awards, including the "Person of the Year-2011" award, the UN award "THE WOMAN NOBEL PRIZE 2021," and the "The Best Employers Luca Awards" (Great Britain). She is recognized as one of the TOP-100 Outstanding People and Brands that modern Ukraine is proud of. Additionally, Nataliya is a co-founder of SUP (Union of Entrepreneurs of Ukraine) and a member of the Successful Women's Club. She is 51 years old and resides in Kyiv.

PART TWO:
THE WAR

At 4:30 a.m. on February 24, 2022, I heard a powerful explosion. I thought to myself, "Again, probably just training in a nearby military unit." I went to the window, but there was no visible smoke, so I assumed it wasn't anything serious. I returned to bed and lay down.

At 5:00 a.m., I received a call from my daughter in London:
"Mom! The war has started!"
"No way! It can't be!"
"All of the media in Great Britain are reporting that there is a war in Ukraine!" she cried into the phone.

At 6:00 a.m., we started evacuating patients, and within a day the clinic was transformed into a military hospital. We opened medical storerooms, relocated surgical and postoperative tables to the reception area, and prepared everything necessary to accommodate the wounded. I instructed the personnel department to gather all of the doctors' personal files with images, pack them in separate cardboard boxes, and take them to the warehouse to be burned immediately if needed, in case, God forbid, the invaders arrive here.

Yes, we were prepared.

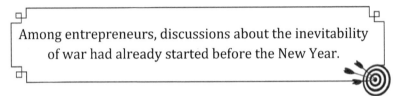

Among entrepreneurs, discussions about the inevitability of war had already started before the New Year.

In the clinic, we had prepared response protocols for emergencies and the evacuation of patients and staff. We conducted such exercises four times in January alone. Everyone had their emergency suitcases and first-aid kits packed, and they ensured their phones were charged and their gas tanks were full. We also purchased medicines worth 6 million hryvnias in case they were needed for the wounded.

But in reality, no one believed that there would be a war.

At that time, we were treating 22 patients. All of them were picked up by their relatives within two days, and our employees assisted in taking them to the railway station and ensuring their departure went as smoothly as possible.

The first wounded person arrived at our clinic at noon, however it turned out that he was a saboteur. How did we find this out? Our deputy chief doctor, who had experience serving in hotspots of armed conflicts, immediately noticed the peculiar nature of the injuries. Only by yourself was it feasible to inflict numerous puncture wounds simultaneously with crossed hands on the forearms and buttocks. During the examination of his shoes, an insole fell out of his sneakers, covered in markings. He responded suspiciously to the police's presence by attempting to flee. Where did the strength come from? He was just dying a minute before, and the next he overpowered four people. When they finally apprehended him and checked his phone, authorities discovered hundreds of photographs of strategic targets.

Every hour, people with severe injuries were brought in.

Their vehicles came under fire, they faced attacks from Grad Multiple Launch Rocket Systems (MLRS), and there were even instances of torture. I vividly recall a married couple who encountered the Kadyrovites. They were asked to disclose the location of Ukrainian military personnel. When the couple responded that they were unaware of it, the woman was shot in the shoulder and arm, while the man suffered two spine fractures.

Military personnel were also brought to us. After giving them some basic medical care, we promptly transferred them to the nearest hospital for further treatment.

On the third day, I gathered the entire 30-person team of the clinic in the bunker and offered anyone who felt it necessary to leave the city the opportunity to do so. They could leave on their own or relocate their children and parents. Nobody, however, wanted to leave. Everyone chose to stay and continue saving people.

We were alerted by the territorial defense that a column of russian tanks was moving toward us. We immediately deployed drones to monitor the convoy's movement. Fortunately, we had drones of our own that we had purchased for the clinic's tenth anniversary celebration. They were initially meant to be used to film the festivities, including guests on the red carpet, singers, spectators, and the banquet.

We had less than an hour to evacuate. In haste, we began burning all the doctors' personal files. All valuable items and equipment that we managed to gather were carried down to the bunker. I issued an order to secure the bunker's entrance by shooting the control point, ensuring that no unauthorized individuals could enter.

I had purchased weapons prior to the outbreak of the war. Although I am not a skilled shooter, I am prepared to use it when necessary to defend myself and my people. I am determined to protect them, even if it means reserving the last bullet for myself.

I will say a few words about our bunker. It has an area of 60 m2 and its walls are reinforced with a thickness of five meters. The bunker is equipped with its own ventilation system. During air raids, we sought shelter in it and even performed operations. Our most important equipment, the neural accelerator, and the CyberKnife, a state-of-the-art radiosurgical system for highly effective cancer treatment, is housed here. In simple terms, it's a robot that eliminates cancer without the need for surgery or anesthesia. This technology represents the future of medical treatment. The entrance to the bunker is secured with a 60 cm thick armored door, and the control point for access is a specialized device that consolidates all cables and electronics.

So, I ordered to shoot at the control point using my weapon. Even if the clinic were to be destroyed, I wanted to ensure that this vital equipment remained intact. Prior to that, a russian tank had already targeted the chemotherapy department.

It was terrifying when the tanks rolled in. We stood frozen, peering through the windows (even though it was not allowed). But it became even more frightening when we heard the sound of automatic gunfire. The Kadyrovites were trailing behind the tanks. I couldn't subject the people to such danger. We made the decision to close the clinic, and all the patients and doctors were transferred to the military hospital in Shpytky. Fortunately, we were able to successfully accomplish this.

How did I end up in Barcelona? I came here for negotiations regarding the establishment of a charity fund to aid people with cancer. In March, 200 oncology clinics were destroyed in Ukraine, leaving the patients in desperate need of assistance.

First, there was the journey to Lviv in a car that had been damaged by the Grad MLRS. Then, I traveled through Poland and Germany. I vividly recall my shock upon arriving in Munich: people were smiling, drinking coffee, and strolling around, oblivious to the terrible events unfolding in our country. It felt as if I had stepped onto another planet.

The negotiations were highly successful, and I returned to Ukraine at the end of May.

As soon as it became possible, the clinic's director gathered everyone who was in Kyiv at that time to restore order. Ten of our employees spent a week cleaning everything: they covered smashed windows with plywood, disposed of garbage, disinfected, washed, and aired the premises. Surprisingly, the clinic remained largely unscathed. While the surrounding area was filled with the remnants of fires and the ruins of supermarkets, gas stations, and hotels, our clinic stood amidst the devastation, having been looted by the occupiers, with broken windows and a collapsed roof.

Our engineers repaired the control point of the bunker door, replacing the damaged parts. With the assistance of our manufacturing partners from Great Britain and Sweden, we remotely launched the linear accelerator and our renowned CyberKnife! Miraculously, all other equipment in the clinic was also functioning properly.

It was essential to gather the doctors, many of whom were men. Thankfully, all of them stayed behind and were safe and in good health. The medical personnel, call center workers, and managers were not elsewhere in Ukraine but within the territory of the Kyiv region!

At the beginning of May, we announced that we had reopened and resumed our operations, ready to welcome patients once again. People started coming.

Cancer patients require a great deal of moral support in addition to medical care. But how can we provide it when we ourselves are broken? Surprisingly, our patients became our source of strength! It is true that in order to help ourselves, we had to help others. Once again, my team demonstrated incredible resilience, unity, and a sense of responsibility, no matter how challenging the circumstances were.

My house was also vandalized and looted, but it was not the russians who were responsible. There were no occupiers in our village. It was the locals who were involved. Neighbors saw young men wearing balaclavas loading my belongings into cars on multiple occasions.

Employees of the clinic also experienced two instances of marauding raids when they came to secure the broken windows with shields and fix the doors that had been damaged by the blast wave.

Almost all valuables had been stolen, cabinets had been turned over, and furniture had been moved. But despite the turmoil, I was filled with an overwhelming sense of happiness that kept me awake throughout the first night.

I was at home! I had a roof over my head. I had a place to return to. I was on my own land! When I told my friends that upon my return I was overcome with joy and ready to kiss the walls and the floor, they all shared the same sentiment.

On June 30 in London, I received the "Luca Awards", a prestigious accolade for entrepreneurs recognizing their outstanding achievements in team development and their field. As part of the Ukrainian delegation, we were viewed as superheroes. People approached us, offering hugs and expressing incredible support.

And when HRH Prince Michael of Kent (Queen Elizabeth II's cousin) asked me how I felt when it seemed like I had lost everything that constituted my life and source of strength, I replied, "I have learned resilience from my patients. These brave people fight for months, weeks, days, and even minutes of their lives."

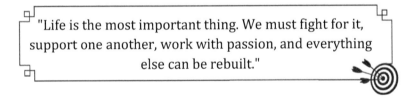

"Life is the most important thing. We must fight for it, support one another, work with passion, and everything else can be rebuilt."

CHAPTER 11

UNKNOWN STORIES OF FAMOUS AND VERY FAMOUS PEOPLE

HOW LICE AND A MAN FROM LVIV SAVED HUMANITY FROM TYPHUS

RUDOLF WEIGL'S STORY

At the beginning of the 20th century, typhus epidemics claimed more lives than wars. All attempts to create a vaccine had failed until Rudolf Wcigl from Lviv took up the task. In the trenches of the First World War (remember: the Great War, as it was then called), he researched typhus, a disease that caused such devastation that combat operations ceased for several months in some areas of the front.

And then, at Lviv University, he subjected himself to dangerous experiments and developed a vaccine against typhus that would later save millions of lives. He discovered that typhus is transmitted by body lice, and the bacteria responsible for the disease can only survive in human cells. It does not thrive in laboratory animals. Weigl then made the decision to feed the lice with his own blood.

He attached matchbox-sized vials with hundreds of lice inside on his thigh and forearm. A thin mesh partition prevented them from escaping while allowing freely feed on human blood.

Once the lice had consumed enough blood, they were removed, infected with typhus bacteria through a microscopic enema, and then killed. The contents of their intestines were turned into a paste, which was used to create the vaccine. All of Weigl's employees, including his wife, participated in feeding the lice.

Thus, in the early 1930s, Lviv became a significant global hub for vaccine production, and Weigl founded the Institute for Typhus and Virus Research, still operational on Zelena Street.

Amazingly, at the beginning of my career I used to sell jewelry in those laboratories. I had wonderful clients there, but little did I know that the history of world medicine was being written and thousands of human lives were being saved!

After Lviv was captured by soviet troops in 1939, Weigl was continuously offered to relocate to moscow. He refused, nevertheless, believing that he would be more useful in Lviv.

History repeated itself when, in 1941, the Germans offered him his own institute in Berlin. The Germans then compelled Weigl to produce a vaccine in large quantities for the front. He reluctantly agreed in exchange for some freedom of action.

It required numerous lice feeders to produce a sufficient amount of vaccine. Weigl enlisted the brightest minds of the Lviv intelligentsia for this task, including artists, doctors, and scientists. Many of them were Jews who, despite wearing armbands with the Star of David, were allowed to live in their own apartments rather than in the ghetto and receive some sort of protection due to their official documents.

Weigl's assistants clandestinely brought the still "soviet" vaccine, which had not been registered by the Germans, into the ghettos and concentration camps under the guise of blood samples for research purposes. In doing so, they managed to save tens of thousands of lives. Weigl became a symbol of goodness and hope for the prisoners, and in the early 21st century, he was honored with the title of "Righteous Among the Nations" by the State of Israel.

Here are just three of the thousands whom Weigl saved. They survived because lice fed on their blood:
- Stefan Banach, mathematician and author of functional analysis;
- Władysław Orlicz, mathematician and author of the theory of linear topological spaces and functional spaces (Orlicz spaces);
- Stanisław Skrowaczewski, conductor of the New York Philharmonic-Symphony Orchestra, Vienna Symphony Orchestra, London Symphony Orchestra, as well as The Yomiuri Nippon Symphony Orchestra, and recipient of The

Ditson Conductor's Award for his contribution to American music.

Rudolf Weigl was twice nominated for the Nobel Prize, but did not receive it on either occasion. The first nomination was in 1942, and he was overlooked because the Germans held a grudge against him for refusing to relocate to Berlin. The second nomination was in 1948, but he faced opposition from the soviets, who accused him of collaboration with the occupiers.

After the liberation of Lviv from the Germans in 1944, the Weigl Institute was transferred to Poland. However, the legendary Lviv man faced persecution both within academia and at the state level. He passed away in 1957, nearly forgotten.

Why did the story of Rudolf Weigl from Lviv, a Pole of Austrian origin who developed a cure for typhus, become personally significant to me?
- Belief in oneself and one's work helps overcome obstacles and achieve the extraordinary.
- It is possible to stand alone against the two most formidable regimes of the century and save thousands of lives.
- Each person's destiny is a matter of their own choice, and there's always a choice.

THE HOLLYWOOD ACTRESS WHO INVENTED GPS AND WI-FI

HEDY LAMARR'S STORY

She appeared nude and simulated an orgasm on camera for the first time in cinema history, left her wealthy husband, became the inspiration for Snow White in Walt Disney's animated film, amassed a fortune, and in her spare time between film shoots and six marriages, she contributed to the development of technology that powers our mobile phones: GPS, Bluetooth, and Wi-Fi.

Hedwig Eva Maria Kiesler, the only child of a wealthy banker and a pianist, was born in Vienna in 1914. She ran away from home at the age of 16, and at the age of 18, she found herself at the center of a sex scandal when she starred in the first erotic film, "Ecstasy." The scene depicting an orgasm (which may seem innocent to us now) shocked audiences in 1932, resulting in the film being banned in several countries.

Frightened parents persuaded their daughter to marry Austrian arms magnate and millionaire Fritz Mandl. Ironically, despite his Jewish origins, Mandl held Nazi views and manufactured weapons for Hitler.

A jealous husband bought all copies of the scandalous film, forbade her to act in movies, and treated his young wife as an expensive possession that added to his collection of cars and horses. After four years of a failed marriage, Hedwig escaped through the back door of their luxurious castle, drugging the maid and taking her clothes.

The future inventor knew firsthand that war was brewing in Europe from her husband and his business partners. Therefore, she headed to Hollywood immediately, where her scandalous film debut was well recognized. She changed her name to Hedy Lamarr and swiftly amassed a fortune of $30 million, which was unheard of at the time.

However, the acting career did not satisfy Hedy. She once said, "My beauty is my curse. I am often cast as empty-headed dolls, and when I ask for serious roles, directors simply laugh at me."

Life handed her a significant role. As fascism gained momentum and as a Jew herself, she was strongly affected by the events unfolding in her native Austria and around the world. It was during this time that Hedy's activism began to emerge.

She had acquired knowledge of anti-ship weapons and navigation systems through her involvement in her husband's business negotiations. While attending his receptions, she not only embellished the events but also attentively listened and quickly grasped the concepts. As a result, when the National Council of Inventors was established as part of efforts to strengthen the United States' defense capabilities, she offered her expertise. In 1942, she successfully invented and patented a system that enabled remote control of torpedoes and ensured secure and uninterrupted communication.

Hedy's ideas were so far ahead of their time that they were only revisited in 1962, when esteemed scientists in classified military laboratories finally recognized the innovations made by the woman who had once boldly appeared nude on screen and depicted an orgasm.

Google a photo of Hedy Lamarr. She is not just a beauty and an exceptional actress who has earned a star on the Hollywood Walk of Fame. She is a woman who changed the world. We have Wi-Fi, GPS, Bluetooth, military satellites, and mobile phones thanks to her.

Even though some "good" people poured buckets of crap on her because of her independent nature, six marriages, and scandalous autobiography, Hedy Lamarr was officially recognized for her discovery in 1997. Her birthday, November 9, is observed as Inventor's Day in the United States.

A PATHETIC FANTASY, OUR BRIGHT ELVEN PAST, AND MY STUDENT SHAME

JOHN RONALD REUEL TOLKIEN'S STORY

"You write in Elvish, the language that Tolkien invented for The Lord of the Rings?"
"Yes, but Tolkien didn't actually invent anything. This is a fictional language for elves who existed in the past and still exist today."

This is how I ruined my reputation in the 90s, during my first year of studies at Ivan Franko Lviv National University, at the height of the book's popularity. I used to pass notes with incomprehensible letters to my group mates during lectures, and one day I timidly asked what language it was. I have a tendency to seek clarity in everything, which often gets me into trouble.

The Tolkienist subculture emerged in the post-soviet space

in the 1990s, and I was there to witness it. With the disappearance of censorship, fantasy literature, attributed to Tolkien as its founder, burst into our lives. My acquaintances and fellow philology students became obsessed with this book. They learned the language invented by Tolkien and wrote to each other in Elvish during lectures, using notes since smartphones and the Internet were not available back then.

I wasn't a fan of Tolkien. To be honest, I read that massive book just to be on trend, as they would say nowadays. However, the enchantment of the magical world and the fairy-tale characters captivated me, as it did millions of people worldwide, with the release of Peter Jackson's film trilogy "The Lord of the Rings" in the early 2000s.

What struck me the most were the facts about the author himself.

- J.R.R. Tolkien knew 14 languages and invented 19 so that each folk in his fictional world could speak their own language.
- Tolkien became an orphan at the age of 12 and lived in dire poverty. He was born in South Africa, where his father passed away while his mother was visiting Great Britain with him and his younger brother. The family faced such hardship that they couldn't afford to attend the funeral and ended up staying in England. This is why the main characters in his books are often orphans; the author himself relied on guardians and moved between other people's homes throughout his youth.
- He refrained from communicating with his beloved for three years because he had given his word to his guardian to devote all his energy to his studies.

At the age of 18, Tolkien fell in love with his neighbor, Edith Mary Bratt, who was also an orphan. However, Tolkien's guardian, Catholic priest Father Francis Morgan, made him promise not to see Edith until he came of age. The reason for this was that she was a Protestant and three years older than John, and falling in love would interfere with his studies, which required all of his strength and time.

- But when he turned 21, Tolkien wrote a letter in which he offered Edith his hand and his heart. Despite not having received any news from him for three years, Edith returned the engagement ring to her prior fiancé, converted to Catholicism, and married Tolkien.

- His beautiful elves were inspired by Edith. He lived with her for 56 years, and they had four children together.
- Tolkien experienced the horrors of the trenches during the First World War, which he later depicted in his works as a realm of darkness.

While they were still neighbors, they invented a secret whistle for exchanging messages. Due to the censorship imposed on the British Army posts during the war, they developed a secret code that they used in their correspondence. This way, Edith could track her husband's movements on the map of the Western Front.

- After the war, from which Tolkien returned disabled, he became the youngest professor at Oxford. However, due to a lack of money — as he was already the father of four children — he took on the task of grading hundreds of exam papers. And one day, when his eyes were already heavy and his brain refused to function properly, he came across an empty sheet of paper in a stack of exams to be graded.

Unexpectedly, Tolkien wrote: "In a hole in the ground, there lived a hobbit." He was surprised by his own words because he had no idea what the word "hobbit" meant or why he had written it. This sparked his imagination, and he began inventing his own world, meticulously crafting every detail. He created several maps of the land and provided intricate descriptions of the various peoples that inhabited it, as well as a comprehensive history and chronology of events from the dawn of time to the final battles.

- At night, he would often tell his children the first story about the hobbit and the world of Middle-earth. Eventually, he decided to write it down because his children noticed that the beloved fairy tale changed each time he told it. Their Dad was confused in his "testimony" ☺.

When a friend of Tolkien happened to see the manuscript of this tale and gave it to the publisher Stanley Unwin, he entrusted the fate of the work to his 10-year-old son. The boy enjoyed the fairy tale, and as a result, the story became a book. It was well-received by readers, who then clamored for a sequel. However, progressing with the sequel proved to be a difficult task. The characters took on the lives of their own, new characters and events emerged, and the story seemed resistant to reaching its conclusion.

The Second World War came to an end. However, it took another 17 years before the novel, which had started as a continuation of the Hobbit's adventures, was finally completed and published.

Two publishers refused to publish "The Lord of the Rings" due to its complexity and volume. However, Tolkien then sent a single copy to the son of one of the publishers, who approved the first story's publication in 1936. As the son got older, he remained enamored with the book and convinced his father to invest in its publication.

- The book was divided into three parts to save on printing costs: "The Fellowship of the Ring" (1954), "The Two Towers" (1954), and "The Return of the King" (1955). "The Lord of the Rings" was published in 1954 and achieved tremendous success, much to the surprise of the publisher. The publisher initially believed the book would be entirely unprofitable and expected significant financial losses, but it turned out to be a huge success.
- When the novel flew off the shelves, critics inundated it with negativity. The mildest criticism claimed it was "literature for teenagers" and accused the author of a "lack of imagination" that they found "pathetic."

The Swedish academics also stood out by rejecting the nomination of Tolkien's work for the Nobel Prize in Literature, stating that "The Lord of the Rings" "cannot, in any case, be considered prose of the highest class." Thus, in 1961, the prize was awarded to a Yugoslav writer, whose name is remembered in history solely because he received the award instead of Tolkien.

- Books and films about hobbits, elves, and orcs fueled the birth of an entire subculture that continues to thrive to this day. Some Tolkienists, like my group mates from the 90s, believe that the world described in Tolkien's books truly existed and actively seek evidence to support this belief. There are even those who claim to have "memories" of that world and identify themselves as elves rather than humans.

Notes from Kalabukha
Escapism is a term used in psychology to describe the act of seeking an escape from reality, mundane daily life, and life's challenges. Escapism can take the form of immersing oneself in a fantasy world through books, movies, or computer games. It can also manifest through active engagement in sports or creative activities, as well as various hobbies.

Role-playing games are particularly popular among Tolkien enthusiasts. They would hold "live-action role-playing games" based on Tolkien's universe. The annual "The Hobbit Games" gained significant popularity in the 1990s, where participants would dress up in appropriate costumes and engage in mock battles using wooden swords.

Then I often heard about how my friends actively participated in such events. Now I find myself wondering why I never joined them or even attended as a spectator.

Board and computer games, plays, musical compositions, and animated and feature films have been created based on Tolkien's works.

The circulation of his books has exceeded 300 million copies in all languages around the world, and the screen adaptations have become the highest-grossing films in the history of cinema. Millions of tourists from all over the world visit Hobbiton, a land built for filming in New Zealand.

Thanks to Tolkien, the words "hobbits" and "orcs" were included in the Oxford Dictionary and became part of the English language.

Orcs are depicted as filthy, ugly creatures prone to violence and meanness, with extremely low intelligence and devoid of most human emotions other than rage. They serve the Dark Lord and reside in the eastern region of Mordor, which translates from the language of the orcs as "the land that dies." Their strength lies not in their individual power but in their sheer numbers, making their army formidable.

Tolkien indeed invented the word and concept of Orcs. It's intriguing to ponder what he would think of the actions of the "Orcs of the 21st century" in Ukraine if he were aware of them.

John Ronald Reuel Tolkien certainly had a profound impact on our world and instilled in us the belief in true friendship, love, and fulfilling one's purpose. He gave us hope and inspiration and created a place where good will always triumph over evil.

ALWAYS!

HOW THE FRENCH QUEEN BRED HAIRY PEOPLE, OR THE TRUE STORY OF THE HEROES OF THE FAIRY TALE ABOUT BEAUTY AND THE BEAST

King Henry II de Valois of France received a renowed gift at his coronation: a cage containing a small boy whose body and face were completely covered with hair. The gift delighted the monarch, who had a fascination for collecting individuals with congenital defects and deformities at his court. However, doubts arose as to whether this boy, who had been brought from the Spanish territories in the Canary Islands, notably Tenerife, was truly human.

Nowadays modern medicine recognizes excessive hairiness as a rare genetic condition known as hypertrichosis. But in those days, children with such a condition were destined for a very unfortunate and, evidently, short life.

But the hairy boy named Pedro González was fortunate. A council of the most esteemed scientists of that time recognized him as a human being. He was removed from the chain, transferred from the cage to a room, ceased to be fed raw meat, and even had his Spanish name changed to a new Latin one — Petrus Gonsalvus. The king, who had a penchant for experiments, ordered that he receive the finest education, comparable to that bestowed upon princes of royal lineage.

And Petrus not only began to study diligently but also demonstrated remarkable scientific abilities. In his teenage years, he already spoke and wrote three languages and comprehended everything that an aristocrat of that time was expected to know. Moreover, he possessed refined manners, a sharp mind, and a sense of humor that endeared him to the king, who made him his favorite and welcomed him into his inner circle. However, despite the comfort of his life at court, he remained somewhat like a pet — an entity devoid of rights and personal freedom.

It is advantageous to be a favorite while the king is alive. And still, this is not always the case. When Henry II died suddenly at the age of 40, France came under his wife's rule, the ruthless and somber Catherine de' Medici (1519-1589). Do you recall when I mentioned her in the Mona Lisa section?

Let's refrain from overlooking her involvement in the death of tens of thousands of Protestants during the St. Bartholomew's Day Massacre, as well as the persecution that led to the demise of countless individuals unfortunate enough to cross her path. I'll just say that this deeply unhappy woman was unquestionably far from being a pleasant person.

Being a genuine daughter of Florentine merchants, Catherine de' Medici meticulously accounted for the money invested in Petrus' education and upbringing, desiring to "recoup" it. Moreover, he had become so widely acclaimed that people traveled from distant lands to see him, as if embarking on a pilgrimage. Consequently, she resolved to replicate him with the intention of selling his children at a lucrative price or presenting them as extraordinary diplomatic offerings.

To accomplish this, it was imperative to marry him off. And not to just anyone, but to "unite" with a pinnacle representative of the human race — a genuine beauty. Naturally, no aristocrat would offer their daughter willingly for a shaggy beast. However, one of the merchants, enticed by prospects of advancement at court and business advantages, might have been inclined to agree.

The bride was swiftly found, and she was assured that the marriage was a tremendous honor, being that the queen herself intended to orchestrate her future. But it wasn't until the wedding that she discovered who had been chosen as her husband. Catherine de' Medici couldn't resist indulging in the pleasure of observing the girl's reaction. What kind of entertainment did she have back then? None at all! Except, of course, for the events like St. Bartholomew's Day Massacre and the subsequent mass executions. But such occurrences were not an everyday affair either.

But then a miracle happened! Petrus succeeded in gaining his wife's trust and, eventually, her love. According to those who lived at the time, this hairy gentleman was an exceptionally delightful individual with impeccable manners. Despite a challenging childhood and an unconventional appearance, he grew up to be a cheerful and kind-hearted person. Moreover, he possessed intelligence and erudition, making his company always engaging and intriguing.

To the astonishment of the French court and the entire Europe, who were watching this affair closely (alas, they didn't have social media back then, but if they did, they would have undoubtedly been a sensation and never worried about a decline in popularity), the beauty fell deeply in love with the "monster." They enjoyed a blissful marriage for 40 years, considering that only a few people reached their thirties at the time. Together, they had seven children, with four inheriting their father's genetic anomaly (three daughters and one son).

The Gonsalvus family embarked on a European tour, showcasing their exceptional education and refined manners, which starkly contrasted with their nearly animalistic appearance. Indeed, they earned money during their travels. However, none of them had any rights or personal freedom in the long run. As planned, their hairy children were still treated as exotic pets and given away to others.

The Gonsalvus family spent their last days in Italy. The narrative of their lives served as the basis for a tale about a Beast, who was indeed an enchanted prince liberated from wicked spells by the power of Beauty's love. However, in reality, Petrus remained regarded as subhuman in the eyes of his contemporaries; he was even denied burial in a regular cemetery. The fate of his children remains unknown.

WHEN A PET IS A ROCK

In 1975, an advertising executive named Gary Dahl, inspired by his friends' grievances about the cost, time commitment, and effort required to care for pets, devised the ideal "pet" — the Pet Rock. After all, a rock doesn't need to be fed, bathed, or walked. Furthermore, it is impervious to mortality.

Imagine a mere stone, akin to those found in our Carpathian rivers *[Carpathian Mountains in Ukraine]*. However, it was marketed and sold in a box equipped with ventilation holes (to prevent suffocation ☺). The package included a 32-page instruction manual detailing how to care for the stone, bathe it, teach it to use a designated area for as a toilet, and even train it to respond to commands such as "lie down" and "listen."

Check it out: "Upon removing the rock from its box, it may exhibit slight apprehension towards unfamiliar individuals. To soothe the stone, gently place it on a layer of old newspapers. The rock is aware of its purpose and will remain stationary until you move it."

A notable section was dedicated to the genealogy of each individual stone (remember, stones are alive!). The lineage traced back all the way to the Egyptian pyramids. Gary Dahl, in his pursuit of effective publicity, spared no expense. He commissioned numerous newspaper articles that contributed to a captivating narrative. As we know, a compelling story in the mainstream media has a snowball effect, then as well as now. When someone writes anything noteworthy about a subject, others eagerly follow suit. After all, media coverage is driven by ratings and intriguing topics.

Thus, the ingenious entrepreneur swiftly gained popularity, receiving invitations to talk shows and exclusive gatherings. The ladies of the United States were captivated, seeking selfies and even romantic encounters with him. PR began in the summer, with sales beginning in time for Christmas. The result was astounding: millions of stone pets were sold at a price of $3.95 each. People bought them for fun, as gifts for friends, and even for people who seemingly possessed everything they needed.

I wonder, if Pet Rock was released now, would people like it?

LEAVING THE MATRIX AND LOVE ON A RAFT

Elon Musk made a statement proclaiming that we live in a matrix, a computer simulation, and encouraged everyone to break free from it. One of the arguments supporting this claim is the occurrence of déjà vu, which occasionally happens when the matrix experience glitches during software changes.

What a surprise ☺. Dating back to the 5th century BC, the philosopher Plato of ancient Athens was the first to recognize that we inhabit an artificial reality. The very same philosopher who wrote about platonic love. By the way, it does not completely exclude sexual intimacy. And, contrary to popular belief, it does not take place on a raft ☺. It represents the union of souls, wherein the sexual connection is indeed highly valued.

Plato believed that all of us are imprisoned, chained within a cave, while the true essence of life unfolds beyond its walls. Regardless of how dismal, uncomfortable, and sorrowful our existence may be, people have convinced themselves that no other reality exists. Furthermore, they are willing to eradicate anyone who seeks the truth and strives to liberate themselves from these chains and confinements of the cave.

"The matrix is a system. However, turn around once you are inside. Whom do you see? Businessmen, teachers, lawyers, workers, ordinary people whose minds we strive to free. You must bear in mind that the majority are unprepared to face reality. They have been so profoundly poisoned and hopelessly dependent on the System that they will fight to defend it." Plato's ideas from the cave myth were the foundation of the legendary film "The Matrix". The first part of the film was released in 1999. The film's creators, the Wachowski brothers, were so moved by its impact that one sibling transitioned, followed by the other, becoming sisters—they underwent a gender change.

And they used to have families and children.

So, my friend's ex-husband, a British entrepreneur, desired change so much that he underwent a gender transition and became a woman. He sold his business and house in London, relocating to Thailand where he now resides in a modest bungalow constructed from unpainted planks. His current job entails teaching English to local children. However, when he turned 50 years old, a multitude of health issues emerged, leaving him in a dire situation without financial stability (totally screwed), comfort, or a thriving business, all within a foreign country and within the confines of a female body. Regrettably, there is no way to return to his previous state, as what has happened cannot be reversed. His own children from the initial marriage, as well as parents and friends, have distanced themselves, leaving only my friend Tanya, his ex-wife, as the sole remaining point of contact.

People! Do not panic. Breaking free from the matrix does not necessarily require a gender transformation or any drastic measures. There are alternative ways to achieve liberation!

Another memorable quote from the legendary film is: "Do your eyes ache? You are using them for the first time." Such revelations often bring discomfort as they unveil the genuine reality of our relationships, work, business, supposed friendships, opportunities, and their absence. It becomes apparent that without making any changes, the current circumstances would remain unchanged.

However, as you begin to see possibilities, paths, opportunities, and guiding signs, it becomes essential to follow them. Follow them to break free from the cycle of going to a job you loathe each day, to stop wasting your life in toxic relationships, to unearth your genuine dreams, desires, and goals, and to live a life devoid of financial constraints, full of joy and support.

The War
Every day is a gift of fate. Maybe this is it, the time when you must finally begin LIVING?

HOW THE ARCHAEOLOGIST EVANS DECEIVED THE WHOLE WORLD AND ENSURED THE INCOME OF THE WHOLE COUNTRY FOR THE NEXT 100 YEARS

Arthur Evans, a British archaeologist, unearthed a distinctive culture on the island of Crete in 1900, unlike anything else previously discovered.

Previously, the tales of King Minos and his daughter Ariadne with the enchanted ball of thread, the bull-headed creature known as the Minotaur, and the architect Daedalus and his son Icarus were regarded as mere fairy tales derived from Greek mythology.

Arthur Evans acquired a hill on the island of Crete where local peasants had been regularly unearthing peculiar fragments in their gardens. Using his personal funds, he employed thirty excavators, and within a week, the world's most renowned newspapers announced the extraordinary discovery: an unknown civilization dating back five thousand years, as well as the legendary Minotaur's labyrinth, had been unearthed in Crete.

Evans himself authored articles that were written in such a captivating manner that newspapers worldwide were quickly sold out, as people eagerly awaited the latest updates and willingly contributed funds for further excavations. Influential figures of the time were specifically invited to give enthusiastic interviews to the press. Within six months, Evans had assembled a team of 300 excavators, and the influx of monetary support from impressed individuals grew with each passing day.

Evans coined the term "Minoan" to describe the civilization and proclaimed King Minos as the presumed ruler of the Knossos Palace, which, according to his findings, housed the labyrinth where the Minotaur was believed to have resided.

Notes from Kalabukha: who was the Minotaur and where did he come from?

Pasiphaë, the Cretan queen, once desired to have sexual relations with a bull. Well, one might say, peculiar desires do exist. However, she unexpectedly gave birth to a bull-headed monster from this union.

To conceal the shame caused by his wife, Minos confined the ferocious monster within an underground labyrinth skillfully constructed by the architect Daedalus. The labyrinth was designed to be so intricate that anyone who entered would be unable to find an escape path.

During that period, Athens was plagued by an epidemic. In an attempt to halt its spread, the Athenians, following the guidance of an oracle, made the decision to send seven young men and seven maidens to Crete as an annual sacrifice to the Minotaur. Rumors circulated that King Minos had bribed the oracle to provide this advice.

And thus, a hero emerged onto the historical-mythical stage — Prince Theseus. Determined to end the sacrificial feeding of Athens' finest individuals to the Minotaur, he set sail for Crete. There, he managed to win the affection of Ariadne, King Minos' daughter, who aided him in his quest to slay the monster. Ariadne gave Theseus a magical thread that guided him through the labyrinth and ensured his safe exit.

The noble Theseus boarded a ship and embarked on his journey back to Athens, carrying the treasures of King Minos with him. However, rather than marrying Ariadne as he had promised, he abandoned her on one of the islands, so as not to hinder his path to heroism.

Cool story, right? And people all over the world were truly captivated and inspired by it. Everyone wanted to see what the palace looked like where such events took place. And Evans gave people that opportunity.

He constructed galleries, rooms, and columns according to his own interpretation. The archaeological community was astounded by Evans' liberal approach to historical accuracy. Not only did he paint murals on newly constructed walls, but he also employed modern technology and even concrete for this purpose! In response to the criticism, Evans argued that the Minoans had actually invented concrete long before the Romans and he was merely replicating their construction methods.

Even the famous red columns, which are considered the palace's trademark, are subject to doubt. This is how the archaeologist envisioned them. Some experts argue that they were constructed from wood rather than stone, and there are even skeptics who question their existence altogether.

Evans, on the other hand, is regarded as hero by the inhabitants of Crete. The Palace of the Minotaur has become a tourist attraction, ranking as the second most visited site in Greece, right after the Acropolis in Athens. The worldwide fascination with antiquity has gripped the hearts of many.

Grateful Cretans erected a monument to Evans, and he was awarded a knighthood by King George V of England. He also received numerous awards and titles, making him a well-known figure. In addition to serving as an example of remarkable PR and the creation of a business on ancient ruins, his efforts provided a tangible place where the heroes of Greek myths found a true home.

LET'S PRAY TO HERMES: THE GOD OF TRADE, CUSTOMS OFFICERS, AND THIEVES

During my trip to Greece, one fact particularly struck me: in 2017, Greek pagans were granted the right to purchase land for their religious buildings, perform rituals for their children (or whatever equivalent exists in their faith), and have legally recognized religious marriages. Surprisingly, this development occurred while Muslims have yet to secure the right to construct even a single mosque in Athens.

Greek paganism (Hellenic religion, as they call it) is becoming increasingly popular.

In Greece, as in Ukraine, the so-called "Slavic native faith" exists. In Lithuania, paganism is recognized as one of the official religions, granting the community the right to perform marriages and hold religious classes in schools upon request from students and parents. So, what should have stopped the Greeks from reviving their faith?

Although I've always wondered how people could worship gods who were often portrayed as flawed versions of humans: shamelessly seducing other people's spouses, engaging in promiscuous relationships with all representatives of flora and fauna, and displaying vengeance, envy, and treachery.

Just remember Arachne's story! The young weaver created a tapestry so beautiful that it aroused the envy of Athena herself. Instead of honing her own weaving skills, the goddess, in a fit of jealousy, turned Arachne into a spider and cursed her, "so that you shall weave for all your days." As a result, people are now afflicted with arachnophobia, the fear of spiders, due to this unfortunate tale.

And what about Medusa, also called Gorgo? She was a virgin priestess who was raped by Poseidon right in Athena's temple. In a shocking twist, it was the victim, Medusa, who was punished by the goddess for desecrating the temple. Athena transformed her into a monstrous creature with snakes for hair, whose mere gaze could turn any living being to stone.

Until now, when Versace made the Medusa Gorgon his logo and people pay a significant amount of money for clothes featuring it. In a way, Versace's use of the Medusa logo can be seen as a rehabilitation of the poor woman's image. It's quite ironic, considering that Athena, the goddess of wisdom and justice, was the one responsible for her transformation.

But who knows? Perhaps it was these gods who provided the ancient Greeks with resilience and hope. Maybe neo-pagans possess knowledge that we are unaware of. Therefore, my entrepreneur friends, just as a precaution, let us offer our prayers to Hermes — the god of trade, travelers, customs officers, and thieves. Who knows, perhaps it does make a difference?

CHAPTER 12

VLADA ALEKSANDROVA'S STORIES

PART ONE:
TOP 5 UNSUCCESSFUL DATES AND WHAT TO DO WHEN EVERYTHING GOES WRONG?

Badoo, Tinder, and Mamba are all well-known platforms, right? Well, you and I haven't had the time or opportunity to look for love elsewhere. After numerous unsuccessful dates, I have something to share with you. I have a few words of caution. Consider the amount of time and Internet data wasted, as well as the amount of coffee consumed as a result of these disappointments.

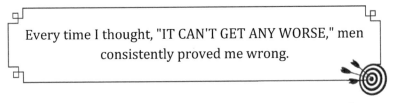

Every time I thought, "IT CAN'T GET ANY WORSE," men consistently proved me wrong.

Actually, it can, but I've learned to live with it, to pick up my self-esteem from the floor each time and try to find my happiness again. Interestingly enough, I actually found it on one of these platforms!

Programmer Sashko and his mother

This meeting had been postponed four times. When we finally met at a coffee shop, the first thing Sashko did (ladies, brace yourselves) was call his mother: "Mom, I'm at a coffee shop on Maidan, I met Vlada, everything's fine. No, I'm not cold. Yeah, I won't be long." For those who didn't catch on, I wasn't on a date with a 10-17-year-old. The guy was 29 years old. I thought, well, maybe he's just a caring son, and they have that kind of relationship.

Within two minutes, a waiter approached us. When asked, "Have you decided on something?" Sashko ordered... nothing. Absolutely nothing. He said, "I already ate at home. My mom says you can't eat at these restaurants. I once had food poisoning after eating out. So, you shouldn't have anything, too." You should have seen the waiter's face. And I wanted to disappear into the ground. Of course, I chose to have a meal after work. I ordered a main course and a light cocktail.

I could tell from Sashko's expression that he wasn't ready for this, so I immediately added, "I'll pay for myself." He started making excuses, saying that his mother controlled all of the money.

I realized that this date was a mistake. I had initially planned to stay for a little while before discretely going home. However, my dinner took 30 minutes to prepare, so I had to endure listening to Sashko's stories about how he and his mother went to Berezynka to buy jeans and how his mother got into an argument with the seller.

And he mentioned that he had dreamed about learning to drive. He had already saved up enough money to buy a car, but his mother always warned him that it was dangerous and discourage him from making the purchase. I could feel my frustration building up inside me.

They brought my food and my drink, and I began to eat. Sashko was looking at me and the food with hungry eyes.

"Do you want some too?" I couldn't take it anymore.
"I've never had anything like this. My mother usually prepares oatmeal for me in the morning, soup or borscht for lunch, and..."
"Alright, spare me the details! Bring another set of utensils."

He started eating eagerly with me. I simply handed him the plate and observed as the child, whose mother had let go of the leash for two hours, indulged in the forbidden act of dining at a restaurant. "I will go hungry, but drunk," I thought.

When Sashko finished eating, he asked for a drink. The cocktail contained alcohol. Little did I know that Sashko would become so intoxicated and I would end up having to drive him home. After dropping off the "child" near the entrance, I hurriedly left the area, fearing that all that might be contagious.

The next morning didn't start with coffee because Sashko

called at eight o'clock in the morning. And he began, apparently, to repeat his mother's words:

"I don't want a girl who drinks and spends recklessly. You'll drag me down. I showed my mom your photo and she didn't like you. We won't see each other again."

"Sasha! But I saw how you were looking at me. You liked me. Remember how much fun we had yesterday? And, by the way, you're not too bad!" I said on the phone, realizing that I wasn't talking to him, but to his mother.

And then I heard the sound of a slap! Sasha got it on the neck from his mother 😊. I felt ashamed of my bitchiness. We didn't see each other again, and I had no intention of meeting someone who was still tightly tied to their mother's apron strings.

A fight in the cinema

For our first date, Pasha invited me to watch "Spider-Man: Far from Home" at the movies. To my relief, the person who showed up matched the 27-year-old boy in the photo on the website. Trust me, ladies, that's already a win 😊. He was pleasant to talk to, and he bought us tickets and popcorn. Everything seemed to be going well. Little did I know how wrong I was!

It was ten minutes into the movie when I noticed that he kept glancing at a particular couple in the theater. They were laughing loudly and hugging in a demonstrative manner.

"Do you know them?" I asked.
"Yeah, that's my ex with some guy," he replied.

Well, it happens. Just a coincidence. But he kept staring at them the entire time. As we entered the movie theater, guess where our seats were? Right behind that sweet couple, of course! I knew this wasn't going to work out, so I decided to at least watch the movie before leaving this crazy place.

His ex-girlfriend and her boyfriend hugged and held hands throughout the film, and Pasha was visibly getting more and more nervous. When her boyfriend started kissing her, she hissed loudly, "What are you doing? How dare you?!" Pasha immediately jumped to her defense, grabbing her boyfriend by the collar, trying to drag him out into the corridor. Their confrontation quickly escalated into a serious fight. Half of the theater-goers ended up following them out: this drama seemed more captivating than any Spider-Man movie.

When they were pulled aside, the ex-girlfriend rushed over to Pasha and exclaimed:

"Pashenka, are you okay? Are you hurt? Let's go home!"

I had just finished my popcorn and my hands were free to applaud her theatrics. Now that's what you call love!

The abandoned gentleman (his name was Denys, by the way) was shocked by what he had witnessed. So I took him to the cinema bar to have some coffee. No, I didn't like him. I just felt sorry for him. Everything was so well orchestrated! It turned out that during their drive to the cinema, the girl was constantly immersed in her phone, showing no interest in Denys whatsoever.

We laughed and went our separate ways. Later that evening, Pasha messaged me, apologizing and confessing his undying love for his girlfriend. Good for him ☺.

What I can say is that a determined woman will always find a way to achieve her goals, even if it means stepping on others (like me and Denys) and causing a commotion in the cinema. I have to give her credit for her ingenuity and the drive to win.

By the way, I watched the movie till the end, but the next time I went, I made sure to go alone. I certainly didn't want to find myself in such a troublesome situation again.

Math test that "I didn't pass"

He was quite mysterious, working in the field of security or something similar. We met up and had coffee together. The guy was pleasant and intelligent, but he seemed completely devoid of emotions. I couldn't tell if he liked me or not. Just as I was considering ending the date, he suddenly asked me whether I was a humanities or a math student. I was actually a humanities student, although I was tempted to say I was a math student for a moment.

He seemed quite enthusiastic for the first time on a date as he asked me to solve a problem: "A bottle with a cork costs 11 hryvnias [*Ukrainian currency*], and the bottle is 10 hryvnias more expensive than the cork. How much does the cork cost?"

I considered various options, but unfortunately, they were all incorrect. So I took out a notebook and a pen and tried to recall my elementary school math lessons. It took me an hour, but I finally figured out the correct answer. And then, brace yourself, he glanced at his watch and remarked, "It took you too long to solve such a simple task."

I felt as though I was being summoned to the board unprepared, and I failed miserably. So, how am I supposed to face him and carry on after such a humiliating ordeal?

That's when I recalled Nadiya Ivanivna, our math teacher, and her advice: "Study mathematics. It will help you later in life." Well, if only I had known that it would also come in handy in my personal life, I would have studied it back then 😊.

Do not get into a car with unknown men
Good manners and error-free writing is my main criterion for selecting men during online conversation. And then there must be photos. There were numerous photos, and all of them featured a car. It felt as if the person was trying to sell their car on Tinder.

He offered to pick me up, but I don't get into cars with strangers. And I don't recommend it to you either. You don't have to believe, as in the movies, when the prince drives the girl in a white Mercedes. And also, remember that the first meeting should always be in a crowded place, no exceptions. No matter how much you communicate on the Internet, keep in mind that you don't really know what kind of person they are.

I suggested grabbing coffee at McDonald's, which was conveniently located near the university where I was studying. We sat down and had a pleasant conversation. He was seven years older than me and claimed to be a businessman, though he couldn't quite explain the nature of his business. Things took a sudden turn when a music video featuring a local singer started playing on the TV. And he exploded! According to him, he liked her, but she "blue-balled" him. Yes, that's right, he used the term "blue-balled." He said it with such arrogance and aggression that it left me speechless.

I hurriedly finished my coffee, intending to make a swift exit. But then he abruptly stood up and exclaimed, "Let's go, they're waiting for us."

"Who's waiting? Where are we going?" I asked, puzzled.

"I'll explain everything on the way. Come on, let's go," he insisted.

Thinking on my feet, I quickly came up with an excuse: I claimed that I had been summoned to the dean's office and had to rush off.

His reaction was nothing short of wild. He snapped, "Stop acting like a fool! Get your things and get into the car. I wasted my time on you. Are you going to bail like that singer?"

I was in shock. But I quickly realized that if I got into his car, I might never come back. In a state of panic, I grabbed my bag and rushed to the McDonald's counter. I explained the situation to the cashier, my hands trembling as I spoke. When the man saw what was happening, he swiftly left the premises, hopped into his car, and drove away.

I waited there for another hour and a half, too afraid to go outside, until my brother finally arrived to pick me up and drive me away. I don't know if I would have shared what happened if I hadn't arranged a date in a crowded place and had gotten into his car instead. Even someone who appears to be a successful businessman with a nice car and good writing skills can turn out to be quite different than expected.

"Looking for a girl between the ages of 21 and 25 to start a family with"

And in his profile, he stated: "I am 29 years old. I live alone and have a college degree. I enjoy traveling and have a fit physique."

Yevhen messaged me first. And it wasn't a typical "Hello, how are you?" message, but rather something that made me want to respond. He wrote, "Let's meet tomorrow at 10:00 a.m. near the civil registry office. Don't forget to bring your passport, and please be on time. I don't want anyone else to snatch you away. I've finally found you."

We exchanged messages for a week and then we spoke on the phone for another week. His voice was simply magnificent. Ladies, I'll be honest, I'm quite picky, but he truly impressed me. He was intelligent and could hold conversations on nearly any topic. He even knew what a trichologist was! Come on, even my mom doesn't fully understand my profession!

Notes from Kalabukha
A trichologist is a practitioner that specializes in hair treatment and restoration.

Did you think these stories were from a psychologist or a women's coach? Well, guess again! In my book "When to Say 'YES", there's also a story about a trichologist. Readers in over 100 countries where my books have been published have sent me photos of tear-stained pages with her story. You should give it a read too. It's filled with experiences and truths. And you can't even imagine what will happen next in this story!

I was eagerly anticipating an invitation for a date. But one thing worried me: I had no idea what he looked like because I hadn't seen a single photo of him. His profile picture on the website was of such poor quality that nothing could be discerned from it.

And then, I received the anticipated text message: "How do you feel about grabbing a coffee now?"

I had been eagerly anticipating this for a week. Of course, my response was a resounding "YES!" However, I had to play a bit hard to get, mentioning my busy schedule at work and such. Persistence is key. A man should be persistent. When you're not interested in someone, their persistence can be annoying. But when a guy shows genuine interest in you, it's delightful! He persisted, and eventually, I gave in. We agreed to meet at 4:00 pm.

I managed to do my makeup at work, style my hair, and my girlfriends even found me a pair of high heels in just 20 minutes. Fully prepared and eagerly awaiting my prince, I arrived at 4:05 pm intentionally a little late. As I scanned the crowd, I couldn't help but size up the men around me, wondering if any of them could be him. Suddenly, someone wrapped their arm around my waist from behind. I turned around and found myself speechless. Before me stood an incredibly handsome man, tall and charming, with a dazzling smile that showcased his pearly white teeth. I was completely caught off guard. Usually, people who post vague photos have something to hide, but in his case, it was quite the opposite. The thought immediately crossed my mind: how could someone like him still be single? However, I didn't ask right away. I was too flustered and embarrassed.

We sat at the table, and he graciously ordered some expensive dishes. He was gallant and attentive, trying to make a good impression. However, his phone kept ringing incessantly, and he continued to decline the calls. At first, I didn't pay much attention to it. We were engaged in conversation and it was as if we couldn't stop talking. It felt like we had known each other for ages. Meeting such an interesting and handsome man was truly a rarity. I was amazed and, to be honest, I was ready to accompany him to the civil registry office the very next morning. But his phone became a source of distraction as he continued to refuse incoming calls.

Finally, I mustered up the courage to ask the burning question that had been bothering me since the start:
"Why are you still single?"

His response hit me like a ton of bricks:
"What made you think I'm single? I have a family. My wife just gave birth to our child two months ago."
"Then why are you playing with my emotions? Sending messages, calling me, and asking me out?"
"My wife is constantly preoccupied with the child, leaving me with little attention. I'm still young and can afford to have a couple more women on the side."

I had to suppress the urge to throw a plate at him. So, there was a wife who believed in him, loved him, and was taking care of their child at home, waiting for him. Yet, instead of supporting her, he was using dating sites and taking other women out to dinner. The only reason I didn't lash out was because at least he told me the truth during our first encounter. He didn't try to fool me when I asked.

I genuinely had feelings for him, and it was evident that he felt the same way about me. But I could never bring myself to be a home-wrecker and destroy someone else's family. I didn't want anything to do with him anymore. That was the end of our communication, even though he persistently tried to reach out to me through texts and calls for a long time.

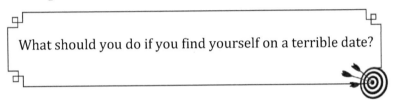

What should you do if you find yourself on a terrible date?

- **How should you react if the guy asks to split the bill equally or suggests that you pay for both of you on a date?**

Run away from him. It will turn out really bad down the road. Do not console yourself with the hope that this is right. If a man takes the initiative, he must take responsibility for his action. In particular, material responsibility. If he can't afford to pay for the coffee himself, he should invite you to the park.

- **What should you do if the guy does not write or call after the date?**

Forget about him. He is not interested in communicating with you. Don't waste your time. Don't even bother.

- **What if a guy begins to talk about his mom on the first date?**

Finish your coffee and go home to feed the cat. Even if you don't have a cat. No, this isn't the case when your chosen one is a good son and worries about his parents. On the contrary, this is an unhealthy case of "mummy's boy". You can stay only if you are ready to raise a 25-50-year-old boy until he reaches the age of maturity. Spoiler alert: he never matures. And remember that a war with his mother awaits you. A never-ending, merciless, and notoriously losing war. Losing for you.

- **Should you go to a guy's house on the first date?**

Listen to your inner voice, as women have a heightened sense of danger. Only go with someone if you are truly comfortable and genuinely want to. However, it's important to inform someone else about your plans, such as a friend. Share his photo and the address of the place you are going to. Remember, the final decision is entirely up to YOU.

- **How to make the best impression on a first date?**
Be yourself. You are unique. You are the best. There is no one else like you. It is much more fulfilling when someone truly falls in love with the real you, without the need to keep secrets or skeletons in the closet. Because, by the way, those skeletons will inevitably come out sooner or later, and always at the most inconvenient time.

> And if it's the other way around, it's not always about you. Most of the time, it's NOT ABOUT YOU. Failed dates should be approached with a sense of humor. Take it lightly and move on.

I finally found a wonderful man on these sites after so many attempts and married him. But now I'm facing a problem: I'm slowly forgetting the stories of my failed dates, and there aren't any new ones. Surprisingly, my husband is against me meeting new people online. Has anyone else experienced this? What should I do about my husband's opposition? 🙂

Vlada Aleksandrova is the owner of two hair care and beauty salons in Kharkiv and Dnipro; author of her own hair reconstruction and restoration technology and the "Guru from Roots to Tips" course, International Hair Straightening and Restoration Championship (2020) judge, mother of two children, 26 years old (!), originally from Kharkiv.

PART TWO:
THE WAR

I was haunted by a bad feeling all day on February 23, 2022, and there was a reason for it: I have two small children, with the youngest being five months old at the time, and we live in Kharkiv, specifically in Saltivka, which is the district closest to Belgorod in the russian federation.

At four o'clock in the morning on February 24, 2022, I was breastfeeding the youngest, when I lay down and heard explosions. Not once, not twice, but every five to seven seconds. I jumped out of bed and said to my husband, "We are being bombed." "No, it's probably just the tram passing," he replied.

When I opened the balcony to the street, I noticed that all the cars down below had their alarms going off, and a missile was flying in the sky above us towards the airfield. I grabbed the kids and carried them into the corridor, away from the windows.

The eldest son, Fedir, who was five years old, asked me in fear:

"Mommy, are those fireworks?"
"No, we are being bombed."
"But, why, mommy?"

I vividly remember this moment. What should I tell a child when he asks why we are being bombed? I burst into tears; I couldn't explain it to him. I ran to pack our suitcases: children's things, bottles, food, and essentials. I gathered the children and led them outside. There were a lot of people there, all with suitcases, all running somewhere, starting their cars, and driving away.

Was there a panic? No, there was a sense that everyone had been preparing for this moment, and it had now arrived. And I had been preparing too: two months before the war I bought a car and filled its gas tank every day so that it was always full.

My children and I traveled to my mother in Dnipro. What was the road like? Everyone was speeding, cutting each other off, in a rush to leave Kharkiv. This behavior was particularly noticeable among drivers of expensive and flashy cars, whose owners often believe they can do anything. As a result, the journey to Dnipro took me three times longer than usual, with just the portion through Kharkiv taking about two hours.

What was it like in Dnipro? Every morning at four o'clock, an air raid alert would sound. We would rush to the basement with the kids three times during the night because we had no idea where the missiles were coming from or where they were heading. I was consumed by hatred and wanted to go and shoot the enemies. I desperately wanted to believe that it will all be over soon.

My beauty salons in Dnipro and Kharkiv are currently closed and not operating. My employees left. Fortunately, I don't have to pay rent as we signed a contract with the owners in December, stipulating that no rent would be charged if martial law was declared. My lawyer recommended including this clause.

A month had passed, yet the situation showed no signs of improvement. I realized that I needed to gradually resume my work and get back into a routine. Furthermore, I couldn't stay in Dnipro any longer; I needed to find a safer place once again.

My husband chose to stay in Kharkiv. After assisting his father and sister in their departure, he visited the Military Commissariat four times, but he was not enlisted. They informed him that he would be called up if necessary. He eventually joined me in Dnipro, and together with my sister-in-law (my brother's wife) and two nephews, we continued our journey.

We arrived in Letychiv, about an hour's drive from Khmelnytskyi, and started looking for accommodation. However, due to the large number of people in our group - seven in total (three adults and four children), we were unable to find anything suitable. At that point, I decided to approach the nearest village council for assistance. They provided us with a house, although it lacked basic amenities. We stayed there for three months with only electricity and a gas cylinder. The toilet was outside and we had to rely on a neighbor for water. It was only in June that we were able to relocate to Khmelnytskyi.

How did I find a job in a new place? Through Instagram. On April 2nd, I posted on my page @volosiki_kharkov for the first time in Ukrainian.

"Hello, Khmelnytskyi! We are from Ukraine, more precisely Kharkiv. Instead of going abroad to work, I want to stay in my homeland, pay taxes, and then return home when everything is over. That's why I came to your city. Who are we? We are the VOLOSIKI_KHARKOV studio, Kharkiv's best studio for taming unruly hair. As long as there is an opportunity, I will work in your city and make you even more beautiful.

Everything will be Ukraine." *[This phrase is used by Ukrainians to convey a unique message that everything will be alright, everything will be "Ukraine."]*

Now I write and speak only Ukrainian, everywhere.

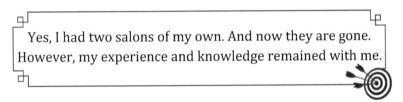

Yes, I had two salons of my own. And now they are gone. However, my experience and knowledge remained with me.

I realized that I would have to start from scratch in a new place without an existing customer base. And that's exactly what I did. I found a place to rent in a salon and ran an ad with a special offer: a 25% discount on the first visit. Furthermore, my followers made dozens of reposts, which quickly filled up my appointment book.

It was the end of March. The salon had just reopened, and clients were already coming in for coloring, haircuts, and manicures. There was a full schedule of clients.

Now I receive four to five clients every day. I haven't changed the profile name on Instagram, only the description (caption). Here's what it looks like now:

Vlada Alexandrova, TRICHOLOGIST
From beloved Kharkiv to Khmelnytskyi
Beauty may not save the world, but it will definitely save Ukraine's economy

One of my clients helped me with finding an apartment. Nobody wanted to rent to us since we had four children. Her husband, on the other hand, agreed and rented us a three-room apartment. My goodness, what a blessing to have a toilet, a bath, and hot water!

As for the children, I am very concerned about my eldest son Fedir. He was greatly frightened by the explosions. Now, in their absence, the consequences have manifested themselves — he has become nervous. Additionally, he has begun to repeat obscene words after hearing them from adults and on TV. For example, "putin khuylo!" *["Khuylo" is a slang term that is considered highly vulgar and profane, roughly translating to an insulting term for a Ukrainian person. When combined with "putin," it becomes an offensive phrase directed at russian President vladimir putin.]* And there is no room for argument here!

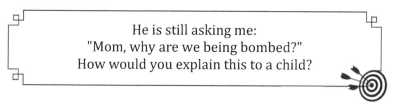

He is still asking me:
"Mom, why are we being bombed?"
How would you explain this to a child?

"Because they are such people. This is such a country. It is in their blood to rob and rape. These are barbarians."

I can see how difficult it is for him; he cannot understand what is happening.

What are my plans for the future? I do not plan to return to Kharkiv yet, as it is still very dangerous there. Instead, I will continue working here in Khmelnytskyi. This city is perfect for me, a charming little town where we have been warmly welcomed. I plan to organize a tour in Europe, as there are many potential customers there. However, I have no plans to permanently live abroad; I want to stay in Ukraine.

Yes, it is difficult. Starting over again can be challenging, especially when you're starting from scratch. But I refuse to give up because I have so much to live for. I have my children, a beloved husband, and my own business where I help girls feel beautiful!

I remember when I was leaving Kharkiv at six in the morning on February 24, a client called me and said, "I have an appointment with you today at 2:00 p.m. Maybe there will be problems with transportation. Will it be ok if I'm late?" Despite our announcement on all social networks that we would be closed that day due to the start of the war, this person was still eager to come. That's why I'm surprised by social media posts asking, "How can people care about hair dyeing or keratin hair restoration when there's a war in the country?"

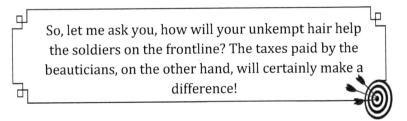

So, let me ask you, how will your unkempt hair help the soldiers on the frontline? The taxes paid by the beauticians, on the other hand, will certainly make a difference!

A Ukrainian woman always strives to be beautiful, even in times of war, tornadoes, or tsunamis. It is our basic need, our resource that gives us the strength to live and prevail. Moreover, it generates funds for taxes, donations, and supports other entrepreneurs. The beauty industry was among the first to be revived and bears the burden with dignity. Once again, everything rests on the fragile shoulders of women.

Beauty may not save the world, but it will definitely save Ukraine's economy.

CHAPTER 13

TETYANA PYLYPETS' STORIES

PART ONE:
FIVE WAYS TO TEACH A CHILD TO LOVE READING

"Books suck and reading is a waste of time" is the most innocent thing I hear from teenagers who are forced to take a library tour.

And I reply:
"Do you want to be paid 350 euros for an hour of conversation? That's how much I used to make when I worked as a special events presenter and had my own event agency."
"Would you like me to share the recipe for success as a good speaker, moderator, or host?"
"Yes!" the children exclaim with interest as I transform the knowledge gained from books into financial success.
"The professional qualities of a good presenter include improvisation, a rich vocabulary, the ability to speak without relying on written scripts, and the ability to adapt the tone of the conversation to each individual. Additionally, a good presenter should also be able to captivate and engage the audience, making them eager to listen and take action. These qualities can be acquired through reading books, which provide valuable knowledge and allow individuals to shape their desired reality. Thanks to books, I am currently living the life of my dreams, influencing the world around me."

This approach has been effective with teenagers. Using this strategy, I have successfully inspired over a thousand children to develop a passion for reading and frequent library visits.

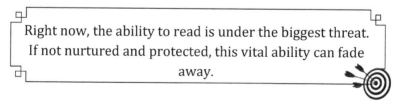

Right now, the ability to read is under the biggest threat. If not nurtured and protected, this vital ability can fade away.

And this will deprive mankind, particularly our children, of important processes necessary for self-realization.

I recently conducted an experiment in which I showed a focus group of 25 young people aged 14 to 18 (from my children's environment) high-quality foreign TV series in the original language but with Ukrainian subtitles. 60% of them were unable to keep up with reading the subtitles in the first one or two episodes. And why is that? It is because they don't have sufficiently developed reading skills; their reading ability lacks fluency.

The situation needs to be rectified immediately! If we do not provide children with the opportunity and encouragement to read, it will become increasingly challenging for them to develop this habit in adulthood.

Five tips on how to teach a child to read

1. **If you don't want your children to smoke, don't show them that you smoke. Similarly, if you want your children to develop a love for reading, lead by example and let them see you reading.**
   And not from a smartphone or a computer screen, but from a physical book. Set aside a dedicated space for reading, such as a cozy chair under a floor lamp or a beautifully decorated windowsill.
   Children should see reading and hear statements such as, "I'll finish this chapter or page, and then I'll be available for you."

2. **Encourage fathers or grandfathers to read to the children before bedtime.**
   The German Book Institute recommends that fathers read to children at night. Father's active involvement in the family can contribute to better connections, increased confidence, and greater success for children later in life.

That is why, in 2017, I became one of the initiators of the UN Population Fund in Ukraine's (UNFPA Ukraine) reading promotion project "Dad, read to me!" Our goal was to engage parents in educational processes in a simple and cost-effective way — by spending time together reading a book aloud.

The project became particularly relevant in the east of Ukraine, where a large number of orphans (both actual and social) have emerged since 2014.

Social orphans, unlike actual orphans, have living parents but, due to various circumstances, are deprived of their care.

Our military personnel began to visit such children in orphanages, boarding schools, or simply in schools and read aloud books by modern Ukrainian authors to them.

3. Introduce your child to a writer.

For what purpose? So that your child does not form the opinion that all writers exist only in the portraits that hang in literary rooms.

You may ask how a person who is not connected to the bohemian scene can meet a contemporary writer. The answer is simple: just attend book presentations in libraries or follow them on social media.

Children do not necessarily need a children's author; they can also be inspired by adult writers. The key factor is that the person is charismatic and a thought leader who can spark their interest in reading and inspire them to aspire to be like them.

4. Turn your child's birthday into a literary celebration instead of going to McDonald's.

Immerse yourself in a fairy tale such as "Alice in Wonderland," "Cinderella," "Harry Potter," or "The Little Mermaid." It's important to highlight, though, that it's not simply about dressing the child up in a costume for a social media photo or getting a themed cake.

Come up with a program where everyone has their own role, quests, and competitions.

You can invite animators, but the biggest mistake parents make is that while their children are being entertained, the adults sit separately, drink, and communicate only among themselves, without actively participating in the event.

How do I know? I have seen this a thousand times.

I worked as an animator starting from seventh grade, playing with children, dressed in costumes of various fairy-tale characters. I continued this career path until I was 35 years old, portraying the character Fiona, which was highly popular at the time. I would walk around the city in that costume, and it felt so natural that even the mayor invited me to a prayer service without realizing I had green makeup on my face.

Join the children's celebration! When adults fail to do so, the hired animators become just another "bribe," like a smartphone or tablet, constantly given to children to keep them occupied and away from the adults.

Spend about 10-15 minutes actively interacting with the child. And if grandparents or godparents are involved, it will be the best gift for the child, one that they will remember for the rest of their lives.

And if this entire experience is based on a book, the child will read with joy and may even suggest topics for future family literary performances or evenings.

5. Enroll your child in the library.

One of the reasons why parents may not encourage their children to read is the cost of books. A good children's book might cost 250-300 UAH *[equivalent to $7-$10]*.

The child begins reading books with enthusiasm, but not every family can afford to buy new books all the time. Therefore, it is important to enroll your children in libraries, where they will have access to a wide range of books and an environment that is highly conducive to reading and development.

Then your child will find joy in reading independently, and books will become a source of support, comfort, and inspiration throughout their life.

***Tetyana Pylypets** is the director of the Roman Ivanychuk Lviv Regional Library for Youth, which, under her leadership, has transformed from a mere "book collection in the sense of a dust collector" into a popular "library of events" and an artistic space in the heart of Lviv. The Ukrainian Library Association has also named the library "Library of the Year 2021".*

Organizer and moderator of numerous literary meetings and presentations, co-organizer and author of the "Kalmius" festival, the First All-Ukrainian Forum of Military Writers, and the Knyzhkova Toloka named after Lyubov Khomchak. 48 years old, resides in Lviv.

PART TWO:
THE WAR

On February 24, 2022, I received an early morning phone call from my niece in Kharkiv. She sounded anxious and asked for our address. I wondered why she would ask for it at 5:00 o'clock in the morning. I asked for an explanation, but she couldn't provide one. She simply mentioned that she needed to leave the city immediately because something terrible was happening there. I turned on the TV and saw footage of explosions in Kyiv. That's when I realized that a major war had started.

When I arrived at work, I knew I needed to keep myself occupied in order to calm down and think clearly about the next steps. I took out the frame that I used for weaving "kikimoras" [*A Kikimora is a creature from Slavic folklore, particularly in Eastern European traditions. It is typically described as a female household spirit. The Kikimora is often associated with mischief and is believed to dwell in the home, particularly in dark corners, under beds, or in the cellar.*] and got to work. As people passed by the library's large transparent door, they saw me and offered their help, wanting to be useful. There was plenty of work for everyone. By the evening of February 24, there were already 300 of us! And so, the Roman Ivanychuk Lviv Regional Library for Youth at 9 Rynok Square was transformed into a volunteer center.

We set up workshops for fabric cutting and dyeing, net weaving, and flag and linen sewing. As the number of people grew and there was no space left, some were directed to other locations to make dumplings, assist with unloading humanitarian aid, and volunteer at the station. Hundreds of people joined us each day, and the collective effort was truly incredible.

When a big influx of forced migrants arrived in Lviv and started coming to us seeking shelter, we set up two rooms for them. Where did we get the mattresses and bedding? They were all generously donated by people and provided by well-wishers. Up to a thousand people per month found refuge in the shelter within our library.

In the early days of the war, I happened to find out that one of my writer friends was running low on ammunition. I reached out to the devoted readers whom I personally knew and we decided to raise funds to purchase ammo for him. It was then that I realized, "My responsibility now is to protect my authors to the best of my ability." Initially, only members of the Association of Military writers contacted me, but later, anyone who knew me and needed assistance began reaching out.

I am grateful to everyone for their trust from the bottom of my heart. With just one post on my Facebook page, we were able to fully meet our collection goal in less than a day. It's incredible to see how many people are eager to help and how generous their donations are. Let me share two remarkable examples: we collected 46,000 UAH *[equivalent to $1,250]* in just a few hours for a weather station and in three days, 84,000 UAH *[equivalent to $2,300]* for a quadcopter.

The camouflage nets we weave are considered the best in Ukraine. By the beginning of August, we had already woven 7,000 square meters of nets!

I am proud that I was able to create such a powerful volunteer center based on our library. People find support, help, and shelter here. We even bring people together, helping them fall in love — we connect hearts!

And most importantly, everyone who donates, weaves nets, works at the fair, or participates in any other way, makes an invaluable contribution to our victory.

> We help the strongest — those whom the whole world looks up to and admires — the Armed Forces of Ukraine.

CHAPTER 14

DZVINA KOVALCHUK'S STORIES

PART ONE:
"SPORTS VISA", TRACTOR DRIVERS, AND THE UNKNOWN WORD "TARGET"

A hotel in the Czech Republic, another working day. I clean the rooms and do hard physical labor while feeling hopeless. The pay is meager, but I save every penny, hoping to someday afford something important and seemingly unattainable.

Next to me are girls and women who haven't seen their relatives in months. It's like an endless Groundhog Day: we come to work, clean the rooms, go back to our rented house, call our kids, and go to bed, only to repeat it the next day all over again. We're in a foreign country, surrounded by strangers. There's a constant fear that even this job might not be available anymore, as we were all working illegally at the time.

Do you know what a "sports visa" is? It's a Polish visa that doesn't grant permission to work in the Czech Republic. You literally try to flee every time you see the police. That's why it's called the "sports visa" because you're constantly running. Even now, in Ukraine, I still get anxious when I see police cars.

Every time I cleaned the toilet or collected condoms after a wild night of guests, I asked myself, "Why am I here? Is this the best I can do? Is this my fate?"

I'm not stupid; I graduated from the foreign languages faculty. Whatever I do, I always strive to do it well.

> I need to find a job where I can use my intelligence to earn a living. I don't want to be nobody and constantly evade the police. I want to live in Ukraine.

So, I returned to Ukraine. My husband and I came back together after working abroad. I was pregnant and searching for a job that I could do from home. I was willing to do anything as long as I could get paid. With the help of Work.ua *[Ukrainian version of Indeed or Monster]*, I became a sales manager in a call center.

What was I doing? I was calling the tractor drivers who were in our database and offered them the opportunity to buy new tractors. My cold call went something like this: "Good afternoon! My name is Dzvina. I'm from Company N. I wanted to inquire if you are in need of a tractor." Yes, I realize now that those were terrible scripts provided by the company. The calls would usually last only a second or two, and I would often be met with curses before they hung up.

I would make 100 calls per hour, while other employees would only make 15-20. I didn't know it at the time, so I called like a maniac just to avoid being fired. Nobody told me about a lunch break either. Despite making every possible mistake (I didn't know any better!), I persevered. I ended up selling more tractors than anyone else, even though I was paid very little. Can you guess how much? 20 UAH per hour (in 2018) *[$1,40]*. Nonetheless, I was still happy to be working from home. My boss was pleased to have such a dedicated employee. He called me and expressed his desire to create an SMM department and asked if I was familiar with the concept of targeting.

"Yes," I answered, sprinting to Google the word I had just heard for the first time in my life.
"Great! I'll buy you some courses to improve your skills."

I attended my first training session the day after giving birth. Because my boss assumed I was knowledgeable about the subject, he bought advanced courses for me. However, I couldn't understand a single word. Not a single one!

I can't even fathom where I found so much strength back then. I had a newborn baby who was suffering from terrible colic, and on top of that, I was studying day and night. Initially, I watched every freely available resource on YouTube on this topic, and then I underwent training provided by my boss and passed the exams. The courses were conducted by renowned target experts who are still active in the industry. However, what disappointed me most about the courses was the complete absence of practical exercises.

The first client I was assigned to in the company expressed dissatisfaction with my work. He felt that the number of followers I brought him was insufficient. As a result, he decided to fire me but did not remove me from the advertising account's administrators. While still in that role, I observed the work of the targeting specialist who replaced me. I grasped the essence of their techniques, started producing results, and was eventually promoted to the position of SMM specialist. Later, I was appointed as the head of the department. Remarkably, all of this progress happened within the same company where I initially sold tractors over the phone.

At that time, I took on the responsibility of recruiting and training new targeting specialists myself. Our department was thriving, with a heavy workload, impressive results, and a fantastic team. About six months later, the majority of the team went on vacation at the same time, leaving only the copywriter and me behind. It was during this period that management requested an assessment of our department's monthly profits. After crunching the numbers, I was astounded to find that we had generated 80 thousand hryvnias *[$2,750]* in revenue. Just the two of us! This was a substantial contribution to the company's earnings.

Do you know how much I was paid at the time? They continued to pay me 20 UAH per hour (2018)! Despite the fact that the workload grew day by day. I started off working four hours a day, then six, then eight. And, when the department was operating at full capacity, I had to work 12 hours a day.

I wondered, what was the reason behind earning so little? Even in the Czech Republic my hourly rate was equivalent to 110 UAH *[$3,80]*. Maybe I should return there to earn money once my daughter grows up. No, that wasn't necessary. It would be better to resign and work for myself so that I could keep all of the 80,000 UAH for myself. That same evening, I created my first Instagram page and began sharing information about target marketing.

To be honest, I was afraid of running out of money. It was unclear when I would start making money from my blog, when at my job I had a small, yet stable income. However, I believed in myself and kept reassuring myself: "You can do it. Everything will work out for you." And it did! On the day I resigned, my first client, with whom I still work, reached out to me.

And what did the company's owner do? He didn't want to let me go. I prepared everything to leave professionally. I handed over all of the projects to my successor, who managed them quite well. At first, he tried to make me feel guilty: "I provided you with everything, taught you everything, paid for your courses. You can't just leave the company so easily, come back!" Then he started making threats: "You won't get away with this, I know where you live."

Do you know how he threatened me? He didn't text me. He sent voice messages on Viber. As soon as he saw that I listened, he would immediately delete them. It was both scary and strange to me that a serious, wealthy adult would threaten me, a girl from Khodoriv (population 12,000), in this manner. And for what? Because I worked so long and so faithfully for him for a meager salary? I would have never left him if I had been paid properly.

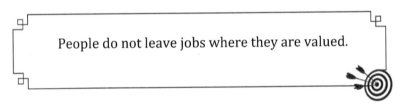

People do not leave jobs where they are valued.

People that are committed to their personal growth and development will not tolerate such disrespect. They are confident in their abilities and recognize their true worth.

"You will crawl to me on your knees, begging to come back, but I won't rehire you. I will make sure to tarnish your reputation so that no one else will hire you!" These were the threatening voicemails I received from my former director, which he promptly deleted. I endured them for another month, but I refused to let them break me. I was no longer crying or living in fear. Instead, I focused on building my own business with the same zeal that I had earlier given to his.

Yes, leaving that company was undoubtedly a frightening

decision. However, not once did I entertain the thought of returning. In an unexpected turn of events, the company itself reached out to me, figuratively crawling on its knees, just as its director had once wanted me to do! As my entire department left one by one, the director's voice messages ceased, replaced instead by pleas from his managers to come back or at least take on one client. However, their arguments remained the same: "The company invested in your education, and now you should help us." But I stood firm and refused to give in.

I had already taken the initiative to find clients, build a team, and earn money on my own.

What would I advise those who work in a toxic team with a toxic manager, where they are not valued, bullied, or taken advantage of? Get the heck out of there!

Why suffer from injustice and unhappiness when there are so many opportunities available? Choose yourself, choose joy in every aspect of your life: relationships, work, and family. But first, build a solid foundation for your departure. Send out resumes, consider how you can make money outside of your current job, and secure your first client before you resign.

Can't think of anything? Learn something new.

I have been working in the field of SMM since 2019. In addition to my Instagram blog, I have a YouTube channel and courses on targeting. I made enough money to get my own house, where I'm finishing renovations. And I have no intention of stopping there.

As for the path I chose, perhaps I had to clean those toilets and make 100 calls to tractor drivers for 20 UAH per hour. But why? To get to where I am now, earning a living with my own skills and knowledge, appreciating the value of my work, and being content with where I am. I am proud to be in my place, right here in Ukraine.

Dzvina Kovalchuk, 26 years old, Khodoriv (Lviv region).

PART TWO:
THE WAR

From February 10, I was certain that the war would begin. Therefore, I began to transition my entire business toward a military focus. I started by optimizing costs. I temporarily halted the development of my YouTube channel, as each video required a significant budget. I reduced my spending on targeted advertising. Additionally, I changed my assistants' salary structure from a fixed rate to a percentage of the projects.

On February 16, we were invited to a birthday party. It was during that event that I had a profound realization that this would be our last moment of joy before the war. At midnight, all of the guests spontaneously replaced the traditional "Mnohaya Lita" ("Many Years") song *[a traditional Ukrainian greeting used to wish someone a long and prosperous life. It is commonly used during celebrations, especially birthdays and weddings, to convey good wishes for a person's longevity and well-being. The phrase is often accompanied by raising glasses and toasting to the health and happiness of the person being celebrated]* with "Batko Nash Bandera" ("Bandera is Our Father") *[a song about Stepan Bandera who was a leader of the Organization of Ukrainian Nationalists (OUN) during the mid-20th century, and he played a significant role in the fight for Ukrainian independence. He is seen as a hero who fought for Ukraine's independence from Soviet and Polish rule. The phrases like "Bandera is Our Father" are used as a way of expressing admiration for his efforts and sacrifices in pursuit of Ukrainian statehood]*. Tears were flowing down the cheeks, and there was a heavy sense of impending doom in the air.

On February 17, I started transforming my rented office space into a headquarters. I cleared out the tables, computers, and moved the sofa. I installed hooks on the walls. Every day, between 60 to 120 people would come to my office to weave camouflage nets. Surprisingly, we had already started weaving these nets before the war began. It was during this time that I connected with experienced volunteers who had been involved in volunteering since 2014. They shared valuable insights about where and how to order supplies. Prior to this, I had no prior volunteer experience.

On February 23, we had a great day. We gathered around 80 people to weave nets and sing Ukrainian songs. The atmosphere was filled with unity and camaraderie. My husband, Roman, brought two liters of homemade wine, and our mothers prepared delicious canapés. It was a joyful and uplifting experience for all of us. We decided to meet again the next day around 9 o'clock to begin our work earlier. I returned home feeling very happy. As we got ready for bed, I asked my husband, "What will happen if the war starts tomorrow?" He remained skeptical and couldn't believe that such a thing could actually happen.

On February 24, 2022, I woke up at 5:30 in the morning. I wasn't in the habit of reading the news, and I wasn't subscribed to any news channels.

When I opened Telegram, all public accounts stated the following: "The war has begun."

Friends from Kharkiv, Kyiv, and Ivano-Frankivsk started to report that they were being bombed.

I started packing two emergency suitcases. I packed my things, my daughter's clothes, and documents in one suitcase. I packed my husband's belongings in the second suitcase. He wasn't supposed to come with me for sure, but he was supposed to stay here to defend Ukraine. My priority was to get the child out of the danger zone.

On March 11, when Ivano-Frankivsk, Lutsk, and Lviv were all bombed on the same day, my husband decided to send me and our child to the Czech Republic.

I'd like to tell you about my journey. I expected to see panic. Roman even hid pepper spray in my jacket so I could defend myself if I was attacked. But there was no panic. Nobody fought or pushed. People allowed mothers with small children to go ahead. And when the pepper spray fell out of my pocket on the bus, the driver remarked, "Oh, it seems that this Ukrainian lady knows how to protect herself."

The Poles provided a lot of assistance when we crossed the border. They brought us hot food, tea/coffee, and toys for the kids.

They even offered help with accommodation if we had nowhere to stay. It was a realization that we were not going into the void, but to a country where we would be taken care of, not judged for seeking refuge, but instead supported. I felt immense gratitude towards all of them, to the point of tears, reaching the depths of my soul.

I was particularly impressed by the Polish border guards at passport control. Just imagine, it was four o'clock in the morning when we got off the bus. There was a table set up with hot drinks, canapés, and sweets. One child accidentally spilled tea, and her mother immediately started apologizing and hurriedly wiping everything with her scarf. The chief border guard on duty came out, reassured everyone that it was fine, and proceeded to clean up the mess himself. It was being handled by the chief border guard!

In the Czech Republic, I was overwhelmed with frustration. I became extremely confrontational, attacking people left and right. It angered me to see them going about their lives, sitting in cafes, playing sports, and shopping, while we were being bombed. I was so overwhelmed by the aggression that I found myself being rude everywhere: at pharmacies, on the street, and even in the subway.

I entered a kitchenware store where Chinese employees were working. I was buying a plate and a friendly cashier asked me in English:
"Where are you from?"
"From Ukraine."
"Oh, that's cool! I know your country is at war. Well, enjoy your time here."

I was so taken aback that I nearly threw the plate at him. How could he tell me to "enjoy my time" when my country was at war? I yelled, "Fuck you!" and stormed out of the store.

Everywhere I went, I made a point to share with others that our country was being attacked by putin and informed them about the situation in Ukraine. russian women with children would immediately leave upon hearing us speak Ukrainian. On the other hand, women from Belarus and Kazakhstan expressed sympathy and support. Initially, I would confront them with grievances as well. However, I eventually realized that we shared a common problem: none of us had chosen to be in this situation. Following the crackdown on protests in January 2022, women from Kazakhstan had faced oppression. People took to the streets to rally against corruption and the rising gas prices, only to be met with violence by russian troops under the guise of a "peacekeeping special operation." Similarly, women from Belarus had fled due to Lukashenko's repressive measures in response to their participation in protests against the fraudulent presidential elections in 2020.

I stayed in the Czech Republic with my dad, who has lived there for 25 years. He went there to make money and ended up settling down. One day, he came to me and expressed that Czechs seemed to be very angry with us because our war had caused a significant increase in prices. When I asked him if he personally knew any Czech people who felt this way, he couldn't name a single one. It became evident that this was a deliberate attempt to spread hostile misinformation, aimed at sowing discord and dividing society.

And I myself had a different kind of encounter. Picture this: I'm at the subway station and a beggar approaches me, asking for money.

"I'm sorry," I say in English. "I don't have any cash on me, only credit cards."
"Where are you from?" she asks.
"I'm from Ukraine," I reply.

Upon hearing this, she stands up abruptly, tears welling up in her eyes, and begins rummaging through her pockets.

"Take it, you need it more, especially with a small child!" she insists.

I politely decline her offer, but she continues to chase us, grabbing my child's hand and insisting that we take the money. We board the train as it arrives, leaving her behind on the platform. As long as she remained within our sight, she made the sign of the cross and fervently prayed:

What Czech people are most concerned about is the fear that the war might reach their country as well. People are debating whether or not we would be able to withstand or fight back against putin. The memories of soviet tanks firing on the streets of Prague in 1968 are still fresh in people's minds. Those so-called "liberators" are well-remembered here.

Notes from Kalabukha

In 1968, the government of the soviet union was not pleased with the actions of Alexander Dubček, the general secretary of the Communist Party of the then-socialist Czechoslovakia. Dubček had initiated various democratic reforms, such as the introduction of freedom of speech and the recognition of the right to private property.

The soviet union decided to intervene and halt these reforms by providing "military assistance" to Czechoslovakia, despite the fact that it was not requested by the Czechoslovak government. Soviet troops were deployed, and within a day, the country was fully occupied. The Czechoslovak government was taken to moscow, and images of soviet tanks firing at civilians circulated worldwide.

This is how the soviet union forcefully suppressed the "Prague Spring" — Czechoslovakia's attempt to establish "socialism with a human face."

As for our refugees, who allegedly tarnish the image of Ukraine, I personally have not encountered such cases. However, there is an issue that bothers me: in some families, such as my father's, men work in the Czech Republic while their wives join them and apply for refugee status in order to receive benefits. This raises concerns as to why they are doing so. There might be true cases where a woman arrives with a child who has truly lost everything, lacking a provider and any means to support themselves. However, due to the limited assistance available to refugees, these true cases may be denied benefits and support, as the funds have already been exhausted by others.

Personally, I did not apply for any financial assistance. From the very first day, I made the decision to resume my commercial activity. And you know how? Right at the cash register in the supermarket!

My dad and I went to the store, and I bought groceries worth 800 Korunas.

Dad said to me:
"Dzvina, my salary is 30,000 Korunas. I still have to pay for the apartment and utilities. We need to save money now that there are three of us."

My thoughts at that moment were as follows: I understand that my father is not used to supporting me because I have been working on my own since I was 18; I will never again become dependent on either my father or my husband.

I gave myself one day to rest after my arrival, and on March 12, I announced that I was resuming work.

I prayed to God, asking Him to send clients so that I could start earning money at least for my team. And God answered my prayer. The first sale was made on the very same day. It was the beginning.

In just one week, we were able to regain the same volume of business as before the war.

I was volunteering while I was in the Czech Republic. I stayed connected with the primary volunteers in Khodoriv and stayed informed about the situation back home. I purchased essential items needed at the front, such as tactical gloves, glasses, and knee pads. People sent me money, and I made sure to report and provide receipts to show how the funds were used.

There is a large military shop in Prague from which couriers frequently visited me. Unlike our Nova Poshta service *[equivalent to UPS/FedEx etc. but without home delivery]*, they offered home delivery. If I ordered two parcels, they would deliver them on two separate trips rather than all at once.

Then I looked for a car that could transport the parcels to the bus heading to Ukraine, where my husband would be waiting. We arranged for him to have a volunteer document so he could drive at night. The most challenging situation was when I had to hand over the thermographic camera at the train station at three o'clock in the morning, while Lviv was being bombarded.

How I wished to return home! Finally, on April 10, the kitchen for our new house, which we had been building for a year, was delivered (it was initially scheduled for February 25). Everything was ready, the kitchen was in place, and the renovations were almost finished. It was time to start living there! I packed my belongings, boarded the bus, and headed home.

Concerning bullying, I witnessed on social media how women who had gone abroad with their children were being judged. They expressed remorse, saying, "I had to do it, please forgive me!" I found this very surprising. On the contrary, when I left for the Czech Republic, I received a lot of support for prioritizing my child's safety. However, upon my return, I was met with criticism, with many claiming that I was setting a bad example and that it might encourage others to come back, which could be dangerous. Interestingly, these opinions were mostly expressed by men.

In Khodoriv, I continued my volunteer work, assisting Roman Tityk, a fellow volunteer who has been involved since 2014. Roman was injured during the shootings of the Heavenly Hundred *[(Ukrainian: Небесна сотня, Nebesna Sotnya) is a term used to refer to the group of people who were killed during the Euromaidan protests in Ukraine in 2014. These protests, also known as the Euromaidan movement or Revolution of Dignity, were a series of demonstrations and civil unrest. The protests were sparked by then-President Viktor Yanukovych's decision to suspend the signing of an association agreement with the European Union in favor of closer ties with russia]* and underwent a lengthy recovery. We make a great team: he advises me on where to buy items and where to submit receipts, I handle finding the necessary funds and making the purchases, and he transports them to the front lines. Roman has taught me everything I know in this regard, and we work together seamlessly.

Recently, I felt compelled to expand my impact, so my husband and I decided to establish the Kovalchuk Charity Fund. Initially, our monthly volunteer turnover was about 100,000-200,000 UAH *[$2,500-$5,000]*, but it has grown to 1-2 million UAH *[$25,000-$50,000]*.

I want to share the story of how we acquired a refrigerator car. One morning, I was in a great mood, feeling on top of the world. Little did I know that such moments of happiness often preceded something terrible. Roman Tityk came to see me, and there was a solemn silence between us. He handed me a phone, and I saw a document stating that our district was responsible for purchasing a refrigerator car to transport the bodies of fallen heroes and bring them back to their hometowns. I asked for clarification, "Is this for the Lviv region?" And he replied, "No, it's for our Zhydachiv district and nearby villages."

The refrigerator car had a price tag of over $9,000, and our dedicated volunteers managed to gather $4,000 towards the purchase. However, we still needed an additional $5,500 to complete the payment. The situation in the eastern regions was dire, with scorching heat exacerbating the need for urgent transportation. Time was of the essence, and we had to find a solution quickly.

I made an announcement on Instagram, expressing the urgent need for the remaining funds. It was challenging for me to find the right words, but the response from people was immediate and heartwarming. They immediately began transferring funds.

> The entire amount of $5,500 (equivalent to 211,000 hryvnias) was collected within a span of 12 hours. I opened the collection at 6 p.m. and it was already closed by 9 a.m. the next day.

For a refrigerator car dedicated to transporting the bodies of fallen heroes from our district. God, how many lives have been lost!

When a russian missile struck the shopping center in Kremenchuk on June 27, 2022, a sense of impending doom enveloped me. The fear of losing my child became my greatest concern. In that state, it felt as if life had lost all meaning. I couldn't find the motivation to pursue personal development, read books, or indulge in anything beyond the bare necessities. The overwhelming emptiness consumed me, and the feeling of helplessness was unbearable. It seemed as though everything had the already predetermined fate.

When I vocalized my inner turmoil to the psychologist, I was taken aback by my own words. I realized that I wasn't facing a terminal illness and that I didn't reside in a continual war zone. Why was I allowing myself to be consumed by such thoughts? I want to live! I will live! I live! From that moment on, I immediately began to accomplish all of my dreams, exploring the mountains, sleeping in tents, and documenting my adventures through vlogs.

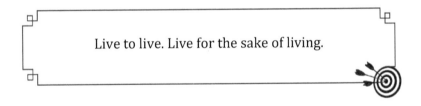

Live to live. Live for the sake of living.

We must take every necessary step to ensure our survival, such as seeking shelter immediately during air raid alerts and seeking medical assistance when we are unwell. In order to minimize psychological trauma, it is crucial to prioritize our physical and mental well-being, as well as the well-being of our children. By caring for ourselves and our families, we contribute to the preservation of our nation. And live for the sake of living.

CHAPTER 15

HOW TO ASK FOR HELP SO THAT IT IS GIVEN?

Ask

Just like in sales. To make someone buy from you, you have to sell. It's not about entertaining, but about consistently communicating the benefits or providing curated selections of interesting films for the weekend. Don't just sit and wait for clients to contact you or come to you for your product. Instead, actively sell it. Be straightforward: "I'm selling this and that, it costs this much, to order — write/press/call here."

The same is true when asking for help. You have to ask for something to be given to you. This is not a sign of weakness, but of strength and trust in the world. Rejection also does not mean that you have failed and will be rejected everywhere. It simply means that those particular people couldn't help for some reason. You have to keep looking for others who can.

However, in order to maximize the chances of getting what you need on the first try, you need to know how to do it correctly.

Your life and the lives of those for whom you ask for depend on it. And the rules are the same as they are in sales.

Phone

Don't ask: "Are you comfortable talking?", "What are you doing?", "How are you?", "Do you have a minute?", "You don't know me..." and other unnecessary phrases that should never be used when making a business call. And even more so now. There's no need to apologize for reaching out or making a request — leave those clichés to professional beggars. IMMEDIATELY state who you are, where you are, and what you need: first, second, and third.

If there is no immediate threat to your life and you have at least a few minutes, be sure to mention where you obtained the contact information from — who provided you with this phone number.

Speak in a confident tone. Don't mumble.

If a person says they can't talk right now and will call back in ten minutes, never agree! If your situation is critical, state the essence of your request clearly and briefly. If you hear background noises such as dogs barking, children screaming, or an engine rumbling, and it seems that the person cannot speak or concentrate on your question at this time, tell them that you will call back in ten minutes.

A million other people, calls, or events can distract a person from calling you back, and they may not do it. You are the one who needs help, money, information, or resources. Perhaps you want to save your own or someone else's life. Always take the initiative and call yourself.

So you've stated the essence of the question. Always end each conversation with a question:
- Can you help?
- Will you send it?
- Will you do it?
- Will you find it?
- Will you provide the contact of the right person?

You shouldn't simply talk and part ways; you should know whether you achieved your desired goal in the conversation or not, and whether you will be helped or not.

This is not about "please/sorry", but about life and death.

Direct messages, private messages, messengers,
never write:
"Hello, how are you?" and then disappear;
"We will be grateful if you listen" and then become silent.

There is no time for idle chat in a world where everyone of us has become an information center, receiving dozens of requests for help every minute through various messengers.

Do you need anything? Put everything in a SINGLE message. Be concise, limiting it to half of the smartphone screen at most. Your lengthy texts with unnecessary explanations are unlikely to be read. Actually, no one ever reads them.

Always, ALWAYS end with a question:
- Will you do it?
- Will you help?
- Do you know someone who can help?

Social media

You can't just write "Urgently need to take the girls to Lviv" without providing specific details such as pickup location, how many girls, and their phone numbers. Sometimes, when people want to help, they may check the profile descriptions on Instagram or Facebook, but even there, the geolocation is often not indicated.

Always include geolocation on your page, even if you operate solely online or work with the Ukrainian market while abroad, or vice versa.

I'm disappointed by children's educational centers and beauty salons that fail to include their location in the page description. Ultimately, people are expected to physically visit these establishments, yet they make it unnecessarily difficult by omitting this crucial information.

Geolocation is an essential aspect of effective sales and a crucial element for building trust. It should always be provided and specified.

And while someone is searching for your location, someone else may have already messaged or called them, liked their page, and you might have lost their attention — and, as a result, a chance to get help. Just as earlier, you used to lose in sales due to communication errors.

How to write the card number so that more money is transferred to you?

If you're collecting money on Facebook, put the card number in the comment. Nothing but the card number itself. This makes it easier for someone to copy it and transfer funds immediately. Also, include the following in your posts: "I put the card number in the first comment."

If you're collecting money on Instagram, put the card number in the post as well as the text "write in Direct, I will send you the card number so that it is convenient for you to copy." Send the card number in a separate message as well, to make it easy for customers to pay immediately.

Simple rules. And here's the result from following them:

"I wrote to my friends abroad based on your advice, and I already have 500 euros for humanitarian aid. I went to my city hall to collect money, remembered your instructions and stories about how you used to go and ask for it. I thought I would go and do it myself. And everything worked out!" Alina, a reader of my books from France, wrote me.

And in her stories, Alina shows boxes of medicine already on their way to Ukraine.

Simple rules save not only your sales, they save lives.

CHAPTER 16

STORIES OF MY JOURNALIST FRIENDS

NATALIYA BALIUK'S STORY: "MAYBE THEY JUST WANTED A DRINK AT MY EXPENSE"

During my first year of university, I was an active freelance writer for the Lviv newspaper "Moloda Halychyna" (formerly "Leninska Molod") *[The name "Moloda Halychyna" translates to "Young Galicia" in English. It is a regional newspaper that primarily serves the western Ukrainian region of Galicia. "Leninska Molod" translates to "Lenin's Youth" in English. It was a newspaper in Ukraine associated with the Communist Party during the soviet era. The newspaper served as a propaganda tool for promoting communist ideology and reporting on the activities of the Communist Party].* In fact, I practically lived there. I was engaged in gymnastics and later in athletics since the age of five, therefore I wrote about sports. When the position of sports correspondent opened up, I was promised that it would be mine. As a third-year student, I'd be a real journalist on the staff of a well-known newspaper! My joy knew no bounds!

"When someone gets hired, there is a custom. The newcomer buys a round of drinks. You go to the store opposite the editorial office, get a drink and a snack, and then you start work the next day," the journalist with whom I had the closest friendship explained the rules of life in their team to me.

Feeling happier than ever, I bought two huge bags of food with all the money from my student stash. The editorial office partied the entire evening. In short, I threw a great party!

That night, I hardly slept in anticipation of my first real working day. In the morning, I put on my best clothes, firmly opened the door to my first grown-up job, and was informed:

"An experienced sports correspondent was hired. You won't be able to handle it because you're still 'green as grass'..."

It wasn't just a blow below the belt. It was, as they say nowadays, "a total betrayal." I don't remember how I got home that day. But I clearly remember crying for two days because of the insult and injustice.

To this day, I wonder if the guys just wanted to drink and eat and decided to do so at my expense in such a cynical way. Did something really change overnight in the universe, so they chose someone more deserving?

Of course, my foot was no longer in that newspaper's editorial office. Regardless, I am grateful to those journalists of the "Moloda Halychyna" who looked after me, helped, advised, and edited my materials. Anyway, I went through the school of life there.

But what is being done is for the better. In my fifth year of university, I completed my diploma internship at the newly created newspaper "Vysokyi Zamok." *[A newspaper published in Ukraine. The name "Vysokyi Zamok" translates to "High Castle" in English]* Stepan Kurpil was the editor-in-chief. Since then, my life has been connected with "Vysokyi Zamok," where I have been working for 30 years. I married Stepan Kurpil, and in 2006, I took over as editor of the favorite newspaper of Lviv residents.

And I often wonder: "If I had been hired at that newspaper, which soon ceased to exist, how would my career and life have turned out?"

__Nataliya Baliuk__ is the editor-in-chief of the daily socio-political newspaper "Vysokyi Zamok," as well as the creator of the YouTube channel "Baliuchi Temy" ["Painful Topics"] (in its two years of existence, the channel became a leader in the interview segment of the Ukrainian-language YouTube). She is 51 years old and lives in Lviv.

ROMAN KOLYADA'S STORIES

PART ONE:
TWO WINGS AND A NICHE BAFFLING PRODUCT

Cairo, Egypt. Concorde Hotel. Our group of journalists had been waiting for accommodation for a long time, and there was a luxurious grand piano in the lobby. I sat down and began improvising. People began to gather around me. During one of the pauses, someone asked:
"Where do you work?"
"On the radio."
"Give up your radio; you'll make a living doing this."

This episode lingered in my mind for a long time, fueling the idea that was already there. I began to consider ways to monetize my musical improvisations.

A business camp in the Carpathians, Ukraine. I was testing a musical portrait as a business idea but received disapproval from one fashionable marketer:
"Cool, but people won't buy it. It's too unique and puzzling."

The next morning, we were having breakfast in the hotel restaurant, surrounded by the Carpathians. The morning sun was breaking through the spruce branches onto the terrace. I sat down at the synthesizer to express my impressions of this morning through music.

The same marketer enters the hall and freezes, listening.
"What did you just play?"
"Improvisation, a musical portrait of this morning."
In an instant, she was sobbing on my shoulder:
"Thank you! It's as if you woke me up from a deep sleep and brought me back to the real me."

They were the same people that I recorded my first musical portrait with. Interestingly, I created it for a man who appeared brutally-looking and stout (a composition was commissioned as a gift for him).

When the final sounds faded, everyone in the room saw him as a refined intellectual, a complex individual, and an interesting interlocutor.

Following that, in the same hall, I received several subsequent orders, which I recorded in Kyiv. For money.

So much for a niche and barely comprehensible product! Turns out that people are really in need of such catharsis. I have realized how meaningful my musical portrait can be.

For years, I was torn between journalism and music. And then I thought, why do I think in terms of "either... or..."? This is something that can and should be combined!

I both constantly give concerts and work at "Suspilne", the First Channel of Ukrainian Radio, the most objective and honest media. I also lead public events. These are my two wings: equal and strong.

What I will say is that if you want to promote your product in the market, no matter how "niche and obscure" it is, go ahead and promote it.

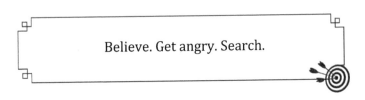

Believe. Get angry. Search.

- ☐ Believe. Believe in yourself, believe in your idea.
- ☐ Get angry. Use anger as a source of energy and potential, not aggression. Let it fuel your motivation, if you don't have any other resources yet.
- ☐ Search. Look for the form, look for the packaging, look for how you can alter yourself and what you can change in the product so that the market wants it.

But don't betray the idea itself.

Never.

Roman Kolyada *is a TV and radio presenter, media expert, pianist, composer, poet, translator, and author of musical portraits of people, cities, and brands. He is 46 years old and based in Kyiv.*

PART TWO:
THE WAR

On February 24, 2022, I woke up to the sound of explosions. The first thing I did was turn on the radio. My colleagues reported that the war had begun.

"Suspilne" Radio is Ukraine's main radio station, a large and serious structure that had been carefully preparing for this. I didn't believe until the end that it would be necessary.

Several backup broadcast points were set up in different locations, independent of each other.

I had clear instructions from management on what to do. Orders were given in the same manner as in the army:
- Arrive at point A; I arrived;
- Go to that basement; I went;
- Check something there; I checked;
- Go up to the studio and broadcast for eight hours; I did;
- Wait for new orders.

We had to maintain the broadcast from the designated points at all costs, even when the fighting was taking place nearby.

In the first days of the war, russists *[a nickname for russians derived from the term "fascist" to express the point of view that both are similar]* targeted transmitter towers in all Ukrainian cities. They tried to destroy centralized radio broadcasting, which is exactly what the Ukrainian "Suspilne" Radio is.

In some occupied territories, our voices were the only ones that could be heard on air. Later, people who ended up there without communication wrote to me: "In the attic, we found an old transistor receiver, listened to you, and understood that Ukraine is fighting and defending itself! So we have nothing to give up; we must survive in these basements and wait for our saviors."

When the first air raids had to be announced, I kept thinking to myself: "Is this for real? Have I lived to see the day when I sit in a bomb shelter and announce air raid alerts to Ukraine?"

There was a room with a grand piano in one of the studios where I was broadcasting at that time, and it was surprisingly in pretty good condition. I began to play, and the flutist, another musician on our team whom I had never met before, came to the sound.

Imagine an air-raid siren wailing while we played Mozart's bright and eternal music and my own compositions. So we formed a flute and piano duet and currently perform all over Ukraine.

We all know that Ukrainian volunteers work wonders. Here's my incredible story about them: I needed a keyboard instrument because you can't carry a grand piano with you and bring it into every studio you work in. I started looking for one, asking everyone whether they had one. Then, in less than a day, I received a fully functional synthesizer.

When I had night shifts, I started playing lullabies on the radio. Starting at around 11:45 p.m., after all the news about the war, I would announce: "And now I'll read you some love poems and play some soft music." This became my signature feature, and I still do it.

People wrote that no matter where they were amidst the horror and chaos of war and evacuation, they were waiting for my lullabies.

And in April, they started ordering my musical portraits! I thought: that's it, with the war and everything, who will need it now, who will pay for it? But it turned out to be necessary!

The first customers were our refugees. They wanted to express gratitude to the people who welcomed them in Malta. Recently I also wrote a musical portrait for the welcoming family in Germany.

It turns out that in difficult and sometimes catastrophic circumstances, people find a way to express their gratitude through such an exquisite art form.

That's how I got a new mission: to embrace it and use this opportunity to tell the European audience about Ukraine.

The war taught me to live in the moment. I used to put everything off for years; rest, joy, meaningful relationships, and fulfilling my dreams were postponed until I achieved the first, second, third, and tenth things, believing that I had to earn and merit the right to begin doing what I truly desired.

Now everything is different. I'm in a hurry to live, and I don't want to postpone anything for tomorrow. The other day, as I was walking down the street, a sudden summer rain started. For the first time in many years, I put my face under the drops with pleasure, enjoying the moment. For the first time in many years, I walked in the rain without any hesitation.

No one knows when such an opportunity will arise again, or whether it will at all.

OLEH HALIV'S STORIES

PART ONE:
LISTEN TO YOUR MOM AND WAIT FOR SOMEONE TO COME OUT OF THE RIGHT DOOR

"Son, you're smart; you should go to Lviv and study there instead of wasting your health working hard," my mother once told me. And I always listen to my mother; she never gives bad advice. So, that's exactly what I did.

Since seventh grade, I haven't missed a single newscast. I learned the names of all prominent politicians and public figures at home, in front of the TV, which we watched together with my grandmother in the village of Staryi Mizun, in the Ivano-Frankivsk region. I was interested in what an ideal society should be like, what democracy aspires to, and what alternatives exist.

When I came to Lviv, I had three goals:
- enroll in journalism;
- make sure to get a full scholarship;
- immediately begin working in my profession.

But how could I do that in a foreign city, where I didn't know anyone? I was seventeen years old. I was a freshman. It was 2014.

Someone told me about "Lviv Radio," where you could get voice training and gain valuable experience. I googled it and found out that it was just next to one of the buildings of Lviv Polytechnic National University, which housed the Department of Journalism and Mass Communication, where I was studying. I went there without any specific strategy, but with a strong desire to work.

A massive iron door with a combination lock separated me from the radio broadcasts. I waited in the freezing cold for two hours, hoping for someone to either come out or go in. And finally, the wait was over.

In the office marked "Director" I announced that I wanted to do my internship there. I was listened to and then sent to the news department. After several of my reports, I was hired.

A year later, I joined the NTA TV channel. It was easier; there was no combination lock on the door. I immediately went to the newsroom, and they hired me! I started working in the news department. I looked for opportunities everywhere: whenever I saw that a project was being created or launched, I immediately submitted my candidacy and participated in the casting.

As a result, I had my first live telecasts at the age of 19. And later, I became the face of the NTA TV channel.

At twenty-four, I became a teacher at the Department of Journalism and Mass Communication at Lviv Polytechnic National University, where I had recently graduated.

What do I advise people who want to study in a city where they don't know anyone and advance in their careers?

Take up residence in a dormitory

Maybe it was a mistake that I rented an apartment. I also witnessed the so-called "apartment market," which had existed since soviet times. What did it look like? A dozen elderly men and women, as well as middle-aged women, were sitting on benches at the tram stop behind the Opera House, near the modern "Dobrobut" market in Lviv. They would instantly recognize and approach "their client," offering accommodation.

That's how, on the very first day, I ended up in an apartment with the owner, a wonderful elderly woman, and another young neighbor, with whom I immediately found a common language. I used to pay 600 UAH per month.

But if I had lived in a dormitory, my prospects for making necessary acquaintances, finding new friends, and working would have been considerably greater. Student friendship and cohabitation help to quickly enter the correct societies and participate in cool projects, as well as be among journalists.

Accept any job

Both in journalism and other domains. It was a very interesting experience. I even worked in a call center, selling satellite TV services over the phone. I made so-called cold calls to people for six hours a day and offered to change their operator. I was told to bugger off. It happened. But it also helped me improve my stress resistance and ability to agree with anyone on anything!

And if you are assigned a project that does not inspire you, you can and should make it interesting and relevant. It can become your business card and a springboard to the top in your field.

Listen to your mother

People who are older than you know and have seen a lot. I turned to my teachers for help and always received useful advice and support, for which I am very grateful.

And most importantly, don't let yourself be disappointed. If it didn't work out here or you were turned down there, gather your courage and try again. Experiment with something new. Knock on every door. They will definitely open for you, despite the code locks and the lack of necessary acquaintances.

Oleh Haliv is the chief news editor of the NTA TV channel, a TV presenter, journalist, media consultant, and lecturer at the Lviv Polytechnic National University's Department of Journalism and Mass Communication. He is 25 years old and based in Lviv.

PART TWO:
THE WAR

February 24 is my mother's birthday. I had planned to go home and celebrate with her. However, I could only greet her over the phone at six in the morning, and it went something like this:

"Happy birthday, and I wish us victory because putin started a war."

Early in the morning, the entire editorial staff was already at work. We were immediately divided into groups: some were responsible for coordinating with the authorities, others with the Armed Forces, and some monitored information from abroad. From 9 o'clock onwards, our TV channel went into special marathon mode. It was crucial to keep people informed clearly and promptly about everything.

From the very first hours of the full-scale invasion, it was clear that we were living in a new reality. Particularly in the professional sense, as we were writing new rules of military journalism.

Previously, during peacetime, it was believed that it was necessary to highlight the positions of both sides of any conflict during the preparation of the material, but now everything is obvious: there is only one truth. And this truth is ours. The statements that "not everything is so clear-cut," which were manipulated by certain mass media before February 24, simply do not exist. russia is a terrorist state. Ukraine is defending itself and waging a war of national liberation.

Ukrainian journalists are now chronicling not only the history of their country, but also forging a new history of world war journalism. It is a story in which reality triumphs over theoretical explanations. We are warriors of truth, and the whole world recognizes our truth.

MARICHKA KURYLO-ALEKSEVYCH'S STORIES

PART ONE:
HOW CAN YOU HIRE TRAINEES WHO LOOK LIKE THAT?

It was the year 2011. Behind me was only an internship at a district newspaper. My friend Yuliya was in a similar situation. But we firmly decided to write articles for Lviv publications. It was the end of the first year, after all!

It was February, wet and gray. I was wearing a black puffy jacket, jeans, and had a large grass-colored bag in my hand. Yuliya was wearing a red puffy jacket, jeans, and carrying a black shoulder bag.

After walking through the yards, we found the right address.

A concerned woman opened the armored door:
"Did you make an appointment?"
"No, we just want to talk."
"Why are there so many of you? Come with me."

We entered a large room. There were many computers and many people. It was very quiet. No one answered our "Good afternoon."

"In her office?" the woman who brought us there asked someone. We heard an annoyed voice from the office:

"What am I, a nanny? I told you that we don't take the first-year students. What do you mean they're already here? Well, call them. But quickly! "

She quickly probed us:
"Where did you publish your articles? Where did you find our address? Why didn't you call ahead of time? There's no way no one answered! Why did you come so early? Why did you decide

we'd hire you?" She was sitting in a leather chair, and we were standing. It was as if we were shrinking in size right before our eyes. We were not offered to sit down, and we would not even consider doing so without permission.

"I don't have time. Write your names, year of study, and phone numbers, and remind me about yourself in March," said "the one who was in her office" and immersed herself in reading on the monitor.

We were closing the door behind us when we heard, as if slapped:

"How can they wear such clothes? Who let them out of the house dressed like that?"

When we reminded her about ourselves in March, "the one who was in her office" said that it was the first time she saw us, we were not on any list, and, in general, "we should have thought about practice in advance, not as we did."

Seven years later, I met her at an editor's meeting.

"Your face looks very familiar to me. Could we have met before?" she asked kindly.

"Yes, I'm the first-year girl with a grass-colored bag who came to you seven years ago with her friend in a red puffer jacket to ask for an internship. You didn't invite us to sit down, made fun of our clothes, and forgot to put us on the list of interns, which caused us problems at the faculty," I thought.

But I said:
"Maybe we've seen each other. This is Lviv. Everyone knows everyone here."

In the four and a half years since I became an editor myself, people have come to me for interviews with restrained hairstyles and combat makeup, with roses in their hands and socks with obscene inscriptions, in classic suits and oversized clothes, scared and self-confident.

Do you know what I thought when I saw these people at my office door? I thought about whether I had taken care of the chair for them and that no one felt the way I did at that interview, regardless of whether we would cooperate or not.

Marichka Kurylo-Aleksevych *is the head of the Lviv Regional Military Administration's (Regional State Administration's) press service. She was formerly the editor-in-chief of the "Galnet" News Agency, a radio host at "FM Halychyna," and a correspondent for the All-Ukrainian newspaper "FAKTY" in western Ukraine, and a tutor at "Media House", the first radio presenter courses in Lviv. Marichka is 29 years old and currently resides in Lviv.*

PART TWO:
THE WAR

At the beginning of February 2022, I changed my professional field. After 12 years in journalism, I became the press secretary of the head of Lviv Oblast and was in charge of the press service at the Lviv Oblast State Administration.

Back in January 2022, half of my Facebook feed was filled with people packing bug-out bags. Some packed their bags, then unpacked them, and stated openly that they had eaten into their "strategic supplies" before February 24. Others didn't pack anything and didn't believe until the last moment that a full-scale war would begin. I was among those who didn't believe till the very last moment.

I couldn't believe it when the invasion was announced for February 16. I did not believe it when on February 21 russia recognized the independence of the temporarily occupied regions of Donetsk and Luhansk. I didn't believe it when the President signed a decree on conscripting reservists on February 22. Even on February 23, when a state of emergency was declared in Ukraine, I still believed that it would not come to that.

On February 24, I woke up to a message in the work chat: "The war has begun." It was about five o'clock in the morning. From noon onwards, dozens, no, hundreds of journalists from all over the world started arriving in Lviv Oblast. I would receive calls from correspondents of The New York Times, The Washington Post, The Wall Street Journal, the BBC, and CNN, both in the morning and in the middle of the night.

I occasionally ask journalists to send me their material for proofreading before publication. I only do this if the person being interviewed has shared information "off the record," meaning something that cannot be published. Such information is disclosed so that media workers have a clear idea of the situation. When reviewing the final version, I check whether the journalists intend to release any important data that the enemy can use.

It's a small world! I met with "that" editor again — I had to proofread her article. She was indignant. She emphasized several times that she hated when someone interfered with her text. I nodded but still insisted on sending it for review. "You're going to get even," my husband said jokingly (or maybe not?).

No, I didn't get even. I didn't cut anything out, I didn't scrap the article. I deleted only the information that could harm important objects of Lviv Oblast. And later, at her request, I arranged two interviews with representatives of the Lviv Regional Military Administration.

That's what happens.

What have I learned about myself as a result of this war?

I've learned that I can abstract and process huge amounts of information, no matter how scary it is.

I discovered that I can work for nearly three months without a single day off. After all, what I do is important. I am valued. I feel a sense of being a part of history as it unfolds right before my eyes, as well as responsibility for everything I do.

That I have my husband by my side, who understands that everyone who calls me even after midnight is one of my co-workers, who also work 24/7.

I have realized that with such a hectic schedule and living in a rented apartment with a wayward cat, getting a dog (a pug evacuated from Irpin) was one of our best decisions. I found time to walk with him! It's some kind of magic — this hour did not exist before, but now it does.

That it is appropriate to travel as much as we did before the war. Now I understand: we could have travelled more.

That everything a person clings to — houses, cars, social position — is not really important. Human life is what truly matters and it is very fragile. We don't know what will happen tomorrow. But we are alive today. And it's a gift.

THE WAR.
LVIV RAILWAY STATION THROUGH MARIYA SHYMANSKA'S EYES

A boy and a girl are stepping over people sleeping on the floor in the waiting room. He grabs her elbow: "Be careful, there's a child!"

"I'm sorry, I didn't mean to!"

"What are you apologizing for?" says a woman holding a baby in her arms with a crack in her voice. "Was it you who kicked me out of the house? Me and my child? It was the damned russia who kicked me out of the house. What are you apologizing for? It's not your fault."

"Please wait in line for the train, I need to inject insulin. I feel bad — I've been standing for five hours, I'm afraid I'll pass out," a woman asks a mother with a child.

"What is it? What do you have to do?" asks the girl.

"A special injection. When there is not enough sugar in the body, a person feels bad and can even die. So I'm asking you and your mother to wait in line instead of me."

"Don't go anywhere, you might be late! You don't need a shot! You won't die — I have one more candy left, take it!"

"She's so pretty," an older woman shows her neighbor a photo of a young beauty on her phone.

"Now her grandmother cut her hair and shaved her head. Dressed her in her father's old clothes. Olechka is a boy now. So that she does not get raped. They are under occupation. God protect them!"

"Do you have space for three people? The mother, wife, and child of our defender. He is a scout, he's at war now."

"Yes, $700."

"Is this a house? How many rooms are there?"

"One-room apartment, new building."

"You want $700 a month just for bare walls? Are you crazy?! For what?"

"But they don't shoot here. There are walls, there are windows, and nothing falls. What else do you need?"

"I have no words. I don't want to know you anymore. Pray to God that this will not happen in your life," the tearful girl ends the call.

"I'm sorry, your phone is so loud. I heard everything. We have two rooms available. I can give them one room. It's not far. If it's appropriate, write down the address. I don't need money."

An air-raid alert signal woke me up late at night in Warsaw. I had forgotten to turn it off. Then the Polish neighbor knocked on the door, screaming: "War! Get up, putin is here! Missiles are being launched at us!" I apologized for causing her stress and turned off the signal. And she said: "God, it's terrible, how I sympathize with your Ukraine."

I ask my relative: "Do the boys need anything? I'm bringing knee pads, combat boots, gloves, and glasses from Poland." And he says: "Everything is there, in general. We need a drone and a car." I will look for them. And money to buy it all. And here comes a neighbor — do you remember Mr. Jacek, a retired physics teacher? — brings me 1,000 euros and says: "Your guys stand not only for Ukraine, but also for a free Poland. Here's the money for your car. Take it."

"We missed the train because of you, we stood in line for a day, where were you?" a young woman yells at a teenage girl. The woman is crying, barely able to speak, and two frightened boys are hugging her from both sides. "We had a chance to leave, to escape the war! We don't know where the missiles will hit next time. And if they come here too? Kyiv is already under siege..."

"Don't cry, Mom!" The girl hugs her brothers and pats her mother on the head. "Dad went to war, how can we leave him here?

So, we don't have to leave. We have to stay in Ukraine. We have to stay, Mother."

Mariya Shymanska *is a journalist, deputy head of the NTA TV channel, author of the interview project "Without Makeup with Mariya Shymanska," winner of the "People and War" contest, recipient of a grant from the National Media Association and the Media Development Fund of the US Embassy in Ukraine, host of "Narodne Talk-Show," 29 years old, from Lviv.*

AFTERWORD

"The air attack has ended..."

Every time I hear this, it's like a new birth: a gift, a celebration of life, a chance, and a right.

As I finish the last chapter, it's a strange feeling, both sad and joyful at the same time, as if a fairy-tale journey has come to an end and you must return to real life. Only now it's pounding in my temple: I need to finish and publish the book on time. The only thing left to write is the Afterword.

I open a pre-war document titled "Seven Types of Liudmyla Kalabukha" — pick your favorite:
1. A girl who lacked confidence, who leaned against the walls throughout all the "slow dances" at school discos and was afraid to even talk to the most handsome boy. A girl who has now grown into such confidence that she breaks through any barriers, commands attention like a rock star, and receives compliments from the most influential men in the country. And when she is reproached for it, she confidently replies, "Thank you, I've worked hard on myself."
2. Ukraine's most effective business trainer (according to her clients), who received a state award — the Order of "Honor of the Motherland" (as written in the diploma — "For honest service to Ukraine and actions aimed at the good of the People and the State") — and a saleswoman who consistently excels in selling and can quickly teach anyone to do the same — with confidence, without discounts, pressure, or begging. I'm certain I've already taught you a great deal!
3. A writer whose stories make people forget about their hungry husbands, children, and cats. They forget to breathe until they finish each chapter and then eagerly dive into the next one. They laugh and cry as they are immersed in the captivating world of the narrative.

The War: *You write that the only books in your emergency suitcase are mine, books that have been transferred across multiple borders because people know that my books would help them earn* *money wherever fate takes them. God, I wrote about sales and funny stories about myself and my friends, but it turned out that people needed them so much, even during the war.*

4. A restless traveler who eats worms, ants, and rotten sharks and walks through criminal areas, volcanoes, and deserts around the world.
5. Cupid's assistant, who has already saved 18 families from divorce, encouraged four guys to confess their love, and helped a supercool businesswoman who suffered from domestic violence to finally divorce, take care of herself, and remarry very successfully.

I consulted people about sales and, as an added bonus, they would receive advice from "psychologist" Kalabukha and find personal happiness.

6. A nerd who can tell stories about kings, leaders, and artists of different epochs and nations as if she lived in the same house with them her entire life. I have been asked so many times: "Why don't they teach history like that in school? Everyone would excel!"
7. An adamant friend and partner who is always there and will fight to the death for her people. Because "your" person is the greatest treasure in your life. Do you have people you consider "yours," and is it mutual? Stay close to them!

Each of the seven types of Liudmyla Kalabukha was with you in sadness and joy, in bed and in the kitchen, on vacation and in public transport, while you were reading this book.

And if any of my stories supported you, inspired you, comforted you, helped you defend your opinion, earn money, or make an important decision, then I would be happy.

This is how I wanted to end this book. That's how we lived. That's what we were.

You can mourn the past as long as you want, but it is gone forever. But there is the now. Today, that is priceless. How much can you fit in it! Our NOW.

"If you're going through hell, keep going," said Winston Churchill. Let's go to the end. To the Victory.

To stop is to give up. NEVER!

My job is to help. Where I can. Where I am strong: to support and develop your sales.

To help find new customers and suppliers, and restore businesses that feed you, wherever you are.

I'll do it no matter what. As each of us does on our respective fronts. For their sake. For your own sake. For the sake of Ukraine.

And your job is to help yourself and the front. And for that, you need to work. Keep your hands and head busy and earn money. In the most difficult circumstances, "put on" a smile and go to people. This is the only way to endure what cannot be endured. That's the only way to get through hell when pain and rage overwhelm you.

We are hard at work. We celebrate life. We laugh. Not because we are having fun, but because we are STRONG.

I'm waiting for your feedback, stories, victories, and questions on social media:

Facebook	Instagram	TikTok
Людмила Калабуха	@kalabukha.l	@kalabukha.l

I am very happy to have you, my close and distant friends, who have thought, said, or written nice things about me at least once.

Yours, #liudmylakalabukha

The book "Start Saying NO: How to Confidently Refuse and Command Respect" covers the following topics:

- How to get rid of the feeling of guilt that is often imposed on us.
- How to encourage clients to make a purchase and handle situations with the help of refusal.
- How to recognize, prevent, and stop manipulation.
- How to maintain good relations with everyone to whom we say "No."
- How to say "No" to parents, social media trolls, and those who ask for money.

Reader's feedback about the book:

"I finished reading your book in one day! This is my personal record. It's not that I really like or dislike reading, but I'm always short on time ☹. *I read the first paragraph of your book, about a conversation with your husband, four times. It's based on my life, word for word. I'm glad I read this book now instead of 20 years later. I'm going to learn to say "no" before it's too late, realize my own ambitions, and not worry about what people will say, just because that's what my parents taught me..."*

"Start Saying NO" is listed among the TOP-10 best books of Ukraine in 2017 in the all-Ukrainian ratings.

Order the book "Start Saying NO"

**The book "When to Say YES: How to Believe in
Yourself and React to Negativity" covers the following topics:**

- How to overcome your personal limitations, avoid burnout, and boost your self-esteem.
- How to deal with criticism, complaints, and negativity in business, life, and social media.
- How to create a successful business in Ukraine without support, money, and connections.
- What to do if the client does not pay.
- Is it okay to accept money from relatives and friends?
- How to find a job for both money and soul.
- How to convince those who are hesitant to buy and help them make a decision.

Reader's feedback about the book:
"Thank you for your incredible books! The stories are both inspiring and captivating. I kept crying and laughing with you. I understand that this is all from real life. All your tips are working. I have now so many orders that I don't have time to fulfill them. Thank you very much!"

"When to Say YES" is awarded the Best Book of Ukraine in the "Readers' Choice" category at the KBU Awards 2020.

Order the book "When to Say YES"
Popular edition

Printed in Poland
by Amazon Fulfillment
Poland Sp. z o.o., Wrocław

26105814R00148